To Have and to Hold

To Have and to Hold

AN INTIMATE HISTORY OF COLLECTORS AND COLLECTING

Philipp Blom

THE OVERLOOK PRESS
Woodstock & New York

For Veronica

First published in the United States in 2003 by
The Overlook Press, Peter Mayer Publishers, Inc.
Woodstock & New York

WOODSTOCK:
One Overlook Drive
Woodstock, NY 12498
www.overlookpress.com
[for individual orders, bulk and special sales, contact our Woodstock office]

NEW YORK:
141 Wooster Street
New York, NY 10012

∞ The paper used in this book meets the requirements for paper
permanence as described in the ANSI Z39.48-1992 standard.

Library of Congress Cataloging-in-Publication Data

Blom, Philipp.
To have and to hold : an intimate history of collectors and collecting / Philipp Blom.
p. cm.
Includes bibliographical references and index.
1. Collectors and collecting—History. 2. Collectors and collecting—Philosophy.
3. Collectors and collecting—Social aspects. I. Title.
AM221 .B58 2002   790.1'32—dc21   2002032183

Printed in the United States of America
ISBN 1-58567-377-3
1 3 5 7 9 8 6 4 2

Contents

CONTENTS

Part IV: The Tower of Fools

List of Illustrations

Acknowledgements

The idea of collecting, the simple question what drives people to amassing things, often of no use, has always fascinated me but it was not until 1998 that I had the opportunity of committing some of my ideas to paper in an article for Elisabeth Bauschmid at the *Süddeutsche Zeitung*. I did not think that many people would be interested in a closer look at this strange and beautiful obsession until I told my agent Victoria Hobbs about it, who showed true flair and insight when she pounced on my idea and then helped me develop it. I was fortunate to find a kindred spirit and eagle-eyed editor in Stuart Proffitt. Sara Fisher also deserves my deepest thanks.

While I was working on my initial idea I was much encouraged by Geert Mak, whose unfailing eye for telling details helped me find my own way. During my research many people allowed me to distil my thoughts by patient listening, or helped me with suggestions that often opened up an entirely new line of inquiry. Hofrat Prof. Dr Maria Teschler-Nicola, Hofrat Dr Rudolf Diestelberger, Hofrat Dr Georg Kugler, Dr Monika Firla and Dr Rudolf Maurer were of invaluable help for the chapters dealing with Vienna, the Habsburg collections and the story of Angelo Soliman. Dr Arthur MacGregor, an unrivalled expert in the field, clarified much about collections in the Renaissance and Baroque periods, Prof. Robert Evans very kindly let me pick his brains about the enigmatic Rudolf II, while Thomas Klinger, Alex Shear, Wolf Stein, Father Thomas McCoog, SJ, David Cahn and Antje Gaiser, Hugh Scully and Anne Heseltine all helped me to gain insight into the mind of collectors. Prof. Jon Stallworthy proved himself a kind and generous friend as well as an excellent adviser in reading the manuscript and suggesting improvements. As ever, the encouragement of my parents, of my sister, Christina, and of Veronica, my wife, were a constant and wonderful support to me.

My final word of gratitude goes to an unknown man: the drunken sage in the Café Bräunerhof who made me think anew and who graciously provides me with an Epilogue. I raise my glass to him, and to everyone whose help has contributed to this book.

PB

Paris, 2001

Every passion borders on chaos, that of the collector on the chaos of memory.

Walter Benjamin, 'Ich packe meine Bibliothek aus'

Three Old Men

When, as a child, I had trouble going to sleep at night, afraid of witches or demons under my bed, I took comfort in imagining my great-grandfather, sitting in his armchair and reading, as I had seen him do and as my mother, who had grown up in his house in Leiden, in the Netherlands, had always described him to me. In my mind's eye he is still sitting there, impeccably dressed in 1940s fashion in a three-piece suit, with a tuft of white hair above his forehead and a trim half inch around the sides of his head, a little brush of moustache underneath his nose (a fashion he had not renounced despite the unloved Austrian who had also sported it). He was dressed correctly rather than elegantly. His suits all old but serviceable and, like his shirts, worn out at the cuffs and collars, testaments to their owner's parsimonious living and Calvinist ideals. He was surrounded by the spines of thousands of books on shelves climbing the wall up to the ceiling.

How much of this image is really memory (he died, aged ninety-four, when I was four), and how much had reconstituted itself in my head out of stories and photographs is impossible to say, but my admiration for his curiosity and learning was such that I never let go of it. It was an image of immense authority and kindness, and I was sure no demon could possibly have the daring to challenge him. He had been, so I had been told time and again, a great collector of books and works of art, a self-made man of immense erudition, and I was intensely proud of him.

Willem Eldert Blom had started life as a carpenter's apprentice and died a rich man – not in financial terms, but having had a life full of improbable adventures and learning, which had led him to master seventeen languages, receive a doctorate in Russian at the age of eighty-five (after which he set out to learn Chinese), and amass a library of some thirty thousand volumes. Some relics of this treasure trove had found their way into our house: old, heavy bibles in stiff leather bindings large as tombstones, classics in Greek and Latin, medical books from the eighteenth century, a wooden traverse flute, which he had played and had taught me to play a little, and some paintings and prints, including one sheet by Rembrandt, which now hangs near my desk. This was the first collection, or memory of a collection, that I remember.

His life, it appears to me now, bears much resemblance to those of other collectors, whose interest in life allowed them to overcome the limitations of their time and upbringing. Having studied Latin, Greek and ancient languages at night, after finishing his day at the carpenter's shop, he became a translator, and then went to New York – as a tea taster, of all things. He returned to the Netherlands to become successively a stockbroker, a manager, a biscuit manufacturer, a stockbroker again, and a feeder of swans. This last innocent occupation was a cunning cover. After retiring from his job, he would leave the house every morning carrying a bag of bread crusts. 'Mother, I'm going to feed the swans,' he would say to his wife, Godefrieda, take a bus to the train station, Leiden Centraal, and from there a train to Amsterdam, where he had an antique shop, De Geelfinck. Godefrieda would have never approved of a man of his position entering into trade, and he had never been keen on domestic arguments. The deception was only discovered years later, when his shop had been burgled and she read about it in the paper.

De Geelfinck, The Yellow Finch, was by all accounts less of a shop than a personal indulgence, a place in which Willem amassed curiosities, works of art and books, which were also for sale, subsidizing his passion for more and rarer items. Those pieces that he did not want to sell he would take home. A photograph from about 1965 shows him in the door of his shop, slightly below ground level, surrounded by things of great value and others of no value at all, bearing testimony both to his collecting passion and to his inscrutable sense of humour: huge keys (nobody knows what to), the back tooth of an elephant (a card affixed to it reads: *Replaces an entire set of dentures*), cardboard messages in verse in touchingly not-quite-colloquial English (*Step in old man/ (Don't call me 'old man')/ Into this jolly old antiques shop/ Old girl (Don't call me 'old') and when/ You've looked around from floor to top/ You'll find it such a jolly old shop/ Where old jolly things in legion abound/ Old Man, Old Girl, look freely around./ (Don't call me old, or I'll call the hound)*). He himself stands next to the *pièce de résistance*: a real Egyptian sarcophagus, which later went to a museum. Inside the shop were hundreds of books ranging from the sixteenth century (bibles a speciality) to modern paperback thrillers, Russian icons and oil paintings, pieces of porcelain, Javanese dolls, African masks, Dutch pewter, Delft tiles, vases, necklaces, antique kitchen utensils, Japanese lacquer and gramophone records. Today the basement where his burrow once was houses a shop for Chinese cooking utensils. The shop to the left sells souvenirs (windmills, painted wooden clogs and gold-coloured plastic Eiffel Towers), the one to the right flowers. In season, the entire space is filled with brightly coloured tulips.

The aura of Willem Blom and his lifelong search for enlightenment in books and old treasure was transferred not just to my parents' shelves and walls; most of his library went to the University of Leiden.

During my school years, my disinclination for sports and woodwork allowed me to spend time in the realm of another collector. The school that I attended was a very odd institution indeed, run according to the principles of that most eccentric of turn-of-the-century sages, Rudolf Steiner, the architect of an assortment of borrowed theories and *idées fixes* which he called anthroposophy, in the grounds of a small castle surrounded by woodland. The castle and land had once been owned by a mysterious man who could still be seen walking up and down the main street of this little community on two crutches, clad in green loden coat and hat, his neck protruding out of the coat almost horizontally, an ancient, turtle-like figure. As children we called him simply the 'Erbprinz', the Heir Apparent, an enigmatic name to a young boy. He was, in fact, Georg Moritz, erstwhile heir to the duchy of Saxony-Altenburg. History had overtaken his father, Ernst II, the last ruling duke of Germany, who abdicated in November 1918. Ernst had been granted the castle, an unromantic building in the middle of

Westphalia, as compensation for giving up his seat in Altenburg and its spectacular family palace, and his son, Georg Moritz, who had come under Steiner's spell, had transformed it and the adjacent agricultural estate into a school.

When I came to know the Erbprinz he was well into his eighties, and I discovered to my delight that the two rooms in the castle which he still inhabited (the rest he had donated to the school where he had also taught) were furnished with antiques and filled with books on history, philosophy and art, a haven from the noise of the boarding school. He gave me a free run of his library, and I spent many a happy sports lesson there, much to the chagrin of the PE teacher, who felt powerless to intervene.

In front of his apartment was a small landing, a neutral space between two worlds. There was the smell of boarding school, of lino, wood polish and washing powder, the hideous pot plants and the atrocious anthroposophic watercolours (plenty of primary colours and swirling shapes). But there was also a fine Biedermeier writing desk crowned by the bust of Ernst, the last duke himself, an austere classicist work in alabaster which frightened me every time I set eyes upon it.

By the time I came to know him, Mr Altenburg, as he was officially called, rarely left his room, which smelled distinctly of old man. There he would sit in his empire bed, propped up by pillows, his translucent skin resembling the complexion of his father's bust. He talked to me about books, about his life and about history. It amused him to have a little young company: he had, after all, spent most of his life among schoolchildren. I lapped up his stories with a sense of wonder but little understanding, for he was truly a messenger from a different time, from a Germany very unlike the one I knew. He had been made a Lieutenant of the Guard in his father's regiment on his fourteenth birthday and had received the education of a future head of state. Occasionally, as his hands were now too uncertain for him to write comfortably, he would also dictate letters to me. These missives were sent to countess this and prince that, with the odd professor thrown in for light relief. A urine bottle hung by the bedside while on a side table his last meal waited to be collected. His bedroom was filled with stacks of books, which made navigating difficult for a lanky teenager.

The other room, the library, seemed large yet intimate, filled with volumes smelling sweetly of old paper and infinite riches. The crowning glory was a morocco-leather armchair with a brass-and-mahogany reading stand set into the left armrest. The chair seemed immense; it would swallow me up entirely while I sat there, devouring biographies or histories, many of which I was too young to understand, or simply looking out of the window at the old trees outside, wishing that I lived in such a room, in such a castle, that I possessed these wonderful books, and was able to read all day without having to think up excuses for missing my lessons.

I can still remember quite acutely when I first realized that collecting could have more powerful, darker connotations than I had witnessed in the collections of my childhood. I had met Wolf Stein in Amsterdam, during synagogue service, which I, not being Jewish, had attended simply out of interest. We began to talk and he invited me to his house for a meal. He spoke Dutch with a slight but unmistakable German intonation. When I arrived at his address, not far from the Rembrandtplein, he welcomed me warmly and asked me to excuse the state of his house. The living room, he explained, was being renovated, a long-term project, as he did everything himself and was not particularly adept at decorating. What I had noticed, however, was not the tools lying about, but the books spreading everywhere like moss on wet stones. Piles of books lined the entire hallway and more were sitting on every step of the staircase leading up to the first floor. Books were creeping up the walls and occupying every inch of free space on the floor, on tables, chairs and other furniture. The rooms were accessible only through narrow canals winding through a mountainous landscape of reading matter in all shapes and sizes. He showed me around the house. There were books surrounding his bed, books on shelves above it, books in front of the bathtub, and books in his study, which also contained a special treasure – his violin, which he said he had not played for many years but always wanted to take up again.

The only room free of this growth of books was the kitchen, a desolate place not only because it was bare in contrast to the other rooms, but also because it was almost devoid of food. The meal we had together was meagre, but Wolf proved wonderfully engaging company and I forgot the sardine sandwiches and tepid tea with which

I was trying to placate an adolescent stomach. He was a curious figure: small and kindly, in his early sixties perhaps, dressed conservatively but somewhat shabbily. His every movement had about it an air of apology, as if he wanted to communicate that he did not mean it like this, that things had just come out this way and that he hoped they might be made up for by his smile and his wit.

He talked about his mother, who was living in an old-people's home and still making great demands on him, and about his medical studies. Was he still studying? I asked him. Yes, he said, he had been studying on and off for the last thirty years, unable to finish, giving up completely periodically and then starting again with new energy. An apologetic smile appeared again. You must understand, he said, I was in hiding for most of the war, here in Amsterdam. When they picked me up I was fourteen and I went straight to Bergen-Belsen. What I saw there made me want to become a doctor, to help people. But, on the other hand, when I see someone with a cut thumb suffering terribly, I cannot help but think back to the mountains of bodies and I simply cannot take the patient seriously. Then I lose all faith in ever finishing.

I learned during that dinner that Wolf Stein had the dubious distinction of having had a fate similar to that of Anne Frank, the difference being that he survived the experience with no diary to show for it. Like the Franks, his parents came from Germany, from Schweinfurt, fleeing to the Netherlands in the hope of finding a bearable life there. Like the Franks, they went into hiding, and, like them, were discovered and deported 'to the East'. Unlike Anne, Wolf came through the hell of the concentration camp. When he was liberated, aged seventeen, life refused to make sense, and ever after he had been trying to make a whole out of the pieces he could gather, tried to gain strength from his life before the catastrophe, from a perfectly normal childhood. His books were part of this project. I asked him why he had accumulated thousands of volumes, some in languages he did not read.

It is stupid, I know, he smiled, but I didn't have much of a formal education in my youth and I always hope I may make up for it if I read all these.

Part I

A Parliament of Monsters

And God said to Noah, The end of all flesh is come before me; for the earth is filled with violence through them; and behold, I will destroy them with the earth. Make thee an ark of gofer wood; rooms shalt thou make in the ark, and shalt pitch it within and without with pitch . . . And of every living thing of all flesh, two of every sort shalt thou bring into the ark, to keep them alive with thee; they shall be male and female. Of birds after their kind, and of cattle after their kind, of every creeping thing of the earth after its kind, two of every sort shall come to thee, to keep them alive.

Genesis 6.13–14, 19–20

The Dragon and the Tartar Lamb

Dragons have always crawled out from their lairs deep in the beginnings of time to test the virtue of the faith of humankind. In legend, they appear before the city gates devouring innocent blood and challenging the greatest and the most pious warriors to defend the order of things by pitting sword against fiery breath.

When a 'fearsome dragon' was sighted in the marshes near Bologna in 1572 it might have stirred these ancient fears. This time, however, the hero of the hour was no knight in shining armour on his way to canonization, but a portly, balding scholar with nothing but a heroic name, Ulisse, to show by way of warlike credentials.

Despite the fact that the pope himself was visiting the city, the Church did not lay claim to what would have been seen only a century before as a victory of Christianity over the devil. Now a collector scientist, the renowned Ulisse Aldrovandi (1522–1605), was thought competent to deal with strange creatures. The deadpan tone in which he relates the capture of the animal is in itself significant:

The dragon was first seen on May 13, 1572, hissing like a snake. He had been hiding on the small estate of Master Petronius near Dosius in a place called Malonolta. At five in the afternoon, he was caught on a public highway by a herdsman named Baptista of Camaldulus, near the hedge of a private farm, a mile from the remote city outskirts of Bologna. Baptista was following his ox cart home when he noticed the oxen suddenly come to a stop. He kicked them and shouted at them, but they refused to move and went down on their knees rather than move forward. At this point, the herdsman noticed a hissing sound and was startled to see this strange little dragon ahead of him. Trembling he struck it on the head with his rod and killed it.[1]

A simple bop on the head with a walking stick was all it took. What exactly this creature was is impossible to say. A large and rare lizard perhaps. Aldrovandi did what a man in his position was expected to do: he had the dragon preserved and set about writing a *Dracologia*, a Latin history of the dragon in seven volumes. It is a scientific treatise, attempting to explain the phenomenon before him as a natural occurrence, not in terms of metaphysics or religion. The animal, he wrote, was still immature, as shown by its incompletely developed claws and teeth. It had moved, he believed, by slithering along the ground like a snake, aided by its two legs. The corpse had a thick torso and a long tail and measured some two feet in all.

Parts of Aldrovandi's museum have survived to our day and are now housed in Bologna's Museo di Storia Nationale in the Palazzo Poggia. Few tourists find their way in here and the wood-panelled rooms with their white cabinets are left in relative silence for much of the time. Two dried crocodiles mounted on the wall are watching over the birds' eggs, strange horns, stone samples, plants and learned tomes. Only the fluorescent lighting serves as a reminder that four centuries have passed. The dragon, which is now lost, had once been part of this display.

Scholars from all over Italy came to visit his collection to see the dragon for themselves. In its heyday the collection attracted scores of visitors, both learned and curious, and Aldrovandi kept an elaborate guest book, which was regularly inventorized and updated. Among those invited to sign the guest book were 907 scholars, 118 nobles, 11 archbishops, 26 'famous men' and 1 single woman. More women had given the great man the honour of a visit, but even Caterina Sforza, the nearest thing Italy had to a queen, who had arrived with an entourage of 'fourteen or fifteen coaches and carriages containing fifty Gentlewomen, the flower of the first families of the city, accompanied by more than 150 Gentlemen',[2] was not thought of sufficient intellectual stature to be asked to sign.

Aldrovandi was at the vanguard of an explosion of scientific and collecting activity in the sixteenth century that emanated from Italy. He saw himself as the new Aristotle and it was his intention to finish what Aristotle and Pliny had started: a complete encyclopaedia of nature. To achieve this he needed facts, and the size of his collection became as much of an obsession to him as the gathering and description of the specimens. The museum held 13,000 items in 1577, 18,000 in 1595 and some 20,000 around the turn of the century.

Many Italian cities around this time had their own great collectors: men like Michele Mercati in Rome, Francesco Calceolari in Verona, Carlo Ruzzini in Venice, Aldrovandi and later Ferdinando Cospi in Bologna, and Athanasius Kircher in the Vatican compiled collections that, classified and catalogued, were instruments of scholarship and realizations of encyclopaedic knowledge. The cabinets of the richest collectors boasted the horns of unicorns, dried dragons with outlandish and fearsome shapes, skulls of strange birds and jaws of gigantic fish, stuffed birds of the most extraordinary colours, and parts of other, as yet unidentified, creatures that seemed to hover between reality and myth, between the hope of rational explanation and the fear of hell. Nor were these collections uniform in their content and orientation. The Veronese Mapheus Cusanus, for example, was known to have a curious predeliction for 'Egyptian Idols taken out of the Mummies, divers sorts of petrified shells, petrified cheese, cinnamon, spunge, and Mushromes'.[3]

This new spirit of Renaissance inquiry was driven by scholars and amateurs, not priests or ancient philosophers, and for the first time it became accepted that a fish market may be a better place to gather wisdom than a library. Fishermen were more likely to have caught in their nets rare and wonderful specimens and to be able to tell of their habits and their names than could any number of Latin manuscripts. It was no longer enough to sit at a desk in a monastery. Aldrovandi himself toured the fish markets for new finds and talked to the fishermen, just as Descartes would make observations about animal anatomy in a Paris butcher's shop a century later.

It would have been anathema to collectors even a century before to seek out objects in places such as these, for until the sixteenth century collecting had been the prerogative of princes, whose interest concentrated on objects that were both beautiful and precious, thus reinforcing their wealth and power. Tut Ankh Amon had collected fine ceramics while Pharaoh Amenhotep III was known for his love of blue enamels, and sanctuaries from Solomon's Temple to the Akropolis as well as the courts of noblemen had always held famous treasures.[4] Ancient Rome had seen a brief blossoming of a culture of collecting, mainly of Greek works of art, but with the empire that, too, vanished.[5]

Throughout the Middle Ages princes of the Church and secular rulers accumulated great hoards of relics, luxurious vessels, jewellery and objects such as horns of unicorns (narwhales) or other legendary creatures.[6] Out of these treasuries developed a more private form of appreciation, the *studiolo*, a purpose-built chamber filled with antiquities, gemstones and sculptures, popular in Italy among men of both means and learning from the fourteenth century onwards.[7] Oliviero Forza in Treviso is thought to have had the earliest recorded *studiolo* in 1335. Collecting works of art and objects crafted from precious metals and stones became a pastime of princes, a diversion that could border on an all-consuming passion.

One day he may simply want for his pleasure to let his eye pass along these volumes [which he had bought and copied for him] to while away the time and give recreation to the eye. The next day ... so I am told, he will take out some of the effigies and images of the Emperors and Worthies of the past, some made of gold, some of silver, some of bronze, of precious stones or of marble and of other materials which are wonderful to behold ... The next day he would look at his jewels and precious stones of which he had a marvellous quantity of great value, some engraved, others not. He takes great pleasure and delight in looking at these and in discussing their various excellencies. The next day, perhaps, he will inspect his vases of gold and silver and other precious material ... All in all then it is a matter of acquiring worth or strange objects – he does not look at the price.[8]

The collector so engrossed in his treasures, Piero de' Medici, known as the Gouty (1416–69), could afford not to worry about the cost of the objects he was acquiring and commissioning wherever he could find them. Several of his descendants, most notably Francesco and Lorenzo the Magnificent, were also swept up in this passion. Francesco had a *studiolo* built and painted with panels depicting the twelve months and twelve orders of books that were to be found in his library.

There is, however, a world of difference between these 'armories for precious things' and Ulisse Aldrovandi's museum some 100 years later. Antonio Averlino Filarete, who observed Piero de' Medici in his *studiolo*, notes the kinds of possessions assembled here: antiquities, gems and works of art, as well as a few 'noteworthy and strange objects'.[9] The significant distinction between the medieval treasuries and the new *studioli* was the privacy inherent in the idea of a study. In their programme and structure, however, little had changed. The walls that both shut out and represented the outside world with their symbolic order of things still resonated with the memory of plainchant and the vibrancy of heraldic emblems. The *studiolo* with its statues, painted panels and gems from antiquity expressed a love of art and beauty, and with beauty came virtue, faith, and what Umberto Eco called 'a kind of ontological humility before the primacy of nature'.[10] The overwhelming curiosity that made collectors hunt not for what was beautiful and emblematic but strange and incomprehensible, that made them pit their wits and their erudition against that of the authors of antiquity, was still far away.

How, the French Huguenot pastor and America traveller Jean de Léry had asked in 1578, could he ask his French readers to 'believe what can only be seen two thousand leagues from where they live; things never known (much less written about) by the Ancients'?[11] *Things never known by the Ancients* – this phrase would echo though-out Europe until it had shaken its very intellectual foundation. With the exploration of new continents, of the planetary macrocosm and the microcosm of the smallest things, Europe was stepping out of the shadow of antiquity and its authors which had circumscribed what was known for more than 1,000 years. During the Middle Ages and the early Renaissance it had been thought certain there was no natural phenomenon, no culture, no animal and no sensation that had not already been dealt with conclusively by Aristotle and Pliny, by Cicero or Pythagoras. The rest, so the scholastics had asserted, was merely commentary and reinterpretation in the light of the gospels.

Now, however, a century after the discovery of America, new dis-coveries on earth and in the skies kept pouring in seemingly every day. Knowledge exploded as age-old horizons were expanded beyond all

that had been thought possible. 'Neither Aristotle nor any other philosopher and ancient or modern naturalist has ever observed or known
[these things],'[12] Francesco Stelluri exclaimed confidently after observing a bee under a microscope; another, Federico Cesi, wondered aloud
what Pliny might have said had he had a chance to see 'the lion-maned,
multy-tongued, hairy-eyed bee'.[13] Collectors in Italy reacted to this
change with an insistence on the empirical study of nature. Across the
Alps, others did not feel that this paradigm offered them everything
they hoped to know and went a different path, combining scientific,
Aristotelian concepts with occult traditions.[14]

With the increasingly scientific spirit of the Renaissance in the second
half of the sixteenth century came a profusion of collections seeking
to explore and represent the world as it was then seen to be. The
studiolo could no longer answer the need to understand the sheer
profusion of the new in all its alien forms. 'It would . . . be disgraceful,'
wrote Francis Bacon in his *Novum Organum* in 1620 'to mankind, if,
after such tracts of the material world have been laid open which were
unknown in former times – so many seas traversed – so many countries
explored – so many stars discovered – philosophy, or the intelligible
world, should be circumscribed by the same boundaries as before.'[15]

Those interested in maintaining these boundaries had put up considerable resistance. Already St Augustine and St Thomas Aquinas
were wary about where curiosity might lead the faithful. Bernhard of
Clairvaux railed passionately against those more interested in things
unknown to them on earth than in the heavens.

Why do the monks who should be devoted to their studies have to face such
ridiculous monstrosities? What is the point of this deformed beauty, this
elegant deformity? Those loutish apes? The savage lions? The monstrous
centaurs? The half men? The spotted tigers? You can see a head with many
bodies, or a body with many heads. Here we espy an animal with a serpent's
tail, there a fish with an animal's head. There we have a beast with a horse
in front and a shegoat behind; and here a horned animal followed with
hind-quarters like a horse . . . In the name of God! If we are not ashamed at
its foolishness, why at least are we not angry at the expense?[16]

Well aware of what curiosity could do to cats, the theologians were
none too sure that faith would fare any better. Curiosity, they decided,

was a bad thing and those who were reluctant to listen to their message could find it reinforced by excommunication and by burnings at the stake.[17] Even Michel de Montaigne, whose insight into human nature was not hidebound by Church teachings, was no friend of too much inquisitiveness. Having met a man who had lived in the New World, Montaigne was unimpressed: 'I am afraid our eyes are bigger than our bellies, and that we have more curiosity than capacity; for we grasp at all, but catch nothing but wind.'[18] Men who spent their lives investigating obscure questions without properly knowing themselves were fools, he thought.

Montaigne's opposition to curiosity as an intellectual form of escapism had a very different motivation to the theologians', who feared that their entire world might be turned upside down. They were right, of course, as some 300 years later collections of curiosities proved a veritable engine of secularization. Collections of *naturalia*, of animals, plants and minerals, mushroomed around Europe, each one a small encyclopaedia of nature, of knowledge not dependent on the Church. Between 1556 and 1560, the Dutch collector Hubert Goltzius itemized 968 collections known to him in the Low Countries, Germany, Austria, Switzerland, France and Italy, while a century later another collector, Pierre Borel, boasted of having seen 63 collections. The Venetian Republic alone had more than 70 notable collections within its borders.[19]

Why was it during the sixteenth century that Europe experienced its first explosion of collecting activity, indeed the first collecting activity not limited to a handful of people known since Roman times?

The answer, it seems, lies partly in this world and partly in the next. The worldly explanation is that the expansion of knowledge in the sixteenth century necessitated new responses, new approaches to new phenomena. Scholars across Europe explored the macrocosm through the telescope and the smallest things through the microscope. Technological innovations, such as the printing press, advances in ship building and navigation facilitated trade across the globe and brought more and cheaper wares to Europe. At home, a more sophisticated banking system smoothed the exchange of goods. With trading empires such as the Dutch and Venetian republics came unprecedented wealth, another crucial factor for a flourishing collecting culture. In order to take objects out of circulation or to devote oneself to finding useless things, one has to be able to afford the time and resources to do so. Indeed, collections flourished wherever commerce did.

Together with these earthly revolutions, though, another, less palpable, one was occurring, a change in the perception of death and the material world.[20] Medieval Christians were forced to choose either to love the physical world and the pleasures in it and suffer eternal damnation, or to renounce it in favour of heaven – for little it profit a man if he gain the whole world but lose his own soul, as the gospel put it. From the perspective of the faithful, death was a transition, a moment of reckoning marked by public spectacle and common ritual. Even for those few able to afford it, accumulating objects without immediate use was acceptable only if they were in accordance with this conception of the world: relics and works of beauty, glorifying God. We do not know of any collection of plants, stones or animals during this time, though individual pieces with seemingly otherworldly properties such as 'dragon bones', usually fossils, often found their way into the treasuries of Church and nobility.

By the increasingly secular and capitalist 1500s attitudes to mortality and to worldly goods had changed. A heightened awareness of the impending end dominated poetry and art, as witnessed by the innumerable *vanitas* still lifes that were part of every wealthy home. In every one of them, the seductive beauty of the here and now is contrasted with its inherent decay. Every blossom was seen to contain the germ of putrefaction, and on every canvas the passage of time was counted down by hourglasses, skulls or burning candles among the sumptuous displays of fruit, precious objects or beautiful flowers. There was no delicate bud without a beetle crawling over it, waiting for it to wilt and die. The Elizabethan poet Robert Herrick (1591–1674) encapsulated this sentiment of futility by appealing to his readers to seize the day:

> Gather ye rosebuds while ye may,
> Old Time is still a-flying:
> And this same flower that smiles today
> Tomorrow will be dying.[21]

Death is only frightening if it really is the end, and if the dying of the flowers suddenly no longer signifies the eternal cycle of God's creation but irreparable loss. In a world in which death was looming larger,  attention was now directed towards the rosebuds themselves, to the material world, and to those who inhabited it. Portraiture asserted itself at the same time as the still life. It was this new conception of life that made collecting possible as it was transformed from an indulgence in *avaritia*, one of the seven deadly sins, and from the rejection of eternal life into a search for God through his creation, into practical theology. For men like Aldrovandi, the awareness of the mortality of the world's splendours only spurred them on to make their collections a testament to future generations.

The new breed of collectors had ceased to appeal to the authority of the Church. As cardinals and bishops flocked to see Aldrovandi's dragon and the other wonders he had assembled in his house, they tacitly acknowledged the validity of his secular approach to nature, and one of the most important collections of this time, that of the Jesuit Athanasius Kircher, was housed in the Vatican. Nature and the arts had broken free from their theological shackles, and the princes of the Church were eager to be part of the excitement, marvelling at the intricacies of human anatomy during dissections, at the mysteries of magnetism and at beautifully woven garments made of asbestos which would not burn even in the hottest fire – all phenomena their teachings had nothing to teach about.

There were, of course, still the great princely collections, immense treasures such as those owned by August, the Elector of Saxony, by Ferdinand II on Castle Ambras near Innsbruck, and of the great royal houses. Beginning during the 1550s, however, a network of scholarly collections spread throughout Europe, as recorded by the Dutch collector Hubert Goltzius. These scholars were in regular correspondence with each other and carried on their arguments about the purpose and order of their collections in learned books.[22] Ole Worm in Denmark, universities such as Leiden in the Netherlands, Oxford, the city museum in Basel, Switzerland, and Pierre Borel in Paris all participated in this exchange of ideas and in the hunt for items that were strange, precious and unknown, ranging from bizarrely formed tree trunks to exotic fruits, nautilus shells and fragments of dragons and mermaids.

With the dissemination of collecting as a serious pursuit another phenomenon appeared: collecting became popular among people who had neither great means nor great scholarly ambitions; ordinary people who had a little bit to spare. The Netherlands were an interesting special case. In this republic, living from its access to the wider world and off its trading connections reaching from the East Indies to the Baltic Sea, the harbours of Amsterdam and Rotterdam were full of wonderful and exotic things. Captains were under instruction from merchants and collectors to note down and purchase everything they thought worth taking home, and sailors commonly increased their wages by hawking stuffed animals, shells or foreign artefacts around.[23]

In a society without aristocracy many people could partake of this plenty and buy objects that they could store in their cabinets and display to friends, evidence of the wonders beyond the waves and of the staggering success their own small and marshy country had made of necessity by turning the hostile sea into its marketplace. There were dealers who specialized in such exotic wares, and apothecaries would commonly store items of curiosity such as Egyptian mummies and dried foreign fish, often leaving it up to chance whether they were to be powdered and taken as medicine or sold intact to become part of a collection. When the Leiden apothecary Christiaen Porret died in 1628, the auction catalogue of his shop itemized a cornucopia that would not have been out of place in any cabinet of its time: 'curiosities or rarities and selected delights of Indian and other outlandish sea horns, shells from the dry land and from the sea, minerals and also strange creatures, as well as some artificially made objects and paintings'.[24]

Long before the famous and fevered speculation on tulips made and broke fortunes on the stock exchange, the admiration of colourful exotica was already established, and the cabinet of curiosities, initially a piece of furniture in which such items could be stored, became a great fashion among the burghers of Dutch cities, so much so that even dolls' houses were not thought complete without their own miniaturized collectors' cabinets complete with tiny sea shells and carvings in drawers no larger than a thumb.[25]

In Amsterdam alone, just under 100 private cabinets of curiosities were recorded between 1600 and 1740, testament to the great prestige collections had acquired and to the availability of objects to fill, according to inclination and purse, individual drawers or entire rooms.[26] The cabinet became an integral part of the Dutch interior, beginning with the mahogany cupboard crowned by oriental porcelain that can still be found in Dutch houses, and culminating in the famous private museums of amateurs such as Nicolaes Witsen, Bernadus Paludanus or Frederik Ruysch. These cabinets really were microcosms behind doors: while poor weather and Calvinist principle meant that wealth could and would not be displayed in the street, be it on the façade of houses or in dress, the same restrictions did not apply to drawing rooms, where objects of interest, fine furniture, carpets and of course paintings defined their owners' status and taste.[27]

When an admirer wrote about the famous collection of Bernadus Paludanus that it contained specimens 'Ut alle hoecken claer, des werelts' ('From all corners of the world'), he did not just use a figure of speech.[28] The sheer variety of items collected as early as the seventeenth century is astonishing and reflects the extent of the Dutch trading empire: from Japanese arms, porcelain and calligraphy, items recorded in Dutch cabinets have their origin in outposts of a mercantile world stretching across China and India, Indonesia, Australia, African regions as diverse as Nigeria, Ethiopia and Angola, the Malaccan Islands, the Caribbean, North and South America, Egypt, the Middle

East and right up to Greenland and Siberia. This profusion of exotica, and the manner in which it was transported, often brought back by seamen unconcerned about the intricacies of preservation, had curious side effects, such as the long-running debate on whether or not birds of paradise had legs (inspiring the beautiful and tragic legend that they were condemned to keep fly-ing until they died – colibris were thought to drill their beaks into trees and stay fixed there if they needed rest), as the overwhelm-ing number of specimens to reach Europe consisted only of the body, usually even without tail and head. Shells and coins, being easy to pre-serve and store, and decorative to boot, were especially sought-after.

While many of these rarities were used for diversion and dis-play, other collectors applied themselves to methodical study and used their collections as repo-sitories of knowledge, comparison, and as an encyclopaedia. Jan Jacobsz. Swammerdam (1606–78) wrote a monograph on 'bloedelose dierkens' ('bloodless little animals' or insects), which appeared sixty years after his death under the title *Bybel der natuure* (*Bible of Nature*), a daring phrase in a pious country. Apart from some 3,000 insects, his collection also contained specimens that were right at the borders of current knowledge, such as 'The fur of a Tartar Lamb which grows out of the earth', a woolly plant, which was thought to turn into a lamb at night to graze off the surrounding plants and to bleed when cut.[29]

Accepting such creatures as at least possible until conclusively dis-proved was good science, not superstition, especially in a culture reared from early childhood on biblical stories and miracles, and on ideas about natural history proposed by Pliny, Plato and Aristotle, which still exerted considerable influence.

Good science and the spirit of empiricism, however, were only one answer to the multiplicity of things pouring into Europe and European minds. While scholars in Italy and the Netherlands were counting beetles, another, infinitely richer, collection was growing in the heart of Europe, at the court of the Saturnine Prince, the Habsburg Emperor Rudolf II.

A Melancholy Ailment

You marvel that this matter, shuffled pell-mell at the whim of Chance, could have made a man, seeing that so much was needed for the construction of his being. But you must realize that a hundred million times this matter, on the way to human shape, has been stopped to form now a stone, now lead, now coral, now a flower, now a comet; and all because of more or fewer elements that were or were not necessary for designing a man. Little wonder if, within an infinite quantity of matter that ceaselessly changes and stirs, the few animals, vegetables, and minerals we see should happen to be made; no more wonder than getting a royal pair in a hundred casts of the dice. Indeed it is equally impossible for all this stirring not to lead to something; and yet this something will always be wondered at by some blockhead who will never realize how small a change would have made it into something else.

Cyrano de Bergerac, *Voyage dans la lune*[1]

It was a magnificent flotilla that landed in Genoa in 1571. The banner of the Habsburgs was flying from its masts, and the cargo being transferred carefully on to the pier of the busy harbour consisted of travel chests full of gifts, weapons, books and precious clothes, and of two princes with their entire entourage of advisers, armed guards, servants and dignitaries. The commander of the ships, Don Juan of Austria, had just defeated the Ottoman fleet in the celebrated Battle of Lepanto; he now oversaw a gentler, peaceful mission. One of the passengers under his care was by all accounts a rather severe young

27

man, who was on his way home from Philip II's court in Madrid, where he had been sent by his parents to spend his formative years. He was Prince Rudolf of Habsburg (1552–1612), soon to become Holy Roman Emperor.

Rudolf had been sent to his uncle's court at the age of eleven, together with his brother, Ernst, one year his junior. His mother, Maria of Spain (the daughter of Charles V), who was also his aunt once removed, had insisted on his going there, in order to take the boy away from the corrupting influence of the Protestant faction at the Viennese court. She was an ardent Catholic, keen on separating the precocious Rudolf from his father, Emperor Maximilian, whose sympathies for the Protestant cause made him unreliable in her eyes, suspicions reinforced by his interest in science and patronage of scholars. Maximilian supported the printing of many books and gave stipends to astronomers and others engaged in the natural sciences, while his diplomats were under instruction to bring him specimens of unknown plants from their postings in foreign countries. It was through Maximilian's ambassador in Turkey, Ghislain de Busbecq, that the first tulips were brought to Europe in 1562, as well as other plants, which were planted in the emperor's gardens in Vienna and Prague. Busbecq, himself a keen amateur scholar and antiquarian, was to become Rudolf's teacher.

These were the influences from which Maria had sought to shield her son. There was no love lost between her and her husband, and the tension between them was mirrored by the constant feuding of papist and Protestant sympathizers at the Vienna court. To have her sons travel to her own country, to Spain, and into her brother's sphere, was a personal triumph for Maria.

Though a staunch Catholic, Philip II was nothing like the religious fanatic of popular myth but rather a worldly king and a skilful politician who did much to open Spain up to new artistic and intellectual movements. The legacy of madness in his family, presumably a result of centuries of inbreeding also evident in the famously protruding Habsburg chin, was to haunt him as well as his nephew Rudolf. Philip's grandmother, Joanna the Mad, had died insane and he himself was given to bouts of melancholy during which he would not receive even his closest advisers.[2] This curse of insanity within the family produced one of the great tragedies of Philip's life, an episode that was seized by Romantic souls like Schiller and Verdi, who reshaped it in their own image.

Don Carlos, the king's only surviving son, was being groomed for government and was due to be sent to cut his teeth in Flanders. A usually gentle and intelligent young man, he had always been beset by episodes of rage, and even by the standards of the time his cruelty to animals caused some concern at court. Misshapen from birth, a hunchback with legs of unequal length and an asymmetrical face, he had difficulties speaking properly and had what was perceived as an unhealthy attachment to the queen, his stepmother, for whom he bought expensive jewels and other presents more suited to a mistress than a mother. When the State Council decided not to send him to Flanders after he had ridden a horse to death, Don Carlos became enraged. He threatened, or, according to some accounts actually tried, to kill the Duke of Alba, the Governor of Flanders, and later threatened to murder his father. He wrote letters to various grandees asking for their support against the king and rapidly became a political liability.

On midnight of 18 January 1567, after consulting with his council, Philip donned his harness and helmet and went to his son's rooms accompanied by a handful of reliable noblemen. They entered silently and seized all weapons and heavy objects in the room. The prince woke up and asked into the darkness, 'Who is it?' to which he received the reply, 'The Council of State.' 'Has Your Majesty come to kill me?' the prince inquired, now fully awake, but was reassured that he was safe. The windows of his room were nailed shut and Philip left his stunned son telling him that he would treat him as a father ought but as a king should. Don Carlos remained a prisoner in his own room, which drove him to distraction. He tried to commit suicide by starving himself to death, swallowing a ring in the belief that diamonds are poisonous, and by putting ice into his bed. Eventually he succeeded. He died on 24 July 1568. The king himself was reported to be terribly shaken by the episode and after Carlos's death he was said to have wept for three days and nights. It is possible that he wept not so much for his son, to whom he had not been as close as to some of his daughters, but for the future of his realm.

Close personal relations generally played an important part in

Philip's life. He had had several mistresses and it was on his initiative that women were allowed to act on stage in Madrid. After two political marriages, to María of Portugal and Mary Tudor, both of whom did not live long, he found companionship in his union with Elizabeth of Valois, and true and deep affection in his marriage to his niece, Anna of Austria. In later life, Philip was a devoted husband known to behave in distinctly unregal fashion. When Elizabeth was in labour in 1566, the king insisted on being present. 'During the night of birth-pains and the birth itself, he never left off grasping one of her hands, comforting her and encouraging her the best that he knew or could,'[3] the French ambassador reported with obvious surprise.

It is important to emphasize this aspect of Philip's character in order to understand the environment in which the young Rudolf found himself. The king was very fond of his nephews and regarded the young princes as possible successors to his throne, as the suitability of his own son, Don Carlos, was already doubtful. Rudolf especially delighted the king, as the boy took a deep interest in his abiding passion: the building of a great collection and of several palaces. These palaces were given the king's attention in every detail. In the accounts and plans for their building and upkeep there are frequent notes in the margins by the king's own inelegant hand, making sure that the plants are watered properly, the gardeners trustworthy ('men who will not steal the birds' nests or the eggs'), and the vegetation chosen with the greatest care and planted at exactly the right time.

The palace that was to express his vision most perfectly was the monastery of San Lorenzo near the village of Escorial, part royal residence and part ecclesiastical complex, and designed to embody the unity and hierarchy of government, learning and faith. It was a *theatro totale*, part monastery and royal residence, part hospital and university, a microcosm of the Christian world. This was to be the setting for a great library, endowed with a royal donation to the monastery of some 4,000 books from the king's own collection, for the relic collection and, in the residence itself, for Philip's paintings.

The king's relics were the most astounding accumulation of such items in Christendom. After the death of his beloved wife, Anna, in 1580, Philip had increasingly sought comfort in religion. He had seen the death of many people close to him, among them his sister, with whom he had a lifelong warm relationship, four wives and three children (though the greatest blow, the death of Catalina, his favourite daughter – a loss more shattering to him than either the death of Elizabeth of Valois or the sinking of the Armada – was still to come). Even before 1580, relics had fascinated him. He had been impressed by the reliquaries he had seen in Cologne and had sent out agents to bring him every relic they could find. At the end of his life the collection amounted to some 7,000 items, including ten whole bodies, 144 heads, 306 arms and legs, thousands of bones, body parts and secondary relics, as well as the usual fragments of the True Cross, the Crown of Thorns, etc., most of which were encased in rich golden settings.

In 1598, when he lay on his deathbed, Philip turned to his relics for relief from his agony. Racked by gout and fever, his terrible pain made it impossible to move him from his bed, even to change his sheets, for five weeks, and the once-magnificent monarch lay dying in his own excrement. His bedroom was filled with holy images and crucifixes and he sent for the arm of St Vincent and a knee of St Sebastian to help soothe his inflamed joints. They did not help him, and he died miserably. Four hundred years later another Spanish ruler, General Franco, was to end his life clutching the arm of St Theresa of Avila, which he had taken with him everywhere he went.

While turning to the heavens when close to death, Philip II was very susceptible to earthly beauty. His galleries boasted masterworks by Italians such as Titian and Frederigo Zuccaro, and Flemish masters such as Rogier van der Weyden and Jan Gossaert, hung side by side with German canvases, and those by his favourite painter, Hieronymous Bosch, whose bizarre visions appealed to Philip's view of the afterlife and eternal damnation. An odd and striking absence from the galleries of the Escorial was the work of the Spanish painter El Greco, whose paintings the king had once admired, at least up until 1582, when he rejected one of them and thereafter ignored the artist altogether.

Back in Vienna, after years of intrigue and feuding at court, Maximilian had finally won the battle, and Rudolf and his brother, Ernst, could return from their Spanish exile. On their way from Genoa to the capital, the young princes and their entourage most probably visited the palace of their uncle the Archduke Ferdinand in Innsbruck. Rudolf would have made a point of staying here, for the Archduke of Styria possessed a famous collection of his own, one of the best north of the Alps. He would have found his uncle inspiring but strangely unfamiliar: unlike his brother the emperor, Archduke Ferdinand II had married beneath himself and was content with his first and only wife, happy to be in Innsbruck and to play no part in high politics. The collection was his great passion, especially his hall of armour, in which he assembled

suits of armour worn by famous men, together with their portraits; a martial reliquary, which he called his 'ehrliche gesellschaft', or 'honest company'. In addition to this, he also had an extensive cabinet of curiosities, comprising, as was the custom of the time, *naturalia* and *artificialia*. The collection was later to move to Ambras Castle, where parts of it can still be seen today.

At court in Vienna, Rudolf soon found himself dealing with intractable religious and national conflicts when he was effectively made envoy between his father and the nobles of the troublesome region of Bohemia. As a diplomatic compromise between them and their emperor, Rudolf was elected King of Bohemia, and crowned with the crown of St Wenceslas on 22 September 1575 in St Vitus's Cathedral in Prague. His residence remained in Vienna.

The new king was twenty-four years old, and his Spanish education had given him little to prepare him for a job that required not so much a monarch as an accomplished diplomat, skilled above all in the art of negotiation. He had some considerable accomplishments, he spoke and wrote German, Spanish, French, Latin, Italian and even a little Czech. His knowledge of courtly life, military strategy and art were excellent, but his distant, Spanish manner did little to endear him to his new subjects. Trying to steer a course between Protestants and Catholics, he ended up pleasing neither. For the former he remained a Spaniard and a Papist; the latter, his mother among them, regarded his conciliatory stance with great suspicion.

It was not until he had fallen seriously ill and had almost been given up for dead that he decided to go his own way. Rudolf recovered and in 1583 moved his court to Prague and threw himself into solving his subjects' practical concerns, such as the reorganization of the faltering mining industry and the stabilization of prices. In the more fundamental political questions, though, his style of rulership embodied the age-old Habsburg virtues of procrastination and avoiding conflict by delaying decisions whenever possible.

Rudolf was crowned emperor in 1575. As the affairs of state kept grinding on, with factional fights between Bohemian and Austrian nobles, Protestants and Catholics, he increasingly involved himself in extra-political activities. He especially devoted himself to adding to the already considerable collection of the Habsburg family, which his father had augmented greatly. As emperor, Rudolf had the means to indulge himself more freely than before. He invited artists and scientists to his court. The castle on the Hradčany Hill and the streets hugging the slopes around it were transformed into a colony of gold- and silversmiths, stone-cutters, watch- and instrument-makers, painters and engravers, astronomers and alchemists. Johannes Kepler worked there alongside the ageing painter Giuseppe Archimboldo, and Giordano Bruno found sanctuary here before going back to Italy (where he was burned at the stake). All of artistic and intellectual Europe was represented in these narrow lanes.

Inside the castle something altogether extraordinary was growing: a collection of such splendour, quality and sheer size that it became the envy of crowned heads throughout the continent. The artists working for the king were granted special dispensation and found almost ideal working conditions, provided they were content to see their patron's cavernous halls gobble everything they could produce as well as the works of art and other objects Rudolf's agents sent back to Prague from all over the world. In artistic terms, the collection was a black hole, sucking in everything that was precious and rare, never to release it.

A collection of mere natural curiosities seemed inadequate to Rudolf and those who thought like him. The 'chamber of artifice', the *Kunstkammer*, too, with its gems, coins and antiquities, was no longer able to contain this new feeling of boundless possibility, and the accompanying threat of disintegration of the limits of the known world that it brought with it. It required a more complex, more sophisticated response, and the sheer multiplicity of objects and ideas streaming in from abroad necessitated the search for a unifying idea or substance at the centre of it all. The 'chamber of miracles', the *Wunderkammer*, was the physical manifestation of this newly emerging mentality, which found its apotheosis in Rudolf's palace and its myth in the abiding legend of the melancholy prince, not ruling, but ruled by dark, Saturnine powers.[4]

Illustrations of these cabinets of wonders display rooms transformed into images of the riches and the strangeness of the world. They were conceived as effusions of the cabinets they had evolved from: small, often richly decorated cupboards with doors, drawers and a multitude of compartments designed to hold cameos, coins, small statues, precious stones.

One of the most famous cabinets of its time was commissioned by the Augsburg merchant and collector Philip Hainhofer and later given to Gustavus Adolphus of Sweden, one of several monarchs and aristocrats to visit the merchant's patrician house. Gustavus Adolphus himself never saw his *Kunstschrank* at his Swedish palace; it was delivered there only after his death. His daughter, the remarkable Queen Christina, made it part of her own collection, though. Today it stands in the chancellor's room at Uppsala University, emptied of the miracles it once contained.

Even without them it is an awe-inspiring work of ingenuity and craftsmanship. The objects in the drawers were arranged as an elaborate allegory to represent the animal, plant and mineral world, the four continents, and the range of human activities, and the front was adorned with hundreds of miniature paintings illustrating the triumph of Art and Science over Nature, and the primacy of Religion over all. Venus crowns the entire creation, but death is never out of sight, depicted in several *vanitas* scenes. The cabinet itself is simple in form despite the ornateness of the ideas underlying its construction. Two central doors on a massive pedestal open to reveal a variety of drawers and compartments fronted by cameos, columns and pilasters. On top of the entire piece is an arrangement of crystals, coral and shells out of which rises a coco-de-mer (or Seychelles nut) set in gold and ship-like in form, carried by an Atlas figure and supporting the statuette of Venus crouching and looking into an imaginary distance.

This outlandish piece of furniture was used, probably by Christina, as a dressing table. The Seychelles nut was not only one of the most valuable objects belonging to the cabinet (the only two islands producing them were not discovered by Europeans until 1768), but was also designed to hold a quart of wine and was thought to possess strong antidotal qualities, while coral was supposed to have the ability to ward off the evil eye. Inside the cabinet was a bezoar, also believed to be a powerful antidote to poison. Bezoars were highly popular and immensely expensive, the property of the very rich. Often set in gold and shaped like cannonballs, they are calcareous concretions formed in the stomachs of *Capra aegagrus*, a Persian goat. Initially extremely rare as their formation depended on the diet of their host, it was later possible to cultivate them like pearls inside furry oysters. Nothing was supposed to be as effective against poison as a bezoar, and no prince of great station would travel without at least one of them in his luggage. Other antidotes and aphrodisiacs contained in the cabinet included powerful and obscure substances such as a musk pouch, cups of *lignum Guaiacum* (a West Indian wood used for medical purposes) and a bowl and mug of *terra sigillata* (a fine clay thought to have magical properties).

Apart from mysterious substances and ancient coins and gems, the drawers also contained objects 'for vexation' such as a pair of gloves without an opening, a cup that one could not drink from and artificial fruit that could fool the hungry. There were anamorphoses, distorted pictures that could be viewed in proportion only when reflected in specially constructed mirrors, and mirrors that would distort the viewer's face. A beautiful pair of portrait pictures, a man and a woman, turned into grinning skulls when turned upside down, thus reinforcing the message that all pleasures and experiences afforded by the *Kunstschrank* were nothing but transient whispers in God's world to be used by the wise as insights into his wisdom and by the foolish as

diversions from his laws. There were also four pictures of heads composed out of fruit and other matter, and, hidden among the crystals crowning the cabinet, an automaton re-enacting an episode from the tenth book of Ovid's *Metamorphoses* in which the hunter Cyparissus is transformed into a tree after shooting a stag. As if this was not enough to dazzle the curious, a virginal concealed in the upper compartment would play one of three tunes when the cabinet was opened, or it would spring into motion every full hour the internal clockwork struck. Those disinclined to leave the automaton to making all the music by itself could take out the virginal and play melodies of their own invention.

Hainhofer's *Kunstschrank* was not just a container of the curious and the precious, it was also an encyclopaedia in objects, a programme of the world in microcosm, a *theatrum memoriae*, in which the individual parts illustrated their place in the great drama of God's mind. Less a piece of furniture than a metaphysical manifesto, it spoke eloquently of a world view dominated by the ideas of metamorphosis and hidden meanings. *Artificialia* and *naturalia* were demonstrated to be two aspects of the same, just as life and death could be seen to change in front of the beholder's eye. A hunter could be transformed into a tree just as a beautiful face could become a skull; ornaments were far from being pleasant only for the eye: they also served a deeper purpose by exerting healing powers and by functioning as allegories. The artist's craft could deceive the eye with enamel fruit and silver beetles, just as what seemed like vegetables in loose arrangement could reveal a portrait – nothing is as it seems, but a hidden order underlies it all.

While the intricate chests from which these new cabinets derived their names were allegories of the natural world and of the principles at work in it, the collection that took their names from them followed a similar programme. An illustration (1622) of the Museum of Francesco Calceolari in Verona displays a scene that is in turns grotesque and highly organized and allows the observer to step through centuries into the museum itself and into the mind that created it.

Stuffed animals are dangling from the ceiling: a porcupine seems to pounce on the visitor, a small leopard, snakes, moonfish, various sharks, a severed, misshapen human head and a crocodile all silently

menace the guest from the roof beams above. Below them, perching on a precipice formed by the top of the ornate shelving running round the room, are stuffed birds, among them a pelican, gulls and a penguin, as well as several animals, starfish and corals. The shelves themselves with their scrolling decoration are filled with shells, beakers and chalices and other precious containers, as well as various animal parts, such as the saw of a sawfish, antlers and snail houses. In the middle of the walls to either side are two statues set in niches, one of Atlas, the other of Minerva with full armour, helmet and shield. At the centre of the far wall, directly opposite the door, is a cabinet built into the wall, containing four rows of small compartments. Doric columns and a simple tympanum frame this inner sanctum. Two small obelisks and a mounted figure are standing on either side. A number of vases, other vessels and books are sorted near to the floor, and the shelves are intersected horizontally by a band of drawers containing cameos.

Calceolari's collection was close to the ideal of a cabinet of art and miracles, combining beauty with strangeness, classical form with riotous excess, scholarship with sheer curiosity. It is a repository of all that is bizarre and exotic (the sharks and crocodiles, the deformed head), all that is venerable (the vases and cameos), and of great and secret knowledge (the books stored below the central 'temple'). The statues and the structure on the middle wall demonstrate that there is order in this chaos, a mind pervading this precocious flourishing of strange forms: Atlas, the carrier of the world, symbolizes the very ambition of the collection to be a microcosm of everything knowable, everything he is supporting on his shoulder, while Minerva, goddess of wisdom, vouches for the fact that the intellect can and will rule over even those alien things and lands that the human mind is only just beginning to grasp. The wealth of the universe and the mind controlling it come together in the central temple and its resonances of ancient knowledge and harmony: the architecture of ancient Greece, and the obelisks, reminding the educated visitor of Egypt, an even more ancient civilization believed to have been in possession of the key to the wisdom of Hermetic philosophy, named after Hermes Trismegistus, the legendary Egyptian priest and teacher of Moses. Here scientific inquiry and the search for truth in alchemy and mysticism went hand in hand. What the scientific method, still in its infancy, could yield was to be used as material for an inquiry into the deeper nature of the universe, into the mind of God.

If Rudolf's collection was such a microcosm, it was so on an infinitely more ambitious scale. In order to contain the ever-growing possessions, the castle was expanded and transformed into a building site for much of his reign. Before taking up residence in Prague the emperor had already ordered the renovation of the living quarters, and then the construction of a summer palace, which he held to be more in keeping with his courtly life. In 1589, the castle was extended by the *Gangbau*, a two-storey gallery set against the old fortifications. New stables and a second large gallery, the Spanish Gallery, were also constructed, linked to the castle by the *Gangbau*. Meanwhile, in 1600, the emperor had taken up a new residence, a palazzo on Hradčany Square, which he had confiscated from Prince Lobkowitz. When it became evident that even this would not be sufficient to contain the collections, yet another building was started, containing stables and more galleries, most importantly, three vaulted rooms or *Gewölbe*. Here the emperor finally established his *Kunstkammer*, the main home of his treasures.

This was not a collection assembled for display. Some of its best and most spectacular pieces were locked up in cupboards and hidden from view by gilt leather boxes. The *Kunstkammer* was a very private universe, containing, among other precious things, a large gallery of paintings, drawings and prints; several Seychelles nuts; ivories and works in gold and silver; carved rhinoceros horns; numerous cups and beakers in precious stone and rock crystal as well as in glass; landscapes inlaid in agate and jasper; glass engraved with great personages and allegorical scenes; medals; exotic arms and armour, among them Japanese and Arabic pieces; works in wax; Islamic art and Mughal miniatures; Chinese porcelain; games and puzzles; bezoars and other items thought to possess magical qualities; globes, sextants, telescopes, compasses, planetaria, astronomical compendia and sundials, clocks, automata and other mechanical devices; books on architecture, astronomy and astrology; printed music and musical instruments that kept coming in from all corners of the Habsburg empire, and filling up every last corner and every inch of free space in the depth of Rudolf's vaults.

While he was an avid collector of antiquities, his great love in the arts was Mannerism, a style which favoured sophisticated posture and allegory over natural representation (Hainhofer's *Kunstschrank* is a Mannerist masterwork). His commissions to artists like Hans von Aachen, Bartholomäus Spranger and Giuseppe Archimboldo often reflect not only his taste in art, but also his legendary fondness for the pleasures of the flesh. Religious contemporaries condemned many of his paintings as immoral: *Cupid and Psyche*, *Neptune and Caenis*, *Joseph and Potiphar's Wife*, *Mars and Venus*, *Apollo and Venus*, *Satyrs and Nymphs*, *Bacchus*, *Ceres and Cupid*, *The Rape of the Sabine Women*, *The Rape of Ganymede*, *Two Satyrs and a Nymph*, *The Suicide of Lucretia*, *Venus and Adonis*, *Hercules and Omphale*, *Leda and the Swan* (the latter attempting to make anatomic sense of legend especially energetically and in many versions) – all good humanistic excuses for titillation and very close encounters.

Rudolf reflected his predilections for erotic themes in his private life. While obstinately refusing to make the advantageous marriage his court was pressing for on account of his belief that there were no women noble enough to be worthy of him (both the Infanta Isabella of Spain, the daughter of Philip II, and Maria de' Medici eventually despaired of his procrastination and accepted other suitors), his sexual exploits were famous, and according to rumour he did actually marry his mistress of long standing, Katharina Strada, in a secret ceremony. He had various illegitimate children from these relationships, but none of them rose to any distinction. Katharina alone bore Rudolf six children, three boys and three girls. Of the latter, one, Carolina of Austria, was recognized by him and was able to marry well. Two others were tucked away in nunneries. Two of his three sons died early, one in childhood and one in battle. The third, Rudolf's beloved Don Juan of Austria, had inherited the Habsburg madness. His sexual excesses, megalomania and Caesarist illusions made him a liability and, despite Rudolf's plans to give him a high office, he was eventually exiled to the imposing Krumlov Castle in southern Bohemia, where he killed a young girl and disfigured her corpse with his hunting knife. It cannot have been lost on Rudolf that he had been forced to act exactly like his uncle Philip had had to with his own son Don Carlos.

While Bartholomäus Spranger and Hans von Aachen were chief purveyors of Mannerist depictions of dubious mythological scenes and of portraits glorifying Rudolf in various heroic poses, the painter Archimboldo had a special place both at court and in the collection. During his stay at Prague, the Venetian artist was in charge not only of a large workshop turning out the grotesque images that made him famous, but he also planned and oversaw large-scale spectacles and celebrations drawing on the entire repertoire of courtly life: lavish banquets, large allegorical processions, painted backdrops, triumphal arches, live animals and fireworks. The emperor was always at the centre of the iconography, cast as a great ruler in the tradition of the Caesars and the great rulers of the Holy Roman Empire.

Archimboldo's paintings have survived, and are a testament to the spirit and the programme of Mannerism. The famous composite heads, symbolizing the four seasons or the four elements by taking objects associated with them and assembling them into an arrangement resembling a portrait, are more than just witty virtuoso pieces. They, too, state that nothing is as it appears, that changing perspectives can transform the random into the purposeful, the unknown into the familiar, a face into a bowl of fruit, that art could be nature and nature art. As in Hainhofer's *Kunstschrank*, the eye was easily deceived while the subtle and occult harmony of the universe stood revealed by the artist's hand. The artist's poetic insight bared the *disegno interno* underlying the divine creation, and this divinity itself was revealed to be an artist. The grotesque and the totality of excess were only the flipside of the simplicity of the eternal truth. The items in Rudolf's *Kunstkammer* bore witness to this conviction: somewhere in their staggering multiplicity and diversity lay hidden that kernel of eternal truth which the alchemists called the Philosopher's Stone. To find it would be to grasp the beating heart of creation itself. The collection itself became an instrument: the greatest alchemistic laboratory the world had ever seen.

For all the dazzling exoticism of the collection, Rudolf was no naïve lover of everything strange. He insisted that the bodies of birds of paradise (thought to be forever airborne as most specimens reached Europe without feet), be drawn and painted with legs, so that the fiction around the object was contrasted with the imagined reality. This scientific bent, though, did not prevent him from collecting magical objects, such as the Paracelsian zenexton, an amulet enclosed by a bejewelled gold case and containing a cake made of toads, virginal menstrual blood, white arsenic, orpiment, dittany, roots, pearls, coral and Eastern emeralds, the recipe for which appeared under imperial privilege in *Basilica chymica* (1609).

Rudolf was especially proud of his unicorns' horns, mandrakes and dragons, which so much impressed the court physician de Broodt that he made a drawing of one of them, adding 'this is the figure of a Dragon which the Emperor Rudolf II has; dried it is this exact size, where it is preserved'. The relics held in the vaults were characteristically not Christian but classical in orientation and included nails from Noah's ark, and the jaw of one of the sirens that Odysseus had encountered.

Among the books in Rudolf's library, symbolic knowledge figured prominently in works on Egyptian hieroglyphs, alchemical, magical and Rosicrucian tracts and other works investigating symbols, magical seals and emblems. It appears that the emperor was well read in this neo-Platonist literature. Other magical texts and books by Jewish Talmudic and cabbalistic scholars added to the library. Rudolf's interest in the magical arts went further than just inviting its practitioners to his court, for he himself was actively involved. In 1609, the Tuscan ambassador sniffed disdainfully, 'for he himself tries alchemical experiments and he himself is busily engaged in making clocks, which is against the decorum of a prince. He has transferred his seat from the imperial throne to the workshop stool'.[5]

Attracted by the emperor's reputation, the English occult scholar John Dee arrived in Prague in 1584. He had been adviser and astrologer to Queen Elizabeth I, had had an influential post at court and was in a good position to pursue his main ambition: to regain the perfect, primeval knowledge that Adam had had, which humankind had lost with the fall, and thus to understand the cryptic correspondences between all things and the universal core of truth contained in them. His hopes of achieving this goal were bound up in a mystic emblem, the *Monas hieroglyphica*, designed to elevate spirits through meditation of its mystical, geometrical and theological connotations. He quickly gained an audience with Rudolf, which lasted for a full hour. Dee outlined his method of gaining arcane knowledge and also told him, according to his own handwritten protocols:

It pleased God to send me *his Light*; and his holy Angels, for these two years and a half, have used to inform me: yea, they have brought me a *Stone* of that value that no earthly Kingdom is of that worthiness as to be compared to the vertue and dignity thereof, etc.

The Angel of the Lord hath appeared to me, and rebuketh you for your sins. If you will hear me, and believe me, you shall Triumph: if you will not hear me, The Lord, the God that made Heaven and Hearth, putteth his foot against your breast, and will throw you headlong down from your seat.

Moreover, the Lord hath made his covenant with me . . . If you will forsake your wickednesse, and turn unto him, your Seat shall be the greatest that ever was: and the Devil shall become your prisoner: Which Devil, I did conjecture, to be the Great Turk. This my Comission, is from God.[6]

The emperor was horrified by this message, and sceptical about the messenger, about the Great Turk and Dee's more personal motives for seeking to take charge of Rudolf's salvation. Dee was never again allowed to appear in front of the emperor and was banned from the Habsburg territories two years later.

As an intellectual approach to the mysteries of the universe, alchemy and magic were seen to be right at the cutting edge of a scientific method which had as yet no way of distinguishing between phenomena such as magnetism and other presumed 'sympathies' between substances, between the existence of iguanas and sea snakes already discovered and the lore of dragons that might still be awaiting discovery in lands as yet unreached. Natural magic, the pursuit of the *prisca theologica*, the first knowledge revealed to Adam and handed down in a hermetic tradition to Moses, Orpheus, Pythagoras and later *magi*, assumed that the key to the understanding of the world lay in deciphering the alphabet in which the universe was written at its creation. There are strong echoes of this in our modern preoccupation with the genetic code and the creative, indeed demiurgical, possibilities raised in understanding and controlling it. It is in itself no less strange than the assumption that all elements were constructed according to an occult 'genetic' code, and that unravelling and changing it would allow initiates to change mud into gold.

To the alchemists and the magicians of the sixteenth century, the dividing line between the natural and the occult was simply that natural phenomena were those that occurred most of the time, according to the 'habits of nature', and manifestly to the senses. Occult phenomena were those that differed from the norm, or those that were hidden from sensory perception. In accordance with this conception, gravity, magnetism and acoustic resonance were all counted among the occult phenomena, together with the *pneuma*, the spirit realm governing the object world, and with the symbols presumed capable of unlocking its secrets. In investigating these, the alchemists were scientists.[7]

The central notion in the alchemical conception of the world was the idea of *pneuma* or *spiritus mundi*, the invisible fluid medium world spirit that linked all elements and entities in the universe whose existence was accepted by scientists and thinkers as different from one another as the author of the *Anatomy of Melancholy*, Robert Burton, who described it as a 'most subtle vapour, which is expressed from the *Blood* and the instrument of the Soul, to perform all his Actions, a common type of *medium*, betwixt the Body and the soule,'[8] and Isaac Newton, who assumed the existence of an aether linking the sublunar realm to the cosmos. The *spiritus mundi* was everywhere, and it is indeed far from vanished from contemporary thinking. It has survived, though transformed, in the political and philosophical traditions of the nineteenth and twentieth centuries in the shape of Hegel's *Weltgeist*, the World Spirit realizing itself in history through the dialectic process; an idea taken up and developed not only by Marx, but also by other thinkers in the Hegelian tradition. Nationalism, the idea that the essence or destiny of a nation can be realized only if uncontaminated by foreign influences and allowed to flourish, is one aspect of Hegel's national spirits through which the World Spirit, the destiny of history, works its mysteries.

Collecting as a philosophical project, as an attempt to make sense of the multiplicity and chaos of the world, and perhaps even to find in it a hidden meaning, has also survived to our day, and we find echoes of Rudolf's elaborate alchemy in every attempt to capture the wonder and magnitude of everything around in the realm of personal possession. A record collector seeking the essence of genius in hundreds of recordings of the same concert or of the same artist continues this tradition in the same way as someone trying to capture beauty itself in everything that is 'rich and strange'[9] – a phrase, incidentally, from Rudolf's day. This practical alchemy is at work whenever a collection reaches beyond appreciating objects and becomes a quest for meaning, for the heart of the matter, a hope to be able to see a grammar if only enough words and phrases are brought together.

Rudolf's Mannerist universe complemented the course taken by Ulisse Aldrovandi and his fellow naturalists. And while, in the age-old opposition of all philosophy, the latter cast himself as a new Aristotle, the mystical orientation of Mannerists followed Platonic ideas. Giovanni Pico della Mirandola summed up this project in one phrase: '*Nam si homo est parvus mundus, utrique mundus est magnus homo*'[10] ('For as man is a small world, the world, by turns, is a large man').

Both the mystical and the critical method of collecting were responses to the challenge of recent discoveries and new horizons. The analytical, Aristotelian rhetoric of the high Renaissance seemed to provide the answer to some, while others found it wanting. They turned to the traditions of Hermetic knowledge promising the single, occult key to a multiplicity of problems. Among the opponents of such neo-Platonist collections, Sir Francis Bacon was particularly trenchant in his critique of the mystical hotchpotch of ideas and correspondences:

There is such a multitude and host as it were of particular objects, and lying so widely dispersed, as to distract and confuse the understanding; and we can therefore hope for no advantage from its skirmishing, and quick movements and incursions, unless we put its forces in due order and array by means of proper, and well arranged, and as it were living tables of discovery of these matters which are the subject of investigation, and the mind then apply itself to the ready prepared and digested aid which such tables afford.

When we have thus properly and regularly placed before the eyes a collection of particulars we must not immediately proceed to the investigation and discovery of new particulars or effects, or, at least, if we do so, must not rest satisfied therewith.[11]

Bacon was on the winning side. The scientists and philosophers, the pan-sophists, eirenists, Hermetists, neo-Stoics and neo-Platonists, Paracelseans and chiliasts were soon dismissed when rationalism began to provide more powerful and verifiable answers to many of the problems that had been exercising European thinkers. Rudolf's policies of balance and indecision, later distorted by paranoid wilfulness, were arguably an illustration of the powerlessness of these ideas to provide solutions to problems in the prosaic realm of human lives. For a brief period, however, the return to neo-Platonism and the search for the great idea seemed to contain the answer that found its expression in the most splendid collection of the period. Only in the twentieth century would the search for the Big Idea be taken up again, and again with catastrophic results.

As his collections, forever unable to satisfy his appetite, grew to legendary size, Rudolf the politician became an increasingly embattled and disputed figure. He had always been a complex man, oscillating between conscientious government and obsessive pursuit of his ideas, great moderation and phenomenal excess, between kindness and fits of rage, approachability and total withdrawal, generosity and paranoia.

During the later stages of his life conjecture and rumour abounded in the streets of Prague and at the courts of Europe as to the contents of the famous *Kunstkammer*, and about its owner's state of mind. As his passion had become known, princes had made it a point of honour, and of policy, to search their own palaces for the finest pieces to be sent to Rudolf. The ambassador from the Duke of Savoy, Carlo Francesco Manfredi, reported with delight that Rudolf had spent 'two and a half hours sitting motionless, looking at the painting of fruit and fish markets sent by Your Highness'.[12] The ambassador was not always so lucky with the emperor's changeable moods. During his second visit, he was made to wait a full nine months before being granted an audience and being allowed to present his gifts of friendship: 'an Indian dagger', a rhinoceros horn encrusted with rubies, three bezoars, 'a large silver ship that contained inside it half of an Indian nut, larger than a man's head', and a crown. This time, however, the bearer of gifts was treated to a tour around the collections, which was conducted by two servants (the emperor himself only showed round other crowned heads). He was especially impressed by a polished stone 'and in the vein of the stone "Christ" was written by nature's hand in big letters', he reported. Nature had spoken to the emperor through the stone.

Rudolf's collection and his widely reported 'ailment of melancholy' increasingly interfered with the business of state, sometimes making it well nigh impossible. Around the change of the century, just after the death of his uncle

Philip II in 1598, a crisis occurred. The emperor's mood swings worsened. When he heard that Isabella of Spain, tired by twenty years of fruitless negotiations, had decided to marry one of his brothers, he exploded in a fit of rage. Soon afterwards he dismissed two of his most trusted administrators, Wolf Rumpf and Paulus Sixt von Troutson. He also seems to have attempted committing suicide with curtain cords and splinters of glass. The emperor was confused and distrustful to the point of paranoia, refused to see petitioners, ministers and ambassadors, and relied for everything on a small group of lackeys and minor aristocrats of dubious stature who effectively constituted his government and held in their hands enormous power. Even the once highly trusted Spanish ambassador San Clemente, Rudolf's link to the court of his childhood and youth, could not gain an audience and was unable to catch a glimpse of the emperor for two years.

By 1600, Rudolf was a changed man and it was commonly believed that he had been bewitched by his enemies, but he could still impress foreign emissaries with his dignity, intellect and charm. The Venetian envoy Soranzo met the emperor in 1607. Rudolf, he said, was

. . . rather small in figure, of quite pleasing stature and relatively quick movements. His pale face, nobly formed forehead, fine wavy hair and beard and large eyes looking around with a certain forbearance, made a deep impression on all who met him. The Habsburg family likeness was evident in their largish lips which curled towards the right. There was nothing haughty in his comportment: he behaved rather shyly, avoided all noisy society and took no part in the usual amusements; jokes pleased him not, and only rarely was he seen to laugh.[13]

Despite being able to summon his old qualities at times, Rudolf was increasingly beleaguered by religious and political problems, and his days as an even remotely effective ruler were now numbered. His politics had long been hostage to his indecision and to the hatred he felt for Matthias, his ambitious brother who had forged strong alliances with Protestant and Hungarian nobles. Soon, brother stood against brother, and Matthias swiftly consolidated his advantage by marching into Prague. In an effort to avert his downfall Rudolf, no longer in command of the political situation and manipulated by his entourage, put his fate in the hands of his 23-year-old nephew,

Leopold, who was charged with opposing Matthias. Prague was in a state of civil war, with plundering troops ravaging the Old Town and the Jewish Quarter. At the critical moment, when Matthias approached with his own forces, Leopold's mercenaries abandoned the town and left Rudolf to see his brother crowned King of Bohemia, while he himself was granted an annuity and the ceremonial title of emperor. Having lost all power, he finally had the solitude he craved. But this last period of his life lasted for less than two years, and he died on 20 January 1612. His grand experiment of collecting as practical alchemy had come to an end once and for all.

An Ark Abducted

Few men have changed the way England looks today more comprehensively and with less acknowledgement than John Tradescant the Elder (*c.* 1570–1638), gardener to the Duke of Buckingham and founder of what became known as Tradescant's Ark. His legacy lives on in parks and country lanes, in gardens and in city squares: the horse chestnut, lilac, plane trees, larch, acacia, tulip trees and Virginia Creeper were all imported first by this indefatigable horticulturist, traveller and collector.

Tradescant's first employment was as gardener to Lord Robert Cecil at Hatfield House, where he not only planned the gardens, but also stocked them with plants gathered on his journeys to various European cities. As if this were not enough, he was also required to do odd jobs such as 'setting a pair of soles upon your Lordship's pompes', as his accounts reveal.[1] Indeed, even his employer seems to have felt pity for him at times. One entry in the household book reads: 'To John Tradescant the poor fellow that goeth to London 2s 6d.'

Cecil, Privy Councellor, Secretary of State and Lord Treasurer, was one of the most powerful men of his age. His prestige and immense fortune were mirrored in those of his house and park, which he acquired in 1607 and enlarged to reflect his status. Tradescant himself was sent to the Low Countries in order to procure more plants and set out in 1611, in his pocket six pounds in cash and a small fortune in bills of exchange. He sent back rare plants by the hundred (one shipment contained, among many flowers, fruit trees and other plants, 800 tulip roots, another 400 lime tree saplings), running up enormous costs, which were paid, apparently without demur, by His Lordship.

The European tour was not exclusively devoted to the purchase of plants. From the Low Countries Tradescant travelled on to Rouen, where he bought an 'artyfyshall byrd' for his master. It is quite possible that he visited some of the collections in Amsterdam and in Leiden, where the university had not only a *hortus botanicus* ('botanical garden'), but also the famous *theatrum anatomicum* ('anatomical theatre'), which later flourished into a fully-fledged cabinet of curiosities and university museum. In addition to seeing the botanical gardens and indoor collections he is unlikely to have missed the opportunity to visit some of France's famous parkscapes. Eventually Tradescant had to return to Hatfield, chalking up on the ferry from Gravesend to London one shilling 'to the boyes of the ship to be Carefull of the trees'.

While the garden at Hatfield was rapidly becoming one of the richest and most beautiful in England, the king himself, James I, took great interest in another of Tradescant's discoveries brought to his attention by his faithful Lord Cecil: among the plants imported from Rouen were mulberries, which, it struck the monarch, might be the beginning of a very profitable line in silk production. The Secretary of State, incidentally, had a patent on the importation of the trees and promised not to take more than a penny per plant, of which more than a million were to be imported every year. The scheme, which would have paid Cecil amply for his generosity towards his gardener, came to nothing, but to this day many of England's older gardens still contain ancient mulberry trees as silent witnesses to the ingenious but stillborn plan.

The double responsibility of Secretary of State and Lord Treasurer proved too much for the fragile constitution of Tradescant's master, and in early 1611 the 'crook-backed earl', then forty-eight, found his health collapsing under the strain of his duties. A laconic entry in the Tradescant's Hatfield accounts for April that year tells the remainder of the story: 'for mowing of the Coorts and East Gardyn against the funerall 4s'. Robert Cecil, Earl of Essenden, never saw the completion of his garden or his house.

Tradescant was passed on to William Lord Salisbury, his former employer's son, and continued working at Hatfield and the other estates inherited by his new master, but in 1615 he accepted the employ of Lord Wotton at Canterbury, in whose service he went to Russia as botanist to a diplomatic party. He kept a journal during this expedition, in which he recorded not only the course of the journey ('being Inglishe and strangers 7 sayls bound for Archangell'), but also the customs and of course the plants of his Russian hosts, remarking among other things: 'For ther streets they be paved with goodli timber trees, cleft in the midell, for they have not the use of sawing in the land, spedtiali in that part whear I was, neyther the use of planing with the plane, but onlie with the shave,' an image still vivid in the great Russian novels of the nineteenth century. On leaving Archangel the English party fired a salute with their ships' cannon, thanking their hosts for the hospitality they had received. One of the cannon was unfortunately loaded and ripped a large hole in a harbourside house, leaving the hosts 'gaping and in great perplexity'.

Tradescant, unfaltering plant collector that he was, found botanical specimens to bring back to England. In addition, a second interest now gripped him. Years later, his son published the *Musaeum Tradescantianum* (1656), which contains entries to remind us of his father's expedition: 'A Russian vest; Boots from Russia; Boots from Muscovy; Duke of Muscovy's vest wrought with gold upon the breast and arms; Shoes from Russia shod with iron; Shoes to walk on snow without sinking; Russian stockings without heels; Boots from Lapland.' Tradescant's interests were no longer confined to plants or to observing the living arrangements of other countries: he had become a collector of foreign rarities, and while the living specimens were tended to in the gardens and greenhouses under his care, the other objects became part of an ever-growing collection of curiosities, which, in time, would make his name just as much as his horticultural skills.

While John Tradescant laboured in gardens and on foreign expeditions, his son, John the Younger, was attending the King's School, Canterbury, where he received an education superior to his father's, and was already helping with his work. The boy cannot have seen much of him, as the elder Tradescant was enlisted in 1620 on a mission to hunt down the Corsairs of Barbary, Algerian pirates threatening the trade routes of the Mediterranean. This sudden enthusiasm for naval warfare was not as dramatic a career change for the gardener as it may seem, for he was drawn to volunteer not by the promise of battle and the spoils of war, but by accounts of a wonderful golden apricot that was to be found in Algiers. There might be a war on, he decided, but the opportunity of bringing back a rare and delicate fruit was simply too good to miss.

From the horticultural point of view (not a perspective taken, incidentally, by the captain of the vessel, who was sceptical about taking this expert on European flora on combat duty) the journey was a resounding success. The captain's collection, too, was swelled by Tradescant's unscheduled exploits. He was able to bring back plants and artefacts from Portugal, Spain, the southern coast of France, Rome, Naples, the Greek Islands and Constantinople (where he picked up lilac) before even reaching Algiers, and from Mount Carmel, Damascus, Alexandria, Crete and Malta on the way back. The later *Musaeum Tradescantianum* lists, in the orthographically more orthodox spelling of John the Younger: '*Barbary* Spurres pointed sharp like a Bodkin, A *Moores* Cap, A *Portugall* habit, 2 Roman Urnes, An *Arabian* vest, and Divers sorts of Egges from *Turkie*: one *given* for a Dragons Egge.'

John Tradescant the Elder had made a great reputation for himself and it is hardly surprising that he was snapped up by another man who had made his own fortune: George Villiers, Duke of Buckingham, the royal favourite who had charmed himself from a relatively humble background into the high nobility and a position of great power. For the horticulturist and his son, Buckingham's gardens were a new challenge: whole avenues had to be planted and plants imported on a lavish scale from overseas. Indeed, trees and flowers were not His Lordship's only pleasure. On 31 July 1625, John Tradescant wrote to Edward Nicholas, Secretary to the Admiralty:

Noble Sir

I have Bin Comanded By My Lord to Let Yr Worshipe Understand that It Is H[is] Graces Plesure that you should In His Name Deall with All Marchants from All Places But Espetially the Virgine & Bermewde & Newfownd Land Men that when they Into those Parts that they will take Care to furnishe His Grace Withe all maner of Beasts & fowells and Birds Alyve or If Not Withe Heads Horns Beaks Clawes Skins Gethers Slipes or Seeds Plants Trees or Shrubs Also from Gine or Binne or Senego Turkye Espetially to Sir Thomas Rowe Who is Leger At Constantinoble Also to Captain Northe to the New Plantation towards the Amasonians

With All thes fore Resyted Rarityes & Also from the East Indes Withe Shells Stones Bones Egge-shells With what Cannot Com Alive My Lord having heard of the Dewke of Sheveres & Partlie seene of His Strang Fowlls Also from hollond of Storks A payre or two of yong ons Withe Divers kinds of Ruffes Whiche they theare Call Campanies this Having Mad Bould to present My Lords Comand I Desire Yr fortherance. Yr Asured Servant to Be Comanded til he is John Tradescant
Newhall this 31 of July 1625

To the Marchants of the Ginne Company & the Couldcost Mr. Humfrie Slainy Captain Crispe & Mr. Clobery & Mr. John Wood cape marchant.
   The things Desyred from those parts Be theese in primis on Ellophants head with the teeth In it very larg
on River horsses head of the Bigest kind that can be gotten on Seacowes head of the bigest that Can be Gotten on Seabulles head withe hornes of All ther strang sorts of fowelles & Birds Skines and Beakes Leggs & phetheres that be Rare or Not knowne to us
of All sorts of strng fishes skines or those parts the Greatest sorts of shellfishes shelles of Great flying fishes & sucking fishes withe what Els strang of the habits weapons & Instruments of ther Ivory Long fluts
of All sorts of Serpents and snakes Skines & Espetially of that sort that hathe a Combe on his head Lyke a Cock
of All sorts of ther fruts Dried As ther tree Beanes Littill Red & Black In their Cods whithe what flower & seed Can be Gotten the flowers Layd Betwin paper leaves In a Book Dried
of All sorts of Shining Stones or of Any Strang Shapes
Any thing that Is strang[2]

Any thing that Is strang. It may be assumed that Buckingham had seen Tradescant's already considerable collection of curiosities and liked what he saw. He was in the process of furnishing a house at Newhall and was looking for interesting objects to join the works by Michelangelo, da Vinci, Holbein, Raphael and Rubens, the antiquities and other precious pieces already in his possession. Tradescant was to be his agent, or one of them, as Buckingham had several scouring the world for treasures. The ducal director of gardens was by now living in South Lambeth, a relatively convenient place from which to keep an eye on his employer's various properties, and for keeping in touch with ships docking in London bringing new and exotic items into the country.

Buckingham's star was at its zenith. It was to plummet even faster than it had risen. On his way back to London in 1627, after a bungled effort to relieve the Huguenots at La Rochelle, the formerly English port on the French mainland reoccupied by France, he was assassinated. Tradescant, once again without an employer, quickly found himself appointed to his most prestigious post yet as Keeper of His Majesty's Gardens, Vines and Silkworms at Oatlands in Surrey, twenty miles from his home. While administering the royal gardens the Tradescants proceeded to order their own collection, to breed and classify the plants they had, and set forth on their great enterprise whose very name testified to their ambition: Tradescant's Ark.

This museum was to become famous all over Europe; later no educated traveller would visit London without knocking at its door. One of these pilgrims, a merchant captain by the name of Peter Mundy, recorded his impressions after a visit in 1636:

Having Cleired with the Honourable East India Company, whose servant I was, I prepared to goe downe to my friends in the Countrey . . . In the meane tyme I was invited by Mr. Thomas Barlowe (whoe went into India with my Lord of Denbigh and returned with us on the Mary) to view some rarities att John Tredescans, soe went with him and one friend more, there wee spent the whole day in peruseings and that superficially, such as hee had gathered together, as beasts, fowle, fishes, serpents, wormes (reall, although dead and dryed), pretious stones and other Armes, Coines, shells, fethers, etts. Of sundrey Nations, Countries, forme, Colours; also diverse Curiosities in Carvinge, painteinge, etts., as 80 faces carved on a Cherry stone, Pictures to bee seene by a Celinder which otherwise appeare like confused blotts, Medals of Sondrey sorts, etts. Moreover a little garden with divers outlandish herbes and flowers, whereof some that I had not seene elsewhere but in India, being supplyed by Noblemen, Gentlemen, Sea Commaunders, etts. With such Toyes as they could bring or procure from other parts. Soe that I am almost perswaded a Man might in one day behold and collecte into one place more Curiosities than hee should see if hee spent all his life in Travell.[3]

Mundy, incidentally, took the time to visit other sights in London, among which was a 'unicorn's horn' on exhibition in the Tower of London. While the Ark in Lambeth could, like its biblical antecedent, boast 'beasts, fowle, fishes, serpents' and 'wormes', unicorns were the pick of the desirable creatures and among the first of all objects of curiosity. In his *History of Four-Footed Beasts*, Edward Topsell described its curious habits: 'It is sayd that Unicorns above all other creatures, doe reverence Virgines and young Maides, and that many times at the sight of them they growe tame, and come and sleepe beside them, for there is in their nature a certaine savor, wherewithall the Unicornes are allured and delighted.'[4] Tradescant, aware of the fact that he was lacking a unicorn's horn for his collection, managed to get his hands on one himself, even though he catalogued it, with a confusion characteristic for his time, as *Unicornu marinum*, 'sea unicorn'.

A visitor from Nuremberg, Georg Christoph Stirn, paid a visit in 1638, the year of John Tradescant the Elder's death. Among the items described by the German traveller were:

The hand of a mermaid, the hand of a mummy, a very natural wax hand under glass . . . a picture wrought in feathers, a small piece of wood from the cross of Christ . . . pictures from the church of S. Sophia in Constantinople copied by a Jew into a book . . . many Turkish and foreign shoes and boots, a toad-fish, an elk's hoof with three clawes, a human bone weighing 42 lbs, an instrument used by the Jews in circumcision, the robe of the King of Virginia . . . a S. Francis in wax under glass . . . a scourge with which Charles V is said to have scourged himself . . .[5]

The young Tradescant carried on his father's work, both on the Lambeth estate and as Keeper of His Majesty's Gardens. He went as far as Virginia to collect plants and rarities for the Ark. Under Cromwell's rule he was left to his own devices, something that must have relieved a man whose family was so closely allied to court and nobility.

One man became a regular visitor to the Tradescant Ark: Elias Ashmole, a lawyer, gentleman scientist and passionate collector. He cultivated John the Younger, wining and dining him and drawing up his horoscope, inviting him to see witches tried at the Assizes, financing the publication of the *Musaeum Tradescantianum*, and even contributing various gifts to his new friend's collection. Ashmole was well connected and it was easy for him to gain John's ear. The Ark, he told the collector, should be preserved for posterity, well beyond the life of either himself or his wife, Hester. These words reverberated in John the Younger's mind when his own son, John, heir to the family enterprise, suddenly died in 1652 and was buried next to his grandfather.

Elias Ashmole was at hand with advice and good counsel. He was concerned for John and Hester in their grief, and for the collection, for their legacy. Little by little he warmed them to the idea that only he had the means and the connections to ensure its survival. Finally, in 1659, he noted in his diary that the couple 'at last had resolved to give it unto me'.[6] He quickly moved to finalize the arrangement with a document signed in front of witnesses. Hester would later protest that there had been no time even to read what was stipulated in it, but Ashmole would pour scorn on this idea. The collection would be his, purchased for a symbolic shilling.

Once she had recovered from the shock, Hester used all her cunning to make the deed undone, to make her husband understand that he had signed over all his possessions to a false friend without knowing the consequences. The deed was in her possession (she had tricked Ashmole into giving it to her), and she cut off the seal. John resolved not to think of the matter any longer. In his will he bequeathed his rarities 'to my dearly beloved wife Hester Tradescant during her naturall life, and after her decease I give and bequeath the same to the Universities of Oxford or Cambridge, to which of them she shall think fit'. On 22 April 1662, he followed his father to the family grave. The inscription on the tombstone in the graveyard of St Mary at Lambeth reads:

> Know, stranger, ere thou pass, beneath this stone,
> Lye John Tradescant, grandsire, father, son,
> The last dy'd in his spring, the other two
> Liv'd till they had travell'd Orb and Nature through,

As by their choice Collections may appear,
Of what is rare, in Land, in sea, in air;
Whilst they (as Homer's Illiad in a nut)
A world of wonders in one closet shut,
These famous antiquarians that had been
Both Gardiners to the Rose and Lily Queen,
Transplanted now themselves, sleep here: and when
Angels shall with their trumpets waken men,
And fire shall purge the world, these three shall rise
And change this Garden then for Paradise.

This, of course, was not the end of it, and for Hester Tradescant
paradise seemed far away. Ashmole was well aware what a prize lay
in his grasp. By now a barrister, a Windsor Herald and a Fellow of the
Royal Society, he also knew that there were ways of securing it for
himself. He took the newly widowed Hester to court at the Chancery,
where the case would be heard by the Lord Chancellor, Lord Clarendon, whom Ashmole knew from his position as Windsor Herald. The
case was found in his favour and it was decided that he was 'to have
and enjoy all and singular the said books, coins, medals, stones,
pictures, mechanics and antiquities'. Unwilling to let go once he had
won, Ashmole continued to humiliate his friend's widow with all
means at his disposal, which included bringing a suit of libel against
her, forcing her to acknowledge publicly 'that I have very much
wronged Elias Ashmole, Esquire, by several false, scandalous, and
defamatory speeches, reports, and otherwise, tending to the diminu-
ation and blemishing of his reputation and good name'. The document
goes on listing in the greatest detail a number of complaints against
her to which she now confessed.[7] On 4 April 1678, Ashmole noted in
his diary: 'My wife told me, Mrs Tredescant was found drowned in
her pond. She was drowned the day before about noon, as appeared
by some circumstances.' He had finally destroyed the woman who had
almost succeeded in preventing him from securing the greatest prize
of his career. As Hester was buried in the family tomb, Ashmole lost
no time in removing the collection from the Tradescant house, starting
with the family portraits. He later modestly resolved to give the
collection to Oxford University, where parts of it can be seen still

today, in the museum named after him. The Ashmolean Museum should by rights be the Tradescantian Museum. It is ironic that Hester Tradescant, too, had the intention of bequeathing the collection to Oxford.

The Exquisite Art of Dr Ruysch

From the wonders of nature is the nearest intelligence and passage towards the wonders of art: for it is no more but by following and as it were hounding Nature in her wanderings, to be able to lead her afterwards to the same place again.

Francis Bacon, *Of the Proficience and Advancement of Learning Divine and Human*[1]

The boy watches the proceedings with great attentiveness. Unlike the other figures in the painting he is not dressed in black, but in a brown jacket with green trimmings, a chestnut waistcoat and a lace collar, which is slightly stained. He holds a cap under his left arm. His right hand is placed lightly but protectively around a delicate, wooden pedestal. Mounted on this is a small skeleton frozen in a gesture that seems half dance, half blessing. The boy's auburn curls are in stark contrast to the tiny skull, its fontanelle still unclosed. To the boy's right, around a table, stands a dignified group of burghers, doctors all, in the black clothes of Calvinist piety, a corona of heads with flowing hair and white lace collars. One of them is bending forwards, almost tenderly, over the bundle on the table: the corpse of a newborn child.

It is the hands that make this picture; by no means unconventional in their elegant and unnatural delicacy, as we know them from innumerable portraits, pointing to whatever is deemed significant of the sitter: an open book perhaps for a scholar, a map for a geographer, a bible for a pious merchant, an instrument for a musician, or a skull

for everyone wishing to acknowledge publicly the transitoriness of his good fortune, thus adding modesty and contemplation to his already considerable attributes. The hands in this painting are themselves allegorical. The boy, his gaze fixed on the adults, points to the little skeleton in front of him, while one surgeon extends a graceful hand towards the dissected infant and another points out the placenta lying next to it. Only one figure shows both of his hands: the man next to the boy, dressed in plain, almost clerical, clothes, and wearing a hat. Poised between the thumb and index finger of his left hand is the dead infant's umbilical cord, while the right is directed palm upwards towards the bystanders. This is Dr Frederik Ruysch (1638–1731), the great embalmer and anatomist, founder of one of the most extraordinary collections Europe has seen. The boy by his side is his own son, Hendrik, who was already twenty years old at the time of the painting, but was depicted as an embodiment of innocence, a poignant link between the infant corpse and the adult physicians, a beautiful child personifying his father's abiding preoccupations with youthful grace, with purity and with *vanitas*.

Anatomy lessons were favoured genre pieces made to order for surgeons' guilds eager to dignify a profession in the process of emerging from the shadows, the backrooms of barbers' shops, into the radiance of science and of the Academy, and, with this canvas, the Amsterdam guild honoured a master of great renown. When it was painted, in 1683, Ruysch was a famous man, Praelector of Anatomy at the Surgeons' Guild of Amsterdam and Professor of Botany at the Leiden *hortus botanicus*.

Anatomists and others daring to make the human body not only subject but also object of the collecting passion have staged some of the most dramatic productions in the theatre of memories. While collectors in Italy dramatized nature and art, and while Rudolf II acted out his own inclination towards melancholy as a cosmic drama, the men pictured in this group portrait and those who shared their passion went further than anybody else by putting on stage the last frontier of an increasingly secular world: mortality. By collecting and investigating parts of human bodies in the name of science they dropped, reluctantly at times, the last mediation between the human condition and the material world by focusing on the fact that bodies could themselves be objects, dead matter. Always in part a striving for eternity, for memory, and for transcending death, collecting was put before the public here more naked than at any other time. Public dissections of criminals were seen as a recognized form of entertainment and as part of the sentence spoken over them, a posthumous punishment, part grizzly spectacle, part moral drama, part revelation, and were performed throughout Europe.

The dissections they were based on often were dramatically and highly staged occasions held in a *theatrum anatomicum*, hence the modern term 'operating theatre'. On an early seventeenth-century engraving we see a dissection at Leiden University. The circular theatre is lit by scented candles, and members of the expectant public are jostling for space in the galleries while in the first row ambassadors and members of the nobility are protecting themselves from the smells with their fine handkerchiefs. A young nobleman in the foreground looks on, his dog seemingly waiting for whatever may come his way. Herbs are scattered on the ground to mask unpleasant odours. On a table in the centre of the room is the body of a criminal, just cut from the gallows. The anatomist points into his already emptied ribcage. Three skulls arranged around the base of the table set the moral tone, which is taken up by a skeleton presiding over the proceedings.

The anatomists of Calvinist Holland had happily accommodated themselves with their Church; dissections were seen as a valuable moral lesson, and executed criminals and paupers who had drowned in the canals (a common occurrence in a city without street lights) provided ample material for the practice of their art. Most universities and major cities throughout Europe had public dissections of their own – though medical men (famously in Edinburgh) often had to rely on body-snatchers for a steady supply of specimens.

The anatomical demonstrations were supplemented by experiments with microscopes and by debates on medical and moral questions, all of which could be attended by the paying public. The revenues from all this edifying activity paid for a banquet for the surgeons. Ruysch was the most important anatomist of his time and by his death at the age of ninety-three he had conducted more than thirty public dissections.

The inevitability of decay limited these occasions to the cold season. In summer, no cadaver could be left lying open for any length of time without nauseating the public with its stench. During the summer months the anatomy theatre was therefore transformed into a cabinet of rarities. The Leiden *theatrum anatomicum* was supplemented by an *ambulacrum* (pleasure walkway) or *hortus botanicus*, a physic garden featuring a large number of exotic animals shivering in the inclement Dutch climate and lending some oriental splendour to their sober surroundings of canals and brick façades. The cabinet of rarities of the anatomy theatre constituted a Calvinist parable on existence in this vale of tears, a Museum of Mortality for the edification of students and burghers alike. Six human skeletons, taken from executed criminals, stood on the visitors' galleries, holding placards admonishing the visitors: *Memento mori*; *Homo bulla*; *Pulvis et umbra sumus* ('Remember you must die'; 'Man is a soap bubble'; 'We are but dust and shadow'). Today this theatre stands reconstructed in the Museum Boerhaave in Leiden, the very place where it used to be, and the visitor can gauge the sense of foreboding and of drama standing amid the steeply rising rows of spectators, which are almost overwhelmed by the skeletal messengers on its crown: a rider of the Apocalypse mounted on a horse, other figures seemingly dancing around the imaginary assembly of dignitaries, grinning mockingly at their stubborn adherence to life and its accoutrements of status, wealth and faith. There were other exhibits around the theatre in its heyday. The label appended to one of the criminals' skeletons thus allowed to play a constructive role in God's world, at least posthumously, read *The skeleton of an English pirate whose body was dissected in 1615 when the dissector was the Honourable Doctor Sebastian Egberts.*

Then, as now, an entire skeletal Garden of Eden is spread before the eyes of the reluctant public: a cow, a rat, a ram and a swan, an eagle with gilt talons, and, in the middle of it all, Adam and Eve standing beside a tree. The theatre also displayed the rearticulated bones of a sheep-stealer from Haarlem, a woman strangled for theft, and, with dramatic flourish, *The Sceleton of an Asse upon which sits a Woman that Killed her Daughter* near to *The sceleton of a man, sitting upon an ox executed for Stealing Cattle.* After 1620, this three-dimensional *vanitas* tableau was expanded into a true cabinet of curiosities, featuring, apart from the preaching skeletons, a Japanese teapot, Chinese scrolls and African plants, as well as engravings of historical, scientific and philosophical subjects. With the rise of archaeology, Roman sacophargi and Egyptian mummies also went on display. The exhibits were situated throughout the building, and in no particular order. The entrance hall, for instance, featured an elephant's head and, according to the English version of the catalogue, which was published first in

1669, 'a pair of stilts or skates with which the Norwegians, Laplanders and Finlanders run down high snowy mountaines, with almost an incredible swift pace' – a pair of skis.

The *theatrum anatomicum* and the art of the anatomical artist flourished at a time when people were constantly confronted with mortality and were only just discovering the wondrous workings of the human body. In art at least, mortality was imbued with grace and moral purpose and the all-pervading power of Universal Reason was revealed.

Medical knowledge and the art of the still life convene in illustrations  of anatomical atlases of the time: skeletons are holding hourglasses and have one foot, literally, in the grave, *écorchés* ('flayed bodies') hold their own skin as a reminder of mortality or assume the heroic poses of classical antiquity, while others muse over their own internal secrets, holding open with graceful fingertips their abdominal walls or the skin covering the muscles of their back. In one of them, Cowper's *Anatomy*, we find an early piece of medical humour: a vignette of putti at play occurring throughout the text. Only a closer look reveals that the chubby little ones are engaged in the vivisection of a dog struggling to get free.

As with all art, the history of anatomy shows not only what is depicted, but also how it was seen. Anatomical prints from the seventeenth and eighteenth centuries are vivid illustrations not just of the workings of the human body; they also show the mentality of an age in which science was still supposed to reveal the mysteries of divine creation and to demonstrate the beauty and wonderment inherent in all creatures. They also have to be read as still lives, as allegories. A celebrated plate by Albinus shows a skeleton in front of a ruin amid lush foliage. Behind the body standing there in classical contra-post and eloquent pose is a rhinoceros, peacefully grazing from the shrubs.

The inclusion of such an animal into an anatomical atlas makes little sense without the knowledge that medieval bestiaries had associated the rhino with melancholia, rendering this plate another meditation on the transience of human life. Like a dissection an anatomical atlas was a lesson in morals, theology, aesthetics – and medicine.

The life's work of Dr Frederik Ruysch was very much in the spirit of the anatomico-theological exhibits in the museum at Leiden, his home town. He was best known not for his knowledge and adroit public demonstrations, but for his almost superhuman skill in the preser-vation and presentation of human beauty after death. According to a secret method of embalming, developed over many years, he could transform any corpse into a state of timeless peacefulness. He applied this method not to adults, though, but to the bodies of small children, which he would procure from local midwives and, in his capacity as Physician to the Court, from babies drowned in Amster-dam's harbour.

These corpses of the unfortunate and the sick would be turned by Ruysch into objects of aesthetic marvel: an infant hand, exquisitely clad in a lace sleeve made by the good doctor's daughter, Rachel (who would later become a famous painter), holding the tissue of an eye socket in elegant repose, encased in a glass jar and filled with alcohol, little faces in quiet repose or with open, glass eyes, both preserved in jars or embalmed and laid out in little beds, sophisticated arrangements of brains and genitalia, all surrounded by fine needlework that served to hide the anatomist's incisions, stitches and gashes, which would have destroyed the illusion of eternal peace.

There were pathological preparations, too, as in every medical collection, but Ruysch's true passion was what he called his *konst*, his 'art', the union between medicine and sculpture, embalming and allegory, science and beauty. He proudly displayed his collection to colleagues and to other visitors. A German doctor was greatly impressed by

the 'mummy' of an eight-year-old boy, and in 1715 a Hungarian student of theology was given the tour of the collection and heard of a Russian prince who had been so touched by the sight of an embalmed twelve-year-old boy that he had kissed the dead body. Another embalmed child stood upright with its eyes open as if it was still living, and despite his stay of three hours the student decided that he would have had to stay three whole days in order to admire all of Ruysch's works in detail.

Ruysch's programme was more ambitious than a mere play with the rare and the exotic. His *chefs-d'œuvre* were much more elaborate arrangements, which eloquently bespoke his intentions and beliefs. The poignancy of death and rebirth, of excess and *vanitas* are all embodied here.

The Dutch historian of medicine, Antonie Luyendijk-Elshout, analysed one of these tableaux and gives a vivid sense of their composition and their purpose:

With eye sockets turned heavenward the central skeleton – a fœtus of about four months – chants a lament on the misery of life. 'Ah Fate, ah bitter Fate!' it sings, accompanying itself on a violin, made of an osteomyelitic sequester with a dried artery for a bow. At its right, a tiny skeleton conducts the music with a baton, set with minute kidney stones. In the right foreground a stiff little skeleton girdles its hips with injected sheep intestines, its right hand grasping a spear made of the hardened *vas deferens* of an adult man, grimly conveying the message that its first hour was also its last. On the left, behind a handsome vase made of the inflated *tunica albuginae* of the *testis*, poses an elegant little skeleton with a feather on its skull and a stone coughed up from the lungs hanging from its hand. In all likelihood the feather is intended to draw attention to the ossification of the cranium. For the little horizontal skeleton in the foreground with the familiar mayfly on its delicate hand, Ruysch chose a quotation from the Roman poet Plautus, one of the favourite authors of this period, to the effect that its lifespan had been as brief as that of young grass felled by the scythe so soon after sprouting.[2]

All of these tableaux were proclaiming the message of the transience of life, and of the dangers of sin lurking behind every corner.

Ruysch had taken a proud tradition to its logical conclusion: sculptors followed the intricate shapes of their material by using corals and constructing allegorical tableaux, and the famous G. G. Zumbo, the same eighteenth-century wax sculptor who made exquisitely beautiful models for the instruction of medical students in Florence and Vienna, also created allegorical tableaux of tiny wax bodies contemplating human mortality in all its forms, with sarcophagi and elaborate baroque tombs, skulls and chubby infants prematurely taken by the reaper, with titles such as *Funeral, The Plague* and *The Triumph of Time*.

Few of the works of Frederik Ruysch survive today, and almost none in Leiden. The reason for this anomaly is the visit of the 'Russian prince' who had come to see the collection and was so moved by it that he kissed the embalmed body of a boy. The prince had arrived in the Netherlands for the first time as one Pjotr Mikhailov, a simple carpenter seeking work and instruction in the shipyards of Amsterdam. He was intent on keeping a low profile, but this was made difficult by his sheer height, for he stood six foot seven in his heavy boots and towered over the other carpenters like a man-o'-war over a posse of Dutch barges. He was, of course, Tsar Peter the Great (1672–1725), who had come to western Europe with his 'Great Embassy' in 1697–8. When his imposing presence rendered his incognito useless, he became less concerned about preserving his anonymity.

Peter was a voracious collector not only of tools and objects of natural history, but also of natural oddities and freaks. In his *Kunstkamera* in St Petersburg he kept a live exhibit, Foma the Dwarf, who had only two digits on his claw-like hands and feet. Another such attraction, a hermaphrodite, who had been paid an annual stipend of twenty rubles, finally ran away from the impertinently gawking onlookers and from the company of less lively exhibits such as the skeleton of Peter's personal footman, Nicholas Bourgeois, who had been a giant of seven foot and, after his death, was to grace his master's collection as an anatomical specimen.

The first great collector in Russian history, Peter had inherited the former Russian cabinet of curiosities, a small assembly of the usual narwhale's horn, a reliquary plundered from a German town by Ivan the Terrible, and 'a few animals and some Lapp sleighs'.[3] Within

a few years he had turned this modest array of objects into a private museum capable, according to the curator, of filling thirty rooms with just the items kept in storage alone, including exotic animals, monstrosities, arms, tools, ethnographic items and gifts from foreign ambassadors. Later, in 1715 and 1716, it was to be swelled further by two gifts of Scythian gold treasures found in Siberia. Peter, with his relentless modernizing drive, famously the nemesis of Bojar beards, however, was not content to keep these riches enclosed and unseen by all: they were to be an instruction to everyone, and so the collection was opened to the public in 1714 with orders to keep out the rabble, but to serve the better class of visitor, aristocrats and foreigners, with vodka and other refreshments.

In establishing his collection, Peter had, true to his motto, sought instruction from the best, and it was the German philosopher Leibnitz who advised the monarch about what to buy and how to compose his possessions:

Concerning the Museum and the cabinets and *Kunstkammern* pertaining to it, it is absolutely essential that they should be such as to serve not only as objects of general curiosity, but also a means to the perfection of the arts and sciences . . . Such a cabinet should contain all significant things and rarities created by nature and man. Particularly needed are stones, metals, minerals, wild plants, and their artificial copies, animals both stuffed and preserved . . . Foreign works to be acquired should include diverse books, instruments, curiosities and rarities . . . In short, all that could enlighten and please the eye.[4]

In accordance with this injunction, agents had been sent out all over Europe to search for worthwhile objects and 'to visit the museums of learned men, both public and private, and there to observe how Your Majesty's museum differs from theirs; and if there is anything lacking in Your Majesty's museum, to strive to fill this gap'.[5]

Peter's collecting was only one facet in the life of this manic monarch, whose inexhaustible energy pulled the newly shaven court in Moscow and St Petersburg into the present by its few remaining hairs. The tsar was seemingly incapable of standing still. He was merciless against his enemies, both in his twenty-year war with Sweden and in putting down various rebellions with iron fist. When his own son, Alexis, fled from his overbearing father to Austria and attempted there to gain support against him, Peter had him lured back, put on trial and, according to which version one is inclined to believe, had him flogged to death or strangled him himself. Courtiers implicated in the episode were impaled, broken on the wheel or flogged and banished.

The tsar's peacetime efforts were equally uncompromising and exhausting, and he was reputed to be just as hard on his friends as he was on his enemies. Not that he spared himself. He was actively involved in the planning of the new city of St Petersburg, reforming taxes, travelling throughout Europe, visiting other monarchs and working incognito (more or less) as a carpenter on shipyards, carousing regularly with the Drunken Assembly, a mock court devoted to drinking vast quantities of alcohol in which he took on the role of Archdeacon Peter, while modernizing, leading wars, legislating, and collecting what he thought would benefit the culture of his country almost as an afterthought.

His celebrations were always on a large scale, and were affairs not for the faint-hearted. Foreign ambassadors were summarily ordered to attend and enjoy themselves and Russian noblemen unwilling to expose their health to the sheer amounts of vodka consumed during the revels found that the tsar's wrath was as formidable as the generosity he inflicted upon them. One of them was whipped because he had chosen not to be present at a feast despite appearing on the guest list. While wearing out practically all of those he blessed with his hospitality Peter himself seemed quite indestructible. A Hanoverian minister recounts waking up with a hangover in Peterhof in 1715, unable to remember what happened the previous evening, only to find the tsar cutting trees to sober up. Then, the unhappy German wrote, 'we received such another Dose of Liquor, as sent us senseless to Bed'. Peter's drinking habits were notorious among aristocrats and diplomats. The Dane Just Joel was marched back to a 'life-threatening' party from which he had attempted to withdraw in his nightshirt. 'For the foreign envoy,' he lamented, 'these drinking sessions are a dreadful ordeal: he either participates in them and ruins his health or misses them and earns the Tsar's disfavour.'

In his rare quiet moments Peter would devote himself to craftsman-ship, especially turning in wood, bone and ivory, a skill of which he was inordinately proud. Several works by his hand were part of his collection. Some of the passions in which the ruler of all Russians indulged excited bemused comments by visitors. 'His dominant pas-sion is to see houses burn, which is a very common occurrence in Moscow since no one bothers to put one out unless there are 400 or 500 alight,' reported a French observer in 1689.[6] The tsar would insist on directing the fire-fighting himself, always standing at the most dangerous spots. His love of dwarfs and other freaks occasionally found expression in lavish and (to our eyes, at least) cruel festivities, such as the marriage of the Royal Dwarf, Iakim Volkov, for which the tsar ordered dwarfs to be rounded up in Moscow and sent to St Petersburg, where they were shut up like cattle for several days and then received especially tailored clothes in which they had to celebrate Volkov's wedding as one large assembly of Liliputians, while normal-sized onlookers who were standing at the sides did little to stifle their laughter as the unfortunate revellers grew increasingly drunk and found their short legs refusing service. When Volkov died in 1724, all dwarfs resident in St Petersburg were summoned to follow the coffin, and the procession was arranged in pairs according to the mourners' height, with the smallest at the front, and the tallest, the tsar himself among them, following.

Peter had a strong fascination for anatomy, illness and death, and believed himself to be an excellent surgeon. Part of his collection was made up of teeth that he himself had drawn, not always because they needed to come out. Many unsuspecting passers-by had to relinquish molars before their ruler's lust for surgery was satisfied. The teeth in the collection are recorded in the contemporary catalogue as: 'teeth extracted by Emperor Peter from various persons', among them a singer, a person who made tablecloths, a bishop of Rostov, and a fast-walking messenger ('not fast enough', as Stephen Jay Gould remarks).

Peter's interest in anatomical preparations was especially great. When visiting Libau he had written in great excitement to Andrei

Vinius, the Royal Apothecary: 'Here I have seen a great marvel which at home they used to say was a lie: a man here has in his apothecary's shop in a jar of spirits a salamander which I took out and held in my own hands: this is word for word exactly as has been written.'[7] On his second European visit in 1716–17, this time officially as monarch, the tsar made a special point of visiting great collections wherever he went, be it the Tower of London, Oxford's Bodleian Library, private cabinets of curiosities, the famed *Kunstkammer* of the Elector of Saxony in Dresden and, of course, the *theatrum anatomicum* in Leiden and the museum of Dr Ruysch. His enthusiasm for the Dutch embalmer's morbid aestheticism knew no bounds. He bought the entire collection for the enormous sum of 30,000 rubles and had it transported to St Petersburg, where some of the pieces still survive in the *Kunstkamera*. After Peter, collecting was as firmly established among the Russian aristocracy as it was in western Europe. Catherine the Great followed his example in buying up entire collections to fill her winter palace, the Hermitage.

Part II

A Complete History of Butterflies

This Curious Old Gentleman

It is not easy to find the Department of Lepidoptera at the London Natural History Museum. Corridors meander their way through the entire history of the museum; past dignified and all but abandoned mahogany cabinets in the old wing to immense metal storage systems in the new containing tray after tray after tray of moths and butterflies of all sizes, colours, origins, all levels of rarity and beauty. An estimated 68 million specimens are kept there, some 20 million of them butterflies. The collection has become a vast reference base for the taxonomy of new or unknown species, and every day new parcels arrive from all over the world, smelling faintly chemical and containing creatures dried or pinned on to cardboard or suspended in alcohol.

I am shown some truly spectacular examples, delicate things of miraculously rich and varied colour, iridescent apparitions with wings as large as hands, death moths that seem to have skulls etched on their massive backs, and others so small that their intricacy is almost impossible to believe. The speci-mens I have come for, however, are all in one small cabinet in a large room smelling unbearably of mothballs. Here, opened only with a special key, are a few trays containing butterflies in individual glass frames, all labelled by hand and sealed with parchment around the edges. Some of these specimens carry a red dot indicating that they are the reference sample used in the past to describe a species; others have suffered greatly and have all but disintegrated. One in particular,

77

large, with red wings shot through with brown and black, hardly survives at all and is little more than the ghost of a butterfly, skeletized like an autumn leaf, mere hues of colour between the two glass panes holding together what remains.

These fragile remnants once formed part of one of the greatest collections Europe has seen, central not only to the holdings of the Natural History Museum but also to those of the British Museum: the life's work of Sir Hans Sloane (1660–1753).

'I had from my Youth been very much pleas'd with the Study of Plants, and other Parts of Nature, and had seen most of those Kinds of Curiosities, which were to be found either in the Fields, or in the Gardens or Cabinets of the Curious in these Parts,'[1] Sloane remembered about his Irish childhood. Born in 1660 as son of a land agent in Killyleagh, Co. Down, he attended the local Latin school. At sixteen, he developed haemoptysis, a painful condition that caused him to spit blood and was to last for three years, though other sources relate that it plagued him intermittently for his entire life. It is possible that it was this medical condition that forced the young man to turn his hand to more academic pursuits instead of following the countrified life of his family. At the age of nineteen he studied at the Apothecary's Hall in London, and soon came to the attention of Robert Boyle, a distinguished chemist and physicist. The young man cultivated Boyle's friendship by 'communicating to him whatever occur'd to himself, which seem'd curious & important, & which Mr Boyle always receive'd with his usual Candour & return'd with every Mark of Civility and Esteem'.[2]

After four years at the Apothecary's Hall, Sloane went abroad to study in Paris, dividing his time between the Jardin Royal des Plantes and the Hôpital de la Charité. He was a voracious student, as a friend testified:

He enter'd at six in the morning the Royal Garden of Plants with Monsr Tournefourt, who demonstrated the Plants after the Order of Caspar Bahuin ... til eight, when Monsr Duforty explain'd their Virtues till ten; & at two in the afternoon Mons du Verney read upon Anatomy till four, & was succeeded by Monsr Sanlyon, the Chemical Professor, who discours'd in French on the Operations to be perform'd that day by Monr Faveur.[3]

From there the young Sloane went to the most famous school of medicine of that time, to Montpellier. As a Protestant he was debarred from taking a degree in both Paris and Montpellier and so he had to finish his studies in Orange. He received the degree of Doctor of Medicine with distinction. Already a respected man of science, the young doctor returned to England with a letter of introduction to Dr Thomas Sydenham, one of the most notable medical men of the day. On his return he was made a Fellow of the Society of Physicians. The world, at least the small world of respectable London society, was open to him.

In 1687, Sloane accepted a position as physician to the 2nd Duke of Albermarle, recently appointed Governor of Jamaica, probably in order to get him as far away as possible from London. The duke had caused considerable scandal with his dissolute lifestyle, which threatened to ruin not only himself, but also the reputation of his father, General Monck, one of Cromwell's most loyal supporters who had switched allegiance and had been created a duke in recognition of his pivotal role in the Restoration of the monarchy in 1660. In the later political climate of the 1680s, however, under James II, whose Catholic sympathies were plain for all to see, the wayward son of an eminent man who had once supported the opposition was a liability, and best removed from the hub.

The prospect of foreign travel excited the young doctor, especially since it would give him the opportunity of studying foreign plants and drugs. Having sailed to Jamaica on the *Assistance*, a frigate of forty-four guns, Sloane soon settled into a routine of perfunctory duties, which left him plenty of time for exploration. He hired artists to record nature and wildlife, kept detailed notes and also wrote about his adventures to London friends:

[A]fter I had gather'd and describ'd the Plants, I dried as fair Samples of them as I could, to bring over with me. When I met with Fruits that could not be dried or kept, I employ'd the Reverend Mr. Moore, one of the best Designers I could meet with there, to take the Figures of them, as also of the Fishes,

Birds, Insects &c in Crayons, and carried him with me into several places of
the Country that he might take them on the place.[4]

Sloane's West Indian days set a pattern for the rest of his life. While
his position as the duke's physician was not demanding and much of
his time was taken up with explorations and with cataloguing and
preserving his finds, he soon operated a flourishing medical practice
open to the governor's circle and the less privileged citizens of Port
Royal alike. (One of his patients was Sir Henry Morgan, a retired
buccaneer, whose medical trouble turned out to be that he drank so
much that he found it impossible to sleep, an unusual consequence of
excessive consumption of alcohol.)

While not allowing anything to detain him from pursuing his passion, Sloane was aware of the dangers lurking everywhere. 'In that distant Climate the Heats and Rains are excessive,' he wrote. 'The Parts
not inhabited . . . are often full of Serpents and other venomous Creatures . . . The same Places remote from Settlements are often full of run
away Negros, who lyie in Ambush to kill the Whites who come within
their reach.' It was not just rebellious former slaves that endangered his
growing collection; the tropical climate presented added difficulties. 'I
attempted to preserve the Skins and Feathers of Humming Birds, and
was oblig'd, to keep them from Ants, by hanging them at the End of a
String from a Pully fasten'd in the Cielling and yet they would find the
Way by the Ceiling to come at and destroy them.'

Sloane's time as a colonial doctor and collector of rare species was
rudely interrupted when on 16 March 1688 his employer, who had
himself enthusiastically sampled local produce, Jamaica rum, suddenly
died. The duchess, no doubt relieved at finding her exile cut short,
decided to return home. Sloane discovered that his skill at preserving
organisms proved a useful asset as the duke's body had to be embalmed
in order to be taken back to England. The political uncertainty surrounding the increasingly embattled James II prevented the party from
sailing for another five months. The dowager duchess wisely decided
that the England of an ever more intransigent Catholic king was no
place to be. They eventually set sail in August, when it seemed certain
that James II would not last. On arriving in England, the duke, pickled
twice over, was interred in Westminster Abbey.

Back in London, Sloane was quick to exploit his connections and expertise. He set up practice in Bloomsbury Square and soon had among his patients some of the most influential members of society. His reputation, and wealth, rose with the publication of his observations made on his journey to the West Indies. In 1693 he succeeded Isaac Newton as Secretary of the Royal Society and in 1719 he became President of the College of Physicians. The personal physician to Queen Anne, he also received an honorary degree from Oxford University. Despite his position as consultant to the rich and famous, Sloane obviously retained a strong sense of obligation to his profession: he returned his annual salary of £30 as Physician in Charge at Christ's Hospital for the treatment of its patients. By now one honour chased the next. He attended upon Prince George of Denmark, the Consort of Queen Anne in 1708, was created a baronet in 1716, and was made Physician General to the Army in 1722. In 1727, by now sixty-seven, he was appointed King's Physician in Ordinary to George I.

While obviously enormously active and successful as a doctor and a man of science, Sloane was first and foremost a collector of immense curiosity and considerable means. His great wealth did not rest on his success as a physician alone; in 1695 he married a widow he had known in Jamaica, Elizabeth Langley, an heiress to a substantial fortune, who enabled him to pursue his passion and to pay fabulous sums for objects he thought valuable and genuine. As there was nothing that did not excite his interest, nothing so small or insignificant that he would not have attempted to acquire it, Elizabeth found that her famous husband came at a price. When John Evelyn visited Sloane in 1691, only three years after his return from Jamaica, he wrote:

I went to see Dr. Sloane's Curiosities, being an universal Collection of the natural productions of Jamaica consisting of Plants, Corralls, Minerals, Earth, shells, animals, Insects &c: collected by him with greate Judgement, several folios of Dried plants & one which had about 80: severall sorts of Fernes, & another of Grasses: &c: The Jamaica pepper in branch, leaves, flowers, fruits &c: with his Journal, & other Philosophical & naturall discourses & observations is indeed very extraordinary and Copious, sufficient to furnish an excellent History of that Island, to which I encouraged him, & exceedingly approved his Industry.[5]

Sloane did not rely on his own judgement alone. Agents and seamen would bring him rarities, and he would buy entire collections in order to incorporate the best pieces into his own. His rooms in Bloomsbury must have been a remarkable sight: wealthy private patients come to see the great man when he was unable to visit them; other, less distinguished but equally sick, people hoping to be attended to; sailors with plants, animals, alive and dead, antiquities, tribal art and boxes arrived from all the harbour towns of Britain, all vying for space in his increasingly cramped quarters.

The collection took a new direction when Sloane's friend from Montpellier University days, the rich botanist William Courten of the East India Company, bequeathed his specimens to Sloane in 1702, a legacy that was estimated at a staggering value of £50,000.[6] After this, there was seemingly no stopping him. Sloane acquired several entire collections, among them 'a good collection of Roman coins, and a most surprising one of shells, a thousand of several sorts from all parts of the world, curious for their form, size, colour &c'.[7] Not content with objects of science, he became increasingly fond of curiosities, such as parts of the salvage from a Spanish galleon. By now, a constant team of curatorial assistants helped him in the task of cataloguing and preserving the exploding number of specimens in his house.

There are conflicting reports as to the appearance of the collection, encouraged perhaps by the fact that it was in a constant state of flux. Initially it was contained in eleven large rooms in which cabinets for various specimens lined the lower areas of the walls, with three or four tiers of bookshelves above. The cabinets were ordered according to the kind of object they contained: mineral or animal, insects or vertebrae, shells, birds' eggs, and one containing '7,000 different fruits'. There were also cabinets containing shoes and clothing, Egyptian antiquities, fossils, medals and coins, and various objects defying classification altogether. Always generous with access to his treasures, Sloane still expected his guests to take great care. When Händel visited the great man in 1740, he disgraced himself and incensed his host by placing a buttered bun on a rare medieval manuscript.

Eventually the ever-increasing number of items in the house forced Sloane to search for new lodgings. In 1742, he chose to move to Chelsea, where he hoped to accommodate his pieces more adequately. Edmund

Howard, who worked as one of Sloane's assistants, had the task of making an inventory. The catalogue runs to forty volumes in folio, including records of a library of 42,000 volumes. The collection kept growing. Already in April 1743 a visitor recorded about Sloane's new residence: 'His great house at Chelsea is full throughout; every closet & chimney with books, rarity's &c.'

An inventory from 1753 gives a more accurate picture of the extent of the collection. It itemized, among many other categories:

Earths and Salts 1035

Bithumens, Sulphurs, Ambers, Ambergreese 399

Metals and Minerals 2725

Talcs, Micae, etc 388

Corals, or such as are kin to them, as Sponges and other Submarine Plants 1421

Vegetables, and Vegetable Substances, as Roots, Woods, Ruits, Seeds, Gums, Resines, and inspissated Juices 12506

Besides 200 large Volumes of dried Samples of Plants, amongst which are such Speciments as were collected by myself In Europe, The Madera Island, and America, as also those gathered by Dr Merret, Dr Plukenet, Mr Petiver, and other curious Persons all over the known world 344

Insects 5439

Echini, or Sea Urchins, and Parts of them, both natural and fossil, found at Sea and Land 659

Fishes, and their parts 1555

Birds, and their Parts, Eggs 1172

Vipers, Serpents &c 521

Humana, viz. Stones of the Kidneys and Bladder, Anatomical preparations, and the like 756

Miscellaneous Things not comprehended with the foregoing, both Natural and Artificial 2098

Things relating to the Customs of ancient Times, or Antiquities, Urns, Insturments, &c. 1125

Large Seals 268

Large Vessels, Handles, and other Things made of Agats, Jaspers, Cornelians, Chistals, besides many Camei and Seals, excisa, incisa 700

Medals, antient, as Samaritan, Phaenician, Greek, Consular, Roman, &c, and Modern, and coins in all Medals 23,000

Books in Miniature of Colours, with fine Drawings of Plants, Insects, Birds, Fishes, Quadrupeds, and all sorts of natural and artificial Curiosities, Books of Prints &c, Volumes of Manuscripts, the greatest Part of them relating to Physick, and Natural History, &c. ca 50,000[8]

Sauveur Morand, a French man of science, visited Sloane's collection in 1729 and was obviously still under the impression of this vast and strange artifice when he wrote down his description of it:

Mr Sloane's cabinet comprises eleven large rooms, including his library, which is the most complete in Europe for books on medicine; he has 3,000 manuscripts on this subject. In this cabinet are to be seen

Extremely rare anatomical pieces, amongst others many preparations by Ruysch; the foetus which Ciprien removed by caesarian operation on 1694 without causing the death of the mother; various injections of the principal vessels of a body of which the tunics are full of knots caused by a tophaceous matter, produced by the gout; various skeletons, including that of a syphillitic, full of growths; several pieces exhibiting maladies of the bones; stones removed from different parts of the body – there are 400 of them; from the bladder, and several from the intestines

A collection of medals; there are as many ancient as modern, 23,000

Skeletons of leaves of various trees, produced by insects, various birds, amongst others humming birds and 'oiseaux du mogol'

Skins of all sorts of animals

Teeth of all sorts of animals, amongst others elephants' teeth, swollen and distended, having been penetrated by foreign bodies which remain inside; in one is an iron ball.

A great number of Egyptian antiquities

4,000 different insects; the Surinam toad

A complete history of butterflies in glazed boxes. Also there are curious leaves resembling flying insects, which are called folia amulantia

A collection of beetles

A collection of all species of spiders

A large collection of snakes in spirits

The wings of several sorts of flying fish

A series of all sorts of shoes of different nations

Indian clothes[9]

Sloane did not leave all the work in detail to his assistants. He himself labelled the pieces in his possession, recording their history, peculiarities, former owners and appearance. Among the rarer items were 'a breast after being buried [blank] years taken up given to me by Mr. Walpole', 'A piece of the breast of Queen Katherine out of the chest at Westminster abby 7ber [September] 1667 had out of Mr Giffords collections', 'The head of an Egyptian mummy dried in the sands brought from Egypt by Mr Sandys' and 'Part of the hide of a Bashaw that was strangled in Turkey given to me by Dr. Varin.' Not all descriptions were so brief. Some labels contained entire stories:

A ball of bezoar taken out of the gutts of a Schoolmaster in Lancashire who suffered seven years of the colic by it notwithstanding the attempts of Physicians. The center is a plumbstone stuck there with gathered [f]omentum about it wich was found in opening his body by his own direction after death to find out the cause of so great a distemper; A small tumor of fatt voided by a person excessively troubled wh the colic who had swallowed a nail being nailing some laths upon a ceiling. He endeavour'd to gett it up by a whalebone and had a pain in his side about a year when by bleeding & the help of an electuary of conf. Ref. Bals. Locatell & fl. Shlph. Wh pectorall drink he brought it up wh a small couth. The nail wh coagulated blood round it.[10]

As a doctor, Sloane had unrivalled access to the kind of monstrosity so beloved by collectors a century before. His own collection had a good deal of specimens of the kind. 'A monstrous child with 4 arms and 4 legs,' was followed by 'A human monster being two bodies of children joined together in one head it hath 4 arms & 4 legs From Staffordshire.' Other items of anatomy testified to Sloane's more eccentric tastes and habits:

Two cataracts taken out of the eyes of a blind small fox from Greenland. He lived many years wt me in my garden was brown in summer & turned white in winter. In April generally the fox shed the white hair unliss the last year of his life when being sick the white fur continued till its death not changing as usually.

Natural curiosities took up a great deal of space. There were pieces of considerable size, such as: 'The skeleton of an Orang Utang or wild man frm Sumatra in the East Indies by Capt. Sprice. The hands and feet were thrown overboard in coming from the East Indies when this creature died. It was given me by Mr. Maidstone'; 'A stuffed Camel'; and 'The trunk, eyes etc. of the Elephant that died of a Consumtion in the year 1741 at Mile end in Middlesex'; as well as more modestly proportioned exhibits, such as 'A white mouse catch'd in a trap in Hannover square.'[11]

It was not just his zoological collection that was thus described. He wrote about fossils as if they were living, roaming sea and land: 'Palat or mandible of an orbis muricatus dugg up in England. This fish eats shell fish & grinds them between the upper & under manibles w are like millstones.' The descriptions of archaeological remains showed their owner to be a man interested more in medicine than history: 'An incrusted Skull and Sword, they were both found in the Tiber at Roma, on the right side of the Skull is the bone or head of the humerus, and the first rib adhering.'[12]

The Chelsea manor, complete with large and exotic stuffed animals, entire boats and a collection numbering around 200,000 pieces, became a great attraction to visitors. Sloane himself, though, had to consider what would happen to it after his death. His collection, though unrivalled in the world, was attacked by some as old-fashioned. John Woodward, himself an ardent collector, wrote about it: 'Censure would be his due, who should be perpetually heaping up of Natural Collections, with out Design of Building a Structure of Philosophy out of them, or advancing some Propositions that might turn to the Benefit and Advantage of the World.'[13]

Unperturbed by criticism, however, Sloane made up his mind how he would dispose of his treasures. Madame du Bocage, a French visitor, recorded with great surprise: 'This curious old Gentleman intends, as it is said, to bequeath these fruits of his enquiries to the Royal Society of London.' The curious old gentleman did just that. He left to the Royal Society 'my library of books, drawings, manuscripts, Prints, medals and coins; ancient and modern antiquities, seals and cameos, intaglios and precious stones; agates and jasper, vessels of agate, jasper or crystal; mathematical instruments, drawings and pictures, and all other things'.[14] The British Museum was born. Sloane himself, who had suffered from a paralytic disorder since 1739, died on 11 January

1753. He was ninety-two. His collection, together with the library of Sir Robert Cotton and the Royal Library, donated to the museum by George II in 1757, was initially housed in Montague House, Blooms-bury, and opened on 15 January 1759.

An account written by a twelve-year-old boy in 1780 already relates a museum experience that sounds familiar to modern visitors:

The next room was filled with all kinds of serpents and lizards once alive, and some of them with wings. There was a pair of gloves made from the beards of mussels, also some snakes and rattlesnakes and swordfishes etc., and a croco-dile, which was such a monstrous great thing, he could have eaten three or four men for a breakfast. There were thousands of other things, which I have not time to enumerate, and indeed, we could not stay to look at half of them.[15]

The statutes of the museum stipulated that it was to be a 'national establishment founded by Authority of Parliament, chiefly designed for the use of learned and studious men, both natives and foreigners in their researches into several parts of knowledge'. The learned and studious men were obviously keen to keep the treasures for themselves, for when the German historian Wendeborn called on the doors of the newly established institution in 1785 he found reason to complain that 'persons desiring to visit the museum had first to give their credentials at the office and it was then only after a period of about fourteen days that they were likely to receive a ticket of admission'.[16] Even then a visit to the collections was no leisurely affair. A curator, who made it clear that he regarded the visitors' appearance as an imposition on his precious time, would walk his charges through the rooms, hardly giving them a chance to pause for breath, much less to look at indi-vidual objects, which were displayed without much organization, and without labels.

Sloane's collection, more and more overshadowed by other trea-sures, had a chequered history in its new surroundings. A Parliamen-tary Select Committee investigating the conditions of the British Museum in 1835 found that much of the great man's bequest had been lost. George Shaw, Keeper of the Department of Natural History and Modern Curiosities, told the committee: 'Sir Hans Sloane had a method of keeping his insects which was very injurious to them. He squeezed them between two laminae of mica, which destroyed the specimens in most cases, even the wings of the butterfly. A few specimens of these insects remained, and we considered them as rubbish, and such were destroyed with other rubbish.'[17] The few specimens fortunate enough to have escaped this barbarity are now housed in the Natural History Museum, where they continue to remind us of Sloane's disordered riches.

Sloane was probably the last of the 'universal' collectors, a man standing on the cusp of the old tradition of the cabinet of curiosities and the new fashion for scientific collecting and methodical classification (another, even later, time-lagged polymath was the German poet, scientist, collector and politician Johann Wolfgang von Goethe).

Already during Sloane's lifetime the nature of collecting had taken a dramatic turn. The Enlightenment and the rise of academies in which scholars met to discuss and to share their research had led to more methodical ways of approaching the material world and to more specialized forms of collecting. The ambition of collecting everything of note, a natural one for Aldrovandi and Tradescant, had given way to a division of disciplines, and within them a new project emerged: the rational classification and complete description of nature and, eventually, art.

A man in the vanguard of this new way of looking at the world, Carl Linnaeus (1707–78), had visited Sloane's cabinet and voiced his disapproval, declaring the collections to be in 'complete disorder'. Chaotic conflagrations of curios held no interest for him. Linnaeus was a pious man and believed that God's work could be expressed and grasped in more systematic terms.

Born in rural Sweden at Råshult in the parish of Stenbrohult in Småland as son of a pastor and devoted amateur botanist, he had studied medicine and had made his name by recording the plants of Lapland as well as the customs of the indigenous Sami people. From Uppsala, the young man went to the Dutch university of Hardewijk and then, armed with an MD, to Leiden, one of the centres of natural philosophy on the continent. Here he found a patron in the famous physician and humanist Hermann Boerhaave (1668–1738), and worked on various botanical works. When he returned to Sweden in 1738 he had a solid reputation as a botanist but no employment and was forced to settle in Stockholm as a general practitioner. He was finally offered a Chair in Botany at his old university, Uppsala, eleven years later.

Here Linnaeus came into his own, cultivating rare plants in his botanical gardens, lecturing to crowds of adoring students, who later formed a worldwide botanical network and supplied more specimens for his collection, and continuing to catalogue plants according to his system of sexual classification.

Linnaeus found that he could subdivide the kingdom of plants according to the form and function of the reproductive parts of individual specimens. By this method he arrived at twenty-four classes and numerous orders, genera and species for further differentiation.

The Latin name of each plant was to consist of two parts, a binominal classification, one for the class and one for the identification of the individual species.

Linnaeus's collection, most of which was sold to London by his widow and is now kept in drawers in a fortified basement room in Burlington House in Piccadilly, the headquarters of the Linnaean Society, is not very large and is spectacular for botanists alone. With his classification, though, he changed the face of the scientific inquiry into nature. He was not without his detractors, of course,  but he had little difficulty holding his own. When the German botanist Johann Siegesbeck attacked his sexual system as 'loathsome harlotry', the gentle Swede found it fitting to name after him a particularly unappealing weed, still known as *Siegesbeckia*.[18]

A form of intellectual opposition, which was more serious than Protestant prudery, came from a Frenchman, the redoubtable George Louis Leclerc, Comte de Buffon (1707–88), the Director of the Jardin des Plantes. Buffon was everything Linnaeus was not: a flamboyant nobleman and scholar, independently wealthy, well connected and brimming with confidence in his own ability. Today, Buffon is remembered as a mathematician rather than a naturalist. At the age of twenty he formulated the binominal theorem, a significant contribution to mathematics. He also worked on probability and posited a surprisingly accurate way of ascertaining the value of π by throwing pins on a gridded sheet of paper.

In his own lifetime, however, it was the study of nature that occupied the nobleman most. Born in the same year as Linnaeus, he studied law, mathematics and botany, translated Newton into French and also championed the writings of Leibnitz. Forced to abandon his studies in Angers after fighting a duel, he set out on a Grand Tour together with the Duke of Kingston and visited Rome and London, where he was elected a Fellow of the Royal Society. Back in France, he took his father to court for trying to cheat him out of his inheritance and accepted the position as Director of the Jardin de Roi (today the Jardin des Plantes) in 1738. He was thirty-two years old.

He now began working on his *magnum opus*, the *Histoire naturelle, générale et particulière* (1749–1804), projected to run to fifty volumes, though only thirty-six were completed. It was the first attempt made during the Enlightenment to represent systematically all fields of human knowledge in natural history, geology and anthropology. Buffon's system differed radically from that of Linnaeus. Where the binominal classification sought to go into ever more detail and to fix every creature with the intellectual equivalent of a taxidermist's needle, Buffon believed in the instability of species. Redundant features such as the hind toe of pigs, he argued, would eventually be bred out and vanish altogether, as indeed might the species itself. This evolutionary concept led him to posit an age for the earth that was much longer than previously thought and to speak of different periods during which species would have existed that had long since become extinct. The *Histoire naturelle* was a mixture of natural history and philosophy, intended partly to keep the work from becoming monotonous in its description of animals and plants. Style was important to the count: 'Le style c'est l'homme même,' as he famously declared in a lecture to the French Academy.

While Buffon's system of classification according to form and function of plants and animals has not stood the test of time, his ideas about the instability of species, the common ancestry of apes and men, and about evolution in nature in general were to prove far-sighted beyond his own imagination and were taken up a century later by another impassioned collector and expert on worms, Charles Darwin.

The cabinets of the sixteenth- to eighteenth-century collectors had been full of objects and creatures that were extraordinary, out of the order of things. The whole point of this project had been to question and expand the kind of knowledge about the world that was extant in the West; dragons and mermaids, armadillos and blowfish, Indian headgear and Eskimo shoes all pointed to a world that was bigger than had been known, to a reality far beyond what had been thought possible. Classifications were anecdotal and uncertain, and, if not invented on the hoof, gathered with equal readiness from Pliny and local fishermen alike. What mattered was the sheer wonder of each object in itself, a material contradiction of the previously supposed limitations of the world.

The emerging scientific approach to nature turned this approach on its head. Now the objective was to place everything within the order of things, in its allotted place within the great system that was, at least potentially, capable of absorbing everything on earth and in the skies. Nature would bend to its ultimate classification and every last beetle and moss would have its place within the pages of Linnaeus, would appear somewhere in one of Buffon's many tomes. The scientific mind was finally poised to master the order of things; indeed, according to some revolutionary writers, it was the scientific mind that established this order and imposed it on the universe.

The Mastodon and the
Taxonomy of Memory

Charles Willson Peale (1741–1827), the son of a convict shipped to Maryland by the British authorities, started out in life as an apprentice saddle-maker. A gifted draughtsman he quickly rose to become the portraitist of many of the revolutionary heroes of early American history; Lafayette, Jefferson and Washington among them. This was more than just a way of making money. Peale was a convinced Republican, a one-time soldier in the War of Independence and an active participant in the political consolidation of the nation.

Painting and politics, though, were never enough to fill Peale's days. He patented steam baths, bridge designs and a polygraph, which allowed him to copy documents, and he proved indefatigable in tracking down objects and organizing their display, according to the ideas pioneered in Europe by Linnaeus and Buffon, in his museum, the finest such to be conceived in the eighteenth century.

The central part of Peale's museum was a long gallery with natural light in which he displayed his own portraits of great Americans as a frieze running along the uppermost part of the room, while below it, both literally and metaphorically, were the exhibits of the lesser orders of nature: animals and birds skilfully stuffed and exhibited behind glass. Other cabinets contained insects, minerals and fossils.[1] The museum held some 100,000 objects, including 269 paintings, about 1,800 birds, 1,000 shells, etc. Theoretical knowledge was less highly prized: the library numbered only 313 volumes. The exhibits were arranged according to the latest theories; Peale himself explained that every good collection should contain:

The various inhabitants of every element, not only of the animal, but also specimens of the vegetable tribe, – and all the brilliant and precious stones, down to the common grit, – all the minerals in their virgin state. Petrefactions of the human body, of which two instances are known, and through an immense veriety which should grace every well stored Museum. Here should be seen no duplicates, and only the varieties of each species, all placed in the most conspicous point of light, to be seen to advantage, without being handled![2]

The evolution of the idea of what a collection should be like had progressed apace since the days of Sloane's chaotic treasure troves, and certainly since the cabinets of rarities that had flourished only one and a half centuries earlier: *Here should be seen no duplicates.*

As far as possible, Peale's arrangements adhered to simple evolutionary principles which seem to owe more to Buffon's morphological ideas than to Linnaeus. While the Orang Utang was placed closer to monkeys than to humans, flying squirrels, ostriches and bats were considered suitable intermediaries between birds and quadrupeds. Backdrops painted with suitable landscapes augmented the display. Nature and natural representation were of supreme importance and as far as possible the museum was to be a true world in miniature. On the floor of the gallery an entire landscape took shape, complete with a thicket, turf, trees and a pond in which stuffed specimens of the appropriate elements (not filled with straw but stretched over wood to enhance their realistic appearance) were walking, creeping and swimming right in front of the astonished visitors. The large brown bear especially, raised on its hind legs in a threatening pose, must have made a great impression.

The most astonishing piece in the museum, however, came into Peale's possession in 1801, and only after a huge undertaking, which he himself immortalized on a canvas he called *The Exhumation of the Mastodon*. The discovery of the mastodon, a prehistoric mammal, was a sensation in scientific circles. Even before its discovery during digging works on a farm in Newburgh, New York, scientists had written about it as evidence that species could indeed die out, a fact that further strengthened the emerging ideas of natural evolution. Peale and his son Rembrandt (all his children were named after great painters, collectors or naturalists) supervised the exhibition of the gigantic

bones. In the picture, the endeavour has reached a climactic moment: a storm is threatening and the work is continued with great urgency, a large walking wheel powering a chain of buckets, which empty the ground water in the pit.

Peale himself is standing by in almost visionary pose, lit brightly in the foreground and with an anatomical plan of a mastodon leg in his hand. The people depicted around him, his family and friends, are all caught in the great anticipation of the moment, the retrieval of something believed long lost (or non-existent); and, as several people shown in the canvas were in fact already dead at the time of the exhumation, they too are thus retrieved. In this moment of private myth they were as present as they certainly were to Peale throughout his life; the painting echoes motifs of another canvas in his collection, a copy by his own hand of Catton's *Noah and his Ark*. In both cases, the father is helped by his sons, rescuing the glories of creation. The parallels are obvious: death is vanquished, nature tamed and subdued by wisdom.[3] The mastodon was installed in Peale's museum and drew in great crowds wishing to see the remains of the monstrous animal.

To its owner, however, it was not so much a crowdpuller as proof of everything he believed in.

One class of exhibit which Peale dearly wished to have in his museum was never realized. While he considered portraiture an adequate means of granting a form of permanence and immortality, he continued searching for a 'powerful antisepticke' in order to preserve actual bodies and prevent them from becoming 'the food of worms'. Although he never did find an embalming technique that would have allowed him to put his plans into practice with human bodies, events in his private life illustrate his profound beliefs and anxieties connected to death and disintegration. When his wife, Rachel, died, probably during her eleventh pregnancy, he refused to have her buried for four days, for fear of putting her into her grave alive.

Years earlier, he had painted a portrait, *Rachel Weeping*, on which he worked intermittently for four years, and which shows the disconsolate mother grieving over the corpse of their fourth child, Margaret, who had died in infancy, as had the previous three.

The picture shows the mother looking heavenwards, while the child lies in its bed peacefully, dressed for burial. A medicine bottle in the background illustrates both the efforts that were made to save the infant and the powerlessness of human endeavour in the face of fate. The painting was hung behind a curtain, making every time it was revealed a renewed moment of immediacy. Peale was much concerned with arresting the present, and with the eventual but inexorable disappearance of everything he held dear: another of his paintings shows two of his sons, life-size, vanishing through a doorway and up a spiral staircase, walking out of view, a presence that contains an absence. He displayed it so as to make it seem as realistic as possible, fooling many of his visitors in the often dim light before electricity. Peale himself was also permanently there, if not in person then represented by a wax figure of himself, which he had placed in the museum in 1787. His preoccupations, most significantly the collection itself, illustrate his acute and agonizing awareness of mortality, of the inexorable passing of time and of those dear to him. Establishing permanence and thus cheating death of its triumph, through portraiture, through embalming, through scholarship and through remaining present in a museum designed to outlast him and his children, was his primary concern.

Peale's roles as founder of America's first museum and as painter of its greatest heroes coincide in a large self-portrait. It shows him holding up a heavy curtain separating him from the long gallery in which birds stand upright in their glass cases underneath the busts of great men while visitors take in the treasures on show. Peale did not flatter himself: he appears as an old man, slightly bent over, his head bald, one hand held out invitingly (or is it to ward off intruders?) while the other supports the velvet. At his feet is a dead turkey spread over a toolbox, America's national animal in the process of being admitted

to taxidermic eternity, while to his left is the jaw of a mastodon and two further bones leaning against a table, a full skeleton partly visible underneath the lifted curtain. Peale was thus opening his collection to the visitor, offering entrance to wisdom, order and to a life without end.

Angelus Novus

We cannot but wish these Urnes might have the effect of Theatrical vessels, and great *Hippodrome* Urnes in *Rome*; to resound the acclamations and honour due unto you. But these are sad and sepulchral Pitchers, which have no joyful voices; silently expressing old mortality, the ruines of forgotten times, and can only speak with life, how long in this corruptible frame, some parts may be uncorrupted; yet able to out-last bones long unborn, and noblest pyle among us.

Thomas Browne, *Urne Buriall*[1]

Dr Gall's collection of human skulls and plaster casts is kept in the idyllic town of Baden, a little under an hour away from Vienna by slow train, a comfortable ride through the suburbs and the vineyards of the Josephsbahn. The Emperor Francis Joseph liked to come here in the summer and a convenient railway stood at the ready to transfer His Majesty to his place of choice. In Baden, in a rather splendid neo-Renaissance villa, the Gall Collection fills one room, just next to that of Dr Rollet, who amassed curiosities, fabrics, snail houses, cameo casts and insects. A menacing mask leers above the entrance door of the house.

Gall's collection is a curious testament to a scientific mind. In large, old glass display cases rising up the entire height of the wall are rows and rows of labelled skulls, which he got from the local lunatic asylum and from the gallows. They are mounted on simple stands and labelled in a neat hand. 'His folly: Believed he was an emperor', reads one, 'Her folly: Drinking herself to idiocy', another. There are human lives here, slow descents into insanity, alcoholism, crime and misery, each summed up succinctly in a single sentence: She killed all her children; He could not stop singing and laughing; He believed himself inestimably rich, etc.

Apart from the skulls, there are full plaster casts of heads taken from people alive and dead. While the skulls mainly belong to 'deviants', the criminal and the insane, some of the casts depict the great and the good: Napoleon is here twice (once from life, once in Antommarchi's death mask), Goethe and Schiller, and also assorted noblemen, mathematicians and administrators: calm, august and usually bearded incarnations of distinction. Many of the subjects of the casts are long forgotten, some no longer have any names attached to them at all – but here they stand, looking surprised or dignified, pained or impatient (the taking of the cast was laborious and claustrophobic), or, in some cases, obviously already dead.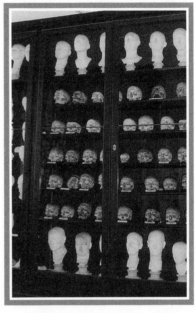

The lasting contribution to science and to the study of the human brain of Dr Franz Joseph Gall (1758–1830) was the discovery that different kinds of brain activity are located in different parts of the brain. This led him to believe that parts of the brain that were especially well developed must be larger than others and must therefore imprint the signature of a person's character and ability on the formation of the skull. It was in an attempt to prove this thesis that Gall chased every head that he considered interesting, from those who had died insane to those who were considered great. His findings were rooted in the Enlightenment. In line with the allegorical thinking of the time, Gall had localized the baser impulses at the base of the skull (the lust for murder, thievery and violence behind the ears), while the highest leanings, faith and theosophy, inhabited the very apex of the cranium.

This science, phrenology, became so controversial and so popular that the Catholic Emperor Franz II forbade Gall to disseminate and teach his materialistic theories in Vienna. With only a few skulls to illustrate his ideas in his luggage Gall left for Germany and finally settled in Paris, where, having been forced to leave behind his collection, he accumulated a second, larger, one, which is now kept in the

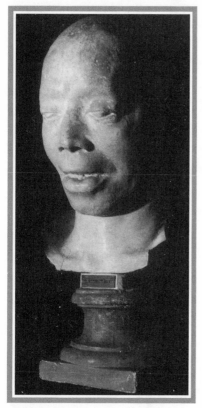

Musée de l'Homme in Paris. His theories were later taken up by eugenicists and given even greater prominence by the Nazis in their illusion of being able to measure their way to a pure and glorious master race.

I had come to Gall's collection to visit an old acquaintance, Angelo Soliman, who had died in 1796 and whose plaster cast had only recently been identified among the heads. The curator and city archivist showed me to the case, though I had recognized Soliman the moment I entered the room. It is the full-head cast of an old man. The left shoulder is missing, broken off some time during the last 200 years.

Soliman does not look at me; his eyes are half closed. He has a handsome, African face, with a well-formed, slightly flat nose, broad cheekbones (the weight of the wet plaster flattened the face), large, almond-shaped eyes and firm, regular lips. He was famous for his appearance, and it is easy to see why. He must have been a sight both dignified and powerful in his lifetime. His hair is short and frizzy and he is bold, an old man. The mouth is slightly opened and the pupil of his right eye protrudes from underneath the lid. He suffered from cataracts in his old age. The mask was clearly made after his death. Gravity was at work on this face, and the corpse was lying on its back when the mask was taken. The skin covering the cheeks has sagged towards his ears, opening and broadening his mouth. There is a skin fold under the left ear and the cheeks are hollowed. The whole face has the emaciated look of a body suddenly without life. When the bust is tipped backwards Soliman's eyes look back at me from underneath their heavy lids and the open mouth makes him look surprised. His death came as a surprise; he died in Vienna, the city that had been his home for most of his life, on the open street, of a stroke.

Angelo Soliman had arrived in Vienna after a long and curious journey. He was born, most likely, in what is today northern Nigeria, at around 1721, and was then enslaved and sold to north Africa and from there to Messina in about 1730. Here Prince Johann Georg Christian Lobkowitz, the Austrian Governor of Sicily, saw the page-boy and requested him as a present when he left to take up his next post as Governor of Lombardy. His wish was duly granted, and the thirteen-year-old Angelo had a new master.

Lobkowitz was a soldier, and his young page became his companion in battle, widely admired for his courage and daring. The years of military campaigns saw the growing boy turn into a young man and took him throughout the Habsburg Empire together with his master's armies: from Italy to Transylvania, to the Czech lands, back to Italy, and then to Hungary. On Lobkowitz's death, he entered the household of Prince Wenzel von Liechtenstein. Now a man of thirty-four, Angelo settled in Vienna for good.

A portrait shows him as a very striking young man in his finest court uniform: a light, fur-trimmed overcoat with a buttoned coat underneath, and a neck scarf.

His regular features are set off by the white turban that he seems to have worn constantly, and in his right hand he holds an ornamental staff in the manner of officers and gentlemen. The handle of the staff is decorated with a lion attacking an antelope, and in the background the oriental theme is reinforced by a palm tree on a hill, as well as two pyramids. Despite this incongruous scenery the figure in the front loses nothing of his dignity. The legend of the image reads with all rococo ceremoniousness: *Angelus Solimanus, Regiae Numidarum gentis Nepos, decora facie, ingenio validus, os humerosque Jugurthae similis. in Afr. in Sicil. Gall. Angl. Francon. Austria Omnibus Carus, fidelis Principium familiaris.* ('Angelo Soliman, from the royal family of the Numidians, a man of beautiful features, great wit, similar to Jugurtha in face and build, dear to all in Africa, Sicily, France, England, Franconia and Austria, and a faithful companion of the prince.')

Angelo was saved from ornamental obscurity by his accomplishments and by the 'great wit' attested to him in the inscription. He may have cut a dash in his silver-trimmed court dress but he was also a soldier of some repute in his own right and had acquired a considerable education. He was fluent in German, French and Italian, and spoke some Czech, English and Latin. Having risen to a position of great respect at court he was accepted into the Masonic lodge *Zur Wahren Eintracht* ('True Unity'), where he became the brother of, among others, Mozart and Haydn. As a Mason, Soliman dealt as equal with the very cream of society, with the same people Mozart himself knew.

Soliman died on 21 November 1796, at the ripe old age of seventy-five. This, however, is not the end of his story. What happened next is related by one of his Masonic brothers, a certain G. Babbée, who writes about Soliman's posthumous fate:

Further it has to be recorded

1. that, on order of the Emperor Franz II, he was skinned,

2. that this skin was fitted on a wooden frame and so resumed Angelo Soliman's former features with great exactitude and was exhibited publicly for ten years,

3. that this skin on its wooden frame or the sculpted shape of our brother Angelo Soliman was consumed by fire and flames 52 years later under great noise, and that at this occasion also his former master of the chair, the cursed

arch heretic, atheist, monk hater and freemason, the imperial and royal counsellor J. von Born was burned *in effigie*.

All this sounds, I must admit, damnably paradoxical, but it will be shown to be entirely true and correct, once I am allowed to explain my words properly[2]

This explanation is relatively simple: Angelo Soliman, page-boy, soldier, companion, courtier and tutor to a succession of princes, had become a star exhibit in the cabinet of natural curiosities of Franz II, a man who had inherited his family's genius for collecting, and few of their other qualities.

A history of the collection describes the former Soliman's new abode as follows:

Angelo Soliman was depicted standing up, his right foot put backwards and his left hand reaching out, dressed with a feather belt around his loins and a feather crown on his head, both made from red, blue and white ostrich feathers in changing sequence. Arms and legs were decorated with a bead of white glass pearls, and a broad necklace braided delicately out of yellow-white porcelain snails (Cyprinid Monet) hung low down on to his chest.[3]

Soliman's temporary resting place, which went by the somewhat cumbersome appellation *K. K. Physikalisch-astronomisches Kunst- und Natur- Thierkabinet* ('Imperial and Royal Physical Astronomical Art and Nature and Animal Cabinet'). The director, Abbé Eberle, had grand plans for the new quarters of the collection in the Josephsplatz near the imperial library. It was to be nothing less than spectacular. When it opened its doors to the citizens of Vienna in 1797 it was part fantasy and part cabinet of curiosities.

The walls of the exhibition rooms were decorated with landscapes commensurate with the habitat of the animals displayed in them. In addition to these grand panoramas, the rooms contained artificial grass and trees, rocks and ponds, glass waterfalls and model oceans with undulating waves. There were fields of grain and whole landscapes dotted with picturesque ruins and a farm with chicken coop. Strong as this arrangement was in effect, its scientific merit was not quite of the same order. The Asian room, a landscape suggesting endless, Siberian forests, displayed a musk-ox and a deer surrounded by singing birds and parrots. The rooms were crammed full with specimens, none of them labelled, but mounted in their artificial surroundings to the greatest possible effect. In one of the European rooms, visitors could admire a hunting scene with a fox fleeing a pack of dogs and a rural idyll with farming implements strewn around as if the labourers had just walked off to have lunch under a nearby tree.

Amid this rococo view of life the 'noble savage' Soliman, for that is what he had become, had a cabinet all to himself, and among the themed splendours of the *naturalia* on display an entire room was dedicated to the effect he created. 'The fourth room in the left wing,' the historian L. J. Fitzinger relates,

> . . . contains a single landscape, a tropical wood with shrubs, watery parts, and canes. Here one could see a water pig, a tapir, some bisam pigs and many American swamp and song birds in different groupings. In the same room, to the left of the exit, from which one can reach the main staircase through a long corridor and through the library, there was a glass case in the corner, painted green. The door, which forms the front wall of the cabinet, was masked with a drape of green cloth and the interior of the case was painted in brilliant red. In this case Angelo Soliman was kept and was shown to the public especially by a servant before they left the department.[4]

The emperor seems to have been well pleased with this artistic new addition and with the advantageous effect of contrasting the handsome figure with the grotesque features of the tapir and the various pigs. The case became an attraction in itself, a fitting grand finale to the tour of the imperial collections.

Abbé Eberle's morbid extravaganza was on display until 1802 when Franz II, tired of his director, appointed a new man charged with the unravelling and proper cataloguing of the collection. The result was a scholarly dampening of Eberle's grandiloquence; the landscapes were not dismantled, but the exhibits themselves were rearranged and labelled in German and Latin. Some scientific displays, such as a series of preparations in twenty-four glass jars illustrating the embryonic development of the chicken, were also added to the collection. A second overhaul finally got rid of the theatrical backdrops.

Angelo Soliman's daughter, Josephine, meanwhile, had carried on a long and desperate battle to have her father's skin returned to her so she could bury it with the rest of his body. Her request remained,

needless to say, unheeded, despite an intervention by the Prince Archbishop of Vienna.

Angelo was not to remain alone; in 1802, a black girl, also stuffed,
a present from the King of Naples, was fitted into the same cabinet,
together with an African male nurse from the hospital of the Merciful
Brothers, and an animal warden from the Schönbrunn Zoo. In 1806,
the new director of the collection, Karl Schreiber, finally found that
exhibiting four stuffed black 'representatives of mankind', as they
were referred to officially, might be unseemly, and they were eventually
moved into the attic. On receipt of an adequate sum servants could
still remember the way and would show visitors to this sad and silent
group of exiles.

The end of Angelo Soliman's second incarnation as wild man, exotic
fiction, scarecrow for small children, money-spinner for servants who
would draw the curtain on receipt of a special gratuity, and as an
object of a collector's unlimited greed, was as dramatic as it was
historically apposite. In the famous year 1848, when democratic riots
shook the German-speaking countries, he was indeed to be 'consumed
by fire and flames . . . under great noise', as the Freemason Babbée had
written, and it was another prince of the Habsburg Empire who
brought about this infernal conclusion.

On 31 October, the troops of Prince Alfred Windischgrätz bom-
barded the inner city of Vienna in order to subdue the revolutionaries.
A single, wayward cannonball hit the part of the roof of the imperial
palace that housed the zoological collection. The entire scientific work
that the eminent Karl Freiherr von Hügl und Agnelli had brought back
from his expeditions was burned, together with other specimens. The
inventory of the catastrophe lists, towards the end, after detailing
damage to cases, butterfly collections and 'other beasts':

[A]lso among humans the negro Salomon Angelo over wood artfully preserved
by the sculptor Thaller, a second negro of chief nurse Narciss, a gift from
the Merciful Brothers, fitted on wood by the sculptor Schrott including
their case, a third, who had been employed by the k.k. Menagerie in Schönbrunn . . . and a stuffed negro girl, who had come as a present from the King
of Naples.[5]

The exhibits were obviously not important enough to have been entered into the inventory with individual numbers.

There are many monuments to our mortality, all preserving death at its most lifelike, in the anatomical collections of hospitals and universities. One such collection is housed in the Narrenturm, or Tower of Fools, in Vienna, which used to be a lunatic asylum before being turned into a museum, a curiously forbidding building in the grounds of Vienna's eighteenth-century general hospital, today the university campus. Half hidden by trees the Narrenturm looms in the furthest corner of the grounds. The plaster is falling off in large lumps from its rusticated façade, especially around the window frames, where the brick is revealed, making it look as though the building is suffering from some terrible skin condition. It has something of a fairy-tale tower or castle air about it, hermetically sealed against the outside world – cruelly appropriate for those of its former inhabitants who, as Dr Gall's collection shows, believed themselves princes and emperors. Its unfortunate inmates have made place for another panopticum of wretchedness: the Federal Museum of Pathology.

This collection, the largest of its kind, was begun in 1796 as a teaching aid for the new hospital. Like the building in which it was to be housed later, it was an expression of a new way of seeing humanity and human illness. Medicine was freeing itself from doctrines laid down by Galen 1,500 years earlier. Surgery was slowly being recognized as a discipline that should not be left to quacks, barbers, horse castrators, butchers and hangmen. The modern hospital embraced these ideas, and work in the mortuary was accepted as an important part of medical science. Johann Peter Frank, who became director of the hospital in 1795, was determined to give a systematic foundation to this new science and to create a repository of specimens that could be used to compare and to instruct. Thirty years later, the collection already encompassed more than 4,000 specimens, either in *spiritus* or as skeletons separated from the flesh with acid. In 1971 it was transferred to the Narrenturm.

Today the tower is part museum part anatomical collection, and visitors enter the building through incongruously modern wrought-iron doors – the tower served as a home for nurses for a while. It is impossible to escape the claustrophobic feeling of the curving corridors and cells and the concentrated misery of the 'preparations', among them Vienna's last remaining stuffed human being: the body of a little girl, standing up, one foot set in front of the other, supported by a staff running through her body, and put unceremoniously among jars of deformities. At the time of her death she had been between four and five, and her entire body is covered by black, fishlike scales. Her face looks like that of a life-sized doll. She is bald and her hands and feet are mummified on their original bones, as the guides relate with solicitous informativeness. She was prepared in 1780 and was later exhibited in the same collection as Angelo Soliman. Nothing is known about her cause of death, or about her identity. The body underneath her skin is cast in wax.

The golden time of the collection, the late eighteenth and nineteenth centuries, provided fertile ground for such displays, when there were as yet few effective treatments for many terrifying illnesses. The devastations of syphilis and leprosy, grotesque tumours and skin conditions are all here, re-created painstakingly in wax and painted after the original. They still look absolutely lifelike. The preparer's skills are also evident from objects such as the head of Georg Prohaska, a groom who survived for a full ten years without a lower jaw after it had been shattered by the kick of a horse. A wax replica of his head, complete with neckerchief, long hair and aimlessly lolling tongue dribbling saliva on to a decorous pedestal, can be compared to the head itself, colourless and suspended in a jar of *spiritus* with a fine glass lid. There are about 50,000 objects, most of them in glass jars or, after the recent acquisition of some smaller collections, in large white plastic buckets.

This museum is no place for women expecting children. Much of the collection consists of deformed newborns who were born dead or died soon after birth. In the crammed former cells and corridors of the asylum, assembled in the form of tiny, floating bodies, is the entire demon world of Greek mythology: cyclops, creatures with bulging eyes and no brains, Siamese twins joined in every conceivable place, bodies with too many extremities, hands with too many fingers, feet with too many toes, claws instead of hands, and the swollen brains of hydrocephali. A special section is occupied by the collection of 'dry preparations': skeletons, largely of people who lived into adulthood. The English Sickness, rickets, has wrought most havoc here, with arms and legs transformed into spiralling growths, powerless appendages to useless bodies. Other specimens illustrate the effects of tuberculosis, tumours, syphilis and spina bifida. A silent assembly of skeletonized Siamese twins seems to be engaged in a grotesquely intimate waltz.

In contrast to the work of Frederik Ruysch and to the graceful anatomical wax models produced in the eighteenth century (some of which are kept a stone's throw from the Narrenturm), this collection speaks of a different attitude to human life, to mortality and to dignity. Human bodies had been deserted by the divine spark and the ideal of beauty once thought inherent in them and in every representation of anatomy. Ruysch's conflation of beauty and mortality and the gracefully instructional *vanitas* tableaux of the eighteenth century had no space here. They had been replaced by a mode of research and teaching that treated bodies quite dispassionately as objects, much like rock samples or beetles. This ideological gap was to widen during the twentieth century and was to reach its nadir in the anatomical collections of Nazi Germany, which would routinely use concentration camp inmates to widen the scope of the specimens. Rumour has it that some of the heads collected by the pathologists of the Third Reich are still held in deep cellars while an embarrassed administration is unsure what to do with them.

Whatever collections try to master it cannot be closer to the bone than collecting the bones themselves. Nature and culture, the past and the present can all be the subjects of collections, of building small ordered worlds amid the chaos all around. If a collection really can promise eternal life then these assemblies of the dead carry this promise by daring us to face them down and learn from the deaths already passed. As graveyards traditionally combine the reality of death with the promise of transcendence and of an afterlife, those collections that had the human body as their object throw down the challenge of the Delphic Oracle: Know Thyself.

The Greatness of Empires

These were wondrous abbreviations and formulae, recipes for civilizations, small amulets allowing one to take the nature of climates and
provinces between two fingers. These were orders drawn on empires
and republics, on archipelagos and continents. What more could caesars
and usurpers, conquerors and dictators possess? Suddenly I recognized
the sweetness of having power over countries, the sting of that avarice
that can be satisfied only by the power to rule. Together with Alexander
the Great I wanted the entire world. And not a hand's width less than
the world.

Bruno Schulz, *The Spring*[1]

This is the world, the buildings say, this is all you need to know.

One can hear this message quite clearly when one is standing in
between the two great museums on Vienna's Ringstrass boulevard,
the grand gesture of a city that was once at the heart of a great empire.
The Ringstrass symbolically unites all institutions that had brought
greatness to Vienna and its dominions. It is more than a little reminiscent of the Great Patriotic Action, the elusive goal in Robert Musil's
Man Without Qualities, in which a host of ineffectual dignitaries are
trying to stipulate the essence and crowning glory of the emperor's
rule. Here the action has taken shape in stone. Apart from assorted
ministries there is the stock exchange; the State Opera; the university,
in Renaissance style embodying the rise of humanism; the City Hall,
its Gothic arches recalling the proud medieval city states; the

Wien.   K. k. Hofmuseum und Maria Theresien-Denkmal.

Burgtheater; the Parliament, splendidly neo-Hellenic. Coachmen are waiting for tourists at all hours of the day on the sweeping expanse of the Heldenplatz. Here is the new wing of the Hofburg, the imperial palace, and directly opposite this heart of the empire are its two museums. To the left the Kunsthistorisches Museum (the Museum of the History of Art), to the right the Naturhistorisches Museum (the Museum of Natural History), and, in between, a square with formal arrangement dominated by a large statue of Empress Maria-Theresia.

It is easy to dismiss these two huge neo-Baroque fantasies as from the patisserie school of architecture, but they are, in fact, rather beautiful in their nineteenth-century grandeur and their historicizing attention to detail: the plaster birds, crocodiles and other creatures on the ceilings of the museum of natural history, the themed grandeur (neo-Egyptian wall paintings in the Egyptian galleries, etc.) of the rooms in history of art, and the dignified secular saints on their façades: scientists, philosophers and artists. Originally designed to contain the burgeoning Habsburg collections, the buildings have been treated with great respect partly for their own antiquarian status, which has been retained for a long time: some galleries in the Museum of Natural History had electric light installed as late as 1992. Behind the scenes is a world that is eternally Habsburg; rambling and cavernous offices overlooking the courtyard in which the august plaster ornaments crumble from brick walls (restoration is in progress), offices in which some of the curators hold the rank of Imperial Court Councillor and sit behind mahogany desks. Computers and coffee machines look like guests from a sadder, poorer future. The female Court Councillor who received me, Dr Teschler-Nicola, was gracious and elegant and gave me the grand tour, the view from the roof, and the skull collection, thousands and thousands of them, assembled for comparison by a more racially minded generation of anthropologists than their predecessors and now filling ten-foot-high walls in a long corridor, part necropolis and part historical curiosity.

Today the arrangements in many of the exhibition rooms in the museum reflect new trends in museology and pedagogy; the upper floor, however, seems almost untouched by time, with its huge mahogany-framed glass cabinets filled with stuffed creatures of the wild: bears, antelopes, tigers and lions, apes and monkeys, all in lifelike poses, by turns frightening and endearing, overwhelming and pitiable in their glass-eyed realism. Opposite, in the Museum of the History of Art, the creatures are less savage and the greatest of them are not locked up behind glass: the Breughels, the Rembrandt self-portraits, the Rubenses. Only downstairs, where sculptures and other objects are kept, glass rules supreme. Here one can see last remnants of the utopian world that the Habsburg Emperor Rudolf II had constructed for himself in sixteenth-century Prague: collector's cabinets, bezoars, sculptures and vessels in marble, gold and silver, isolated messengers of plenty.

Together the two buildings, with the statue of the empress keeping watch, used to talk in one tongue to imperial subjects and to foreign visitors alike who came to see these treasure troves, and their exhibits used to sing in a mighty unison. Everything is here, they say: culture and nature, ordered and displayed by experts, enshrined in glass cabinets and hung along the walls, cleaned, classified and explained scientifically, dusted regularly; all overseen by government. This is the world, this is all you need to know.

In the nineteenth century faith in the ability of collections to be symbolic worlds, to encompass the understanding of the world and of man's place within it, both in space and in time, in a particular place and as part of a particular history, made museums much beloved by Europe's newly formed nation states. They satisfied a need for national history and mythology, especially as displays could be arranged and rearranged to suit prevailing orthodoxies. The *museion*, the place of the muses, housed in temple-like buildings and celebrated like shrines, lent a form of justification and of validity to imperial ambition, national histories, and to traditions that had been invented recently, that was otherwise beyond the reach of even the most canny politician.

The transition from exclusively private or royal collections to public museums was slow, made possible only by a huge conceptual leap in the thinking about the relationship of the private and the public sphere, and by the emergence of the modern state. Semi-public museums belonging to a private collector, to a ruler or ruling house had existed for a long time: Rudolf II was happy to show ambassadors and other dignitaries round his treasure troves at the beginning of the seventeenth century; the Tradescants's was one among many collections that charged entry to the public; Peter the Great stipulated very specifically that 'it is fitting that those desirous of the experience should be educated and made welcome, and not made to pay money',[2] and that 'coffee and zucherbrods', along with vodka, should be served to the nobility.

As the Enlightenment took hold, rulers throughout Europe began to make their collections accessible to their peoples and to a scientific approach that had until then been the domain of natural collections. In 1710, the Pfalz-Neuburger Regent Elector Johann Wilhelm II organized his Düsseldorf gallery, the first public picture gallery in Germany, for the first time according to historical principles. Another milestone was Christian von Mechel's chronological arrangement in 1781 of the Habsburg picture collection in the Belvedere in Vienna.[3] In France, the opening of the royal collections to a wider public was overtaken by history. The royal palace of the Louvre was supposed to be converted into a museum for the nation during the reign of Louis XVI and architects were commissioned to draw up plans for the conversion. The royal bureaucracy, however, all but ground the project to a halt, as it had delayed another plan: the demolition of the Bastille and the building in its place of a pleasure garden for the people of Paris, to be surrounded with colonnades which were to bear the inscription: 'Louis XVI, Restorer of Public Freedom'. Here, too, the royal architects came too late, and the fortress, which by then housed no more than seven prisoners (one of whom was the Marquis de Sade), became a focus of revolutionary anger, its storming a symbol of the Revolution itself.

France's new masters turned the former royal repository of artwork into a public museum only nine days after the fall of the monarchy on 10 August 1792. When it opened exactly one year later, the revolutionary spirit and the ideal of education and elevation of citizens' minds, however, were nowhere to be seen, and the exhibition spaces looked, according to the playwright Gabriel Bouquier, like 'the luxurious apartments of satraps and the great, the voluptuous boudoirs of courtesans, the cabinets of the self-styled amateurs'[4]; all the trappings, in other words, of the lives of those the *citoyens* had so resented, which the Revolution had set out to sweep away in the first place. Something had to be done, and by 1794 efforts were made to bring the displays in tune with revolutionary ideals. Religious works went into storage and were replaced by more heroic, historical canvases. The greatest change took place in 1803 when Napoleon appointed a new director for the museum, one Dominique Vivant Denon.

It had taken a revolution to create the first great museum that did not make access dependent on social status, patronage or the whim of curators and noblemen. Now war intervened to transform the former royal palace into a collector's dream.

Denon (1747–1804) was a figure with less than perfect revolutionary credentials, a former diplomat in the service of the king, a passionate collector and gifted engraver, writer, wit and socialite. He had weathered the murderous storms of the Revolution in Venice, a fact that almost certainly saved his head, for Denon was the very kind of person the Committee for Public Safety was eager to drag to the guillotine. A son of minor nobility from Burgundy, he had come to Paris initially to study law, but he was soon bored by it. Instead of the future his father had had in mind for him, the purchase of a good position in the civil service and an advantageous marriage, the young man found artists' workshops and the theatre far more diverting; his friendship with a group of actresses even enabled him to have a play of his put on at the Comédie-Française, though the play was a comprehensive flop and put a damper on any plans he might have had regarding a career as the new Molière. Undeterred he went to Versailles and, in the absence of any letter of recommendation from a highly placed personage, took it upon himself to make his own introduction to the king during one of the monarch's walks through the endless formal vistas of the park. Louis XV, bored witless by his courtiers and more than likely astounded by the young man's audacity, found the incident quite amusing and appointed him keeper of a collection of gem stones left to the crown by Madame Pompadour. Soon after this, Denon was appointed *gentilhomme ordinaire de la chambre du Roi*, a title which gave him permanent access to the king. From then on there was no stopping his career. Perhaps the court began to bore Louis, too; perhaps he had the good sense to recognize ability when he saw it; in any case, the *gentilhomme* chamberlain was soon travelling the breadth of Europe on diplomatic missions. Between 1772 and 1785 he undertook journeys to Frederick II's court in Berlin and from there on to Catherine the Great in St Petersburg, to Stockholm and, finally (when Louis XVI had already acceded), to Switzerland. Here he took the opportunity to visit the ageing Voltaire, one of the great monuments of the Grand Tour. Sickly and unwilling to be disturbed in his rural idyll, the philosopher declined to see him, whereupon Denon claimed the right to an audience under royal prerogative. Voltaire, amused, yielded to this persistence and received him, only to find himself caricatured by an engraving from Denon's hand, which quickly went into circulation in Paris. Voltaire was stung by such insolence and declined to see the artist-courtier again despite Denon's promise to make a better life drawing.

In 1776 Denon became *chargé d'affaires* in Naples, a difficult and thankless post considering the anti-French bias of the Neapolitan King Ferdinand IV. Unwilling to let work spoil what was promising to be a very good time under the Mediterranean sun, surrounded by the beauty of ancient relics and young women, Denon relished the local attractions as best he could, both the female companionship and his frequent excursions to Pompeii, Herculaneum, Rome, Greece, Sicily and Malta. There was another reason for these travels: he had developed a passion for antiquities, especially vases, and missed no opportunity to add to his collection specimens that seemed to grow out of the ground as abundantly as olive trees. As he was to recount:

A journey to Calabria and Sicily awakened my passion for the arts and made me take up my pen once more and to undertake some excavations in Campania and Apulia. The discovery of a Greek vase or of any vase of new, unknown shape seemed to me a great service on my part to good taste, and I came back to France so laden with pottery that I had not the faintest idea where to put it all.[5]

He found a place, needless to say. Diplomatically, though, his mission had not been a success, though that was put down to circumstance rather than to a lack of diligence on his part. He received an honourable discharge, an *ex gratia* payment of 10,000 livre and an annual pension of 2,000. At thirty-eight, Denon was financially secure, fancy free, and able to pursue his interests at his own pleasure, which is exactly what he did. The years had not been wasted. More than any activity on the political stage perhaps he may have savoured an episode which he had dealt with very discreetly during his time in His Majesty's service; this concerned the writing of a slim novella entitled 'Point de lendemain' that had appeared in the *Mélanges Littéraires ou Journal des Dames* in 1777. It was an elegant but rather explicit short story about an encounter between a young man and a countess, written in the best possible taste and avoiding all vulgar words, and published under a pseudonym, M.D.G.O.D.R., which was not deciphered until well into the nineteenth century. It simply stood for *Monsieur Denon gentilhomme ordinaire du Roi*. This work of aristocratic piquanterie has given its author a reputation as a pornographer, but he was no more guilty of any lapse in taste than that great Enlightenment wit, orator, politician and other writer of erotic novels, his compatriot the Comte de Mirabeau.

Meanwhile, in Paris, honours and diversions filled Denon's days. He was elected to the Académie des Beaux-Arts as an engraver and had a comfortable life. The pleasures of Italy, however, lingered in his mind, and in 1787 he took himself to Venice, where he quickly found access to the better circles of society and intended to write a universal history of painting from the beginnings to his own day. He amused himself by showing the sights to his compatriots, Elisabeth Louise Vigée-Lebrun among them, who had already met him in Paris and who wrote about their meeting:

His *ésprit* and his knowledge of the arts made him a wonderful Cicero [i.e., guide] and I was enchanted to see him again . . . Thus I was led around by one of the most lovable countrymen we have – though not in respect of his physical appearance, as Monsieur De Non had not been beautiful even as a young man, a fact that did not keep a great number of pretty women from liking him.[6]

When the Revolution raged through France, Monsieur De Non (the aristocratic-sounding spelling of his name he had used until then) was safely ensconced in Italy, thinking about the history of the arts and charming the local beauties. He was isolated, unable to return home and regarded with suspicion in Venice, where all Frenchmen who were not exiled dukes were thought to be revolutionaries. In 1793, however, hearing that his fortune was to be impounded along with that of other exiles, he took the great risk of travelling to Paris to save the collection he had left behind in his apartments. Fortunately none other than the painter of the Revolution, Jacques Louis David, vouched for his political reliability, a life-saving lie under the circumstances. From the close proximity of some of Europe's most senior crowned heads, now France's most bitter enemies, Denon, who had absorbed the article 'de' into his name, making it sound less suspiciously noble, found himself being consulted by Robespierre himself on the contribution the arts might make to the reform of public morals and the furthering of virtue.

Their acquaintance was necessarily brief, but Denon had little time to mourn the citizen's demise: this year, 1794, proved to be the beginning of an exciting new phase of his career. Moving in the highest political circles, he met the man of the moment, the young and ambitious general Napoleon Bonaparte, possibly at a dinner in the house of the formidable Foreign Secretary Talleyrand, where the urbane Denon would have had little trouble putting the awkward Corsican at his ease. Their encounter resulted in Denon being offered the chance of accompanying the French army expedition into Egypt in 1801. He jumped at it. Seeing Egypt had always been his life's desire, he said.

In 1802, he published his Egyptian recollections, which won him instant and great public recognition, as Egypt was very much *en vogue* in imperial France and Denon knew to mix scientific fact and gossip, offering both elegant illustrations of the glories on the Nile and exciting titbits, like a story of his shooting a local who had been about to attack him while he was working on a landscape study. Napoleon rewarded Denon's services during the campaigns with an appointment that seemed daring, but turned out to be inspired: he made him Director General of Museums, a position that put the nobleman and newly minted Republican in charge not only of the former royal treasures, but also of the fabulous loot from France's victorious campaigns throughout Europe.

Denon was as delighted as he was daunted by this ultimate of collector's tasks. He wrote to the emperor:

I spend my days trying to familiarize myself with all the things which I have been made master of, hoping that in future I may live up to your opinion of me which you expressed in choosing me, and every time I discover a possible improvement I apply myself to the task wholeheartedly in order to show my gratitude to you.[7]

The fact that the new arrivals at the museum were without exception abducted from other collections did not unduly perturb Denon or his colleagues. On the contrary: 'the reclamation of works of genius and their safekeeping in the land of Freedom would accelerate the development of Reason and human happiness',[8] the French Minister of Justice opined in 1803. In 1794, Jacques-Luc Barbier had found even stronger words to justify the emptying of collections in the Netherlands:

These works of famous men shall find their peace in the hearts of free peoples; the tears of the slaves are not worthy of their greatness, and the honour of kings does nothing but disturb their peace. These immortal works shall no longer be in a foreign land; today they have arrived in the fatherland of the arts and the genius, liberty and equality, in the French Republic.[9]

The collection being amassed cart after ox cart in the Louvre presented its director with an unprecedented opportunity. Denon could create displays of staggering quality that collectors before or since could only dream of. Two weeks after his appointment he invited Napoleon to view the newly designed Raphael Gallery: 'It is like a life of the master of all paintings. The first time you walk through this gallery you will find that this brings a character of order, instruction, and classification. I will continue in the same spirit for all schools . . . one will be able to have . . . a history course of the art of painting.'[10] Instead of writing his universal history of art, Denon was now in a position to arrange it within a museum. In doing so, he was pleased to take an active part in Napoleon's martial acquisition policy:

Sire, there should be in France a trophy of our German victories equal to those we brought back from Italy. If your majesty allows, I would like to draw your attention to some objects . . . in the Kassel collections, which could yield at least forty paintings, such as those by Albrecht Dürer, Holbein, and others, which so far are totally absent from the museum. In Upper Austria there is a collection of medals containing a number of portraits that is available nowhere else. This collection, which one can visit only with great difficulty, would be a welcome addition to the Cabinet impérial of your majesty.[11]

Denon's European travels were coming in handy.

His tenure as Director General of Museums was not just a personal dream come true, it also signified a landmark in the history of displaying works of art, as he arranged the works according to art-historical ideas and methodology, not randomly or purely according to the curators' tastes, as had been the case before. He focused on chronology, on national schools and on the evolution of styles. The *grand système* of the natural sciences had communicated itself to the display of artistic work.[12] One of the most important influences on Denon's arrangements was Johann Joachim Winckelmann, a German historian of art whose ideal of classical beauty and its primacy in aesthetics and art history overshadowed the entire century to come. *Stille Anmut, edle Größe* ('Silent grace, noble greatness') were his aesthetic watchwords and he regarded the overstuffed baroque interiors of many collections with nothing but scorn:

The paintings on ceilings and above doors are usually there only to fill space and to cover areas which cannot be filled up with gilt ornaments . . . Fear of emptiness fills the walls and paintings, empty of thought, are there to replace emptiness.[13]

True beauty, Winckelmann argued, was noble and pure, and the rooms in which works of art were displayed had to reflect not the amount of gilt putti their owner could afford but the intention to serve this ideal above all others. For objects from classical antiquity this approach worked well: many of them, especially marbles, were almost impossible to date. Denon, though, did not follow the German master blindly. Other sections of the museum, especially paintings, were arranged in a rational spirit akin to the work of Linnaeus and Buffon – genera, species, subspecies – as far as this seemed possible.

Denon's dream, and Napoleon's, was not to last. The great museum that had been designed for eternity was dispersed again after the Battle of Waterloo, when representatives of various countries discreetly placed requests for the restitution of their property (though the Tuscan delegates did not trouble themselves with early Renaissance panels in the Louvre and went to retrieve their fine furniture instead). The Director General of Museums, however, was confident that he had justified Napoleon's confidence in him by having been able to use and display with great sensitivity and intelligence the greatest art collection there ever was.

In 1815 Denon thought that it was time for him to retire. His personal collection was waiting for him, after all, in his house on the Quai Voltaire. He had assembled a fine collection of vases and also of paintings, all of which he had bought legitimately – testament to the character of a man in an incomparable position to avail himself of whatever he chose.

Over the course of his collecting career Denon had found several works by old masters such as Ruïsdael and Parmigianino, and had stored in his cupboards thousands of etchings, medals, bronzes, exotic curiosities and works of art. The centrepiece and heart of his collection, however, was a medieval reliquary made of gilt copper and containing an unexpected range of relics, which he itemized meticulously himself:

Splinters of the bones of the Cid and his wife Jimena, found in their grave in Burgos; splinters of the bones of Heloise and Abaelard from their graves in the monastery of Paraclet; hair from Agnès Sorel, who is buried in a hole, and from Ines de Castro from Alcaboça; a part of the moustache of the French King Henri IV found whole during the exhumation of the king's corpse in Saint-Denis in 1793; a part of the shroud of Turennes; splinters of the bones of Molière and La Fontaine; hair from General Desaix. Two other drawers in the side walls contain a signature from Napoleon's own hand, a bloodied part of the shirt worn at the moment of his death, a lock of his hair and a leaf of the willow tree under which he is resting on the island of St Helena.[14]

Dominique Vivant Denon died in 1825, aged seventy-eight, of a cold he had contracted while leaving an auction.

During the nineteenth century, burgeoning museums were thrown into a series of curiously ill-matched marriages: young states wanted long ancestries and tried to invent them spiritually if they could not establish them practically. At the same time the finest achievements of the arts had to be displayed as scientifically as possible; the all-dominating spirit of rationalism, commerce and inquiry was attempting to establish its own mythology.

Many museums throughout Europe set out to achieve what the great Vienna museums were to proclaim in their very architecture: completeness and universality. Rooms filled with plaster casts at the Victoria & Albert Museum still remind visitors that what was not actually there could be recreated in order to show the public all that was great in art, but during the nineteenth century the British Museum, too, filled the gaps in its ranks of Greek and Roman sculpture with plaster casts of great masterworks.

In their new public function, museums assumed the roles of public educator and arbiter of taste and knowledge with the whole-hearted ferocity of a Victorian missionary bringing to childlike natives the gospel and the rules of cricket. As empires expanded into increasingly remote parts of the globe it was felt necessary to display the spoils of this new-found power at home, arranged in a Darwinian, or even Hegelian, progression of civilizations and human types from the primitives who had been found in a pitiful state and blessed with the gift of Christian progress to the very pinnacles of this culture, which happened to coincide (depending on the museum's location) with the life and horizons of the British ruling class, of German Protestantism, of the newly restored French monarchy, or of the liberty of the Americans.

Collections had changed from being instruments of exploration to instruments of conservation, exploratory only in so far as they contained the specimens by which plants or animals, artistic styles or types of minerals were defined. From occupying a place in the intellectual vanguard, questioning the limits and the very quality of human knowledge, the great collections of natural history and of the history of art that had evolved out of the old cabinets became, tendentially at least, profoundly conservative; institutions devoted to classification and representation, and to the prevention of decay and corruption, both material and moral.

The process leading to the opening of the Naturhistorisches Museum in Vienna illustrates this process. When the *naturalia* contained in the former Habsburg cabinets of rarities were amalgamated with the collection of the Florentine scientist Johann V. Baillou, which had been purchased by the Habsburg emperor in 1748, Baillou was made Director of the Imperial and Royal Collections. True to the spirit of the Enlightenment it was no longer thought appropriate to have a large, general collection for the amusement of the nobility alone: the new, scientific displays were intended for instruction and were to be installed in the palace, even if this good intention was not put into practice until some fifty years later. By then the collections of dead specimens were partly supplemented by the menagerie and botanical gardens in Schönbrunn.

After the rule of the fanciful Abbé Eberle and his more sober successor Schreiber, the museum continued to grow apace, boosted by gifts, bulk purchases and the results of several expeditions to South America and other continents. It was a better, more genuinely general, collection now, but it had quickly outgrown its quarters at the

Josephsplatz. The entire city was bursting at the seams, and accommodation inside the medieval city walls had become almost unbearably cramped. Vienna was due for a dramatic reinvention.

On 20 December 1857, Emperor Francis Joseph finally decreed the demolition of the old city wall and the building in its stead of a grand boulevard around the old centre of his capital. Among the buildings to be erected in this symbolic location would be two museums, which would be built by Gottfried Semper and Karl von Hasenauer. The two large museums between the famous stables built by the Baroque genius Joseph Emanuel Fischer von Erlach and the imperial palace itself would form an imperial forum of knowledge, culture and history.[15] Now the collections (which had been separated into zoology, botany and mineralogy in keeping with the scientific thinking of the day) could be once more reunited under one roof and would have space enough to grow and flourish. The new building was administered no longer by the imperial court but by an independent authority, the ministry of education.

Here, finally, everything could be displayed with sufficient space, labelling and explanation, ordered accordingly, catalogued and kept safely behind glass; while in the offices, workshops and laboratories curators and scientists could prepare and restore specimens, determine and classify new additions, and press on with the advance of science. This was to be a home worthy of the greatness of the Habsburg Empire.

The spirit of collecting had come a long way from the cabinets of curiosities of 200 years earlier, which had sought to extend the boundaries, to find and document what was rare and monstrous. Now was the day of the ordinary, not of what was outside human understanding, but what had already been subjected by it. The system was all-important, the objects themselves mere illustrations of the supremacy of the rational mind. When Sir William Henry Flower, Curator of Zoology at the British Museum, described the planning of a new museum in 1898 the priorities are already set:

First you must have your curator. He must carefully consider the object of the museum, the class and capacities of the persons for whose instruction it is founded, and the space available to carry out this object. He will then divide the subject to be illustrated into groups, and consider their relative proportions, according to which he will plan out the space. Large labels will next be prepared for the principal headings, as the chapters of a book, and smaller ones for the various subdivisions. Certain propositions to be illustrated, either in the structure, classification, geographical distribution, geological position, habits, or evolution of the subjects dealt with, will be laid down and reduced to definite and concise language. Lastly will come the illustrative specimens, each of which as procured and prepared will fall into its appropriate place.[16]

This ethos of objectivity, which transformed great collections effectively into catechisms of scientific and imperial greatness, to pillars of empire, was not confined to museums owned by the state. General Pitt Rivers, then still Colonel Lane Fox, the founder of Oxford's Pitt Rivers Museum of ethnography and natural history, had a similarly detached view of his own anthropological objects and their significance:

The collection does not contain any considerable number of unique specimens, and has been collected during upwards of twenty years, not for the purpose of surprising any one, either by the beauty or value of the objects exhibited, but solely with a view to instruction. For this purpose ordinary and typical specimens, rather than rare objects, have been selected and arranged in sequence, so as to trace, as far as practicable, the succession of ideas by which the minds of men in a primitive condition of culture have progressed from the simple to the complex, and from the homogeneous to the heterogeneous.[17]

The journey from one aristocratic owner into professional administration and finally state ownership (the Habsburg collections were nationalized in 1919), mirrors a process that took place all over Europe. Museums were national business, and had to play a role in the formation and perfection of the nation. It had, in the delicious definition of the curator G. Brown Goode's, reached the stage of being 'a collection of instructive labels illustrated by well-selected specimens'.

An Elevator to the Heavens

It was so bulbous that even the most sycophantic of his admirers could do no better than to ignore it altogether; like leavened dough it seemed to expand further and further, a luminous symbol of its owner's capacity of sniffing out important pieces; by the time he reached old age J. Pierpont Morgan's nose had mushroomed to almost grotesque proportions.

Caricaturists had a field day with this organ, reducing its owner to little more than a porous snout with chequebook attached, prowling the world for treasure, or simply attracting the most precious pieces of the Old World with a gigantic, dollar-shaped magnet.

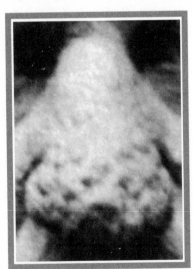

J. Pierpont Morgan (1837–1913) had spent his youth in material comfort and emotional uncertainty. The son of a successful American banker, he changed school nine times and saw little of his father. As a small child, he had suffered from convulsions and ill health stayed with him for much of his life. The boy's diaries show a mind intent on control. While the individual entries ('Mother Ill', 'Dancing school. Ladies to tea', 'Father did not come home'[1]) give no more than a hint at what exercised him, the paraphernalia on the page bring it to life vividly: in addition to the dated entries are lists of days past and days remaining of the year, of places in which he had lived, together with the relevant page numbers of diary entries, the initials of the girls he fancied, and a list of all letters sent and received, including the cost of postage. Pierpont, it was clear, liked keeping track and asserting his control over the small corner of the world in which his will counted for something. His father's busy life, his mother's emotional instability and his own itinerant schooling with the accompanying lack of friends and certainties may have been beyond his power; the cost of postage and the days of the year, however, could not elude him as easily.

His upbringing was dour and unforgiving, as befits a businessman in the making, so a tour to Europe in 1853 proved to be a revelation: the art, the history and the sheer wealth of beauty he saw there fascinated him, and he was happy to find himself back in London three years later, when his father moved there in the latest step on the long path of his career. Pierpont was sent to Switzerland, where he was to attend an exclusive boarding school, the latest and last of the many he had been enrolled in. The boy was not impressed with what seemed to him a trap for paying foreigners, but did enjoy the travelling his new base enabled him to do, duly noting down entrance fees to museums and money spent on alms for beggars, flowers, cologne, confectionary and the like. He made out his accounts in the correct currencies. Doctors' fees made regular appearances.

Morgan had not yet finished the education his father thought necessary for his son. He had learned French in Switzerland and was now sent to Göttingen University. Here Pierpont hired a servant and found the good life, declaring the biggest of his problems to be his inability to flirt in German, though he quickly came to understand that his helplessness endeared him to local girls. The university itself was not unduly burdened with the presence of the young American, who clearly was fully occupied already.

Having finished his education, Pierpont joined the family bank and spent the next few years travelling between Europe and the States. He married, but his wife died of consumption when he was only twenty-four. While his private life was overshadowed by tragedy and his health continued to trouble him, business was booming, and an almost psychic sense for the right investment in a time of tremendous expansion made Morgan a very rich man indeed. As such he lived in great style and with all the trappings of a nineteenth-century tycoon. He married again, and seemed happy in his roles as financier and *père de familie*. It was not until the change of the century, though, when he was in his sixties, that he hit his stride as a collector of European art and books. Once the passion had taken hold there was no going back. His ravenous appetite for all things great and exquisite meant that he himself often had little idea what precisely was in his possession. A note to his librarian inquiring about a sculpture of the infant Hercules, which was attributed to Michelangelo and which Morgan gathered from his account books he had purchased for $10,000, was answered, in green ink, 'This bronze Bust is in your Library and faces you when sitting in your chair. It has been there for about a year.'[2]

Morgan continued buying as if there were no tomorrow. Money was no object, and objects were everything. The collector himself noted sardonically that the three most expensive words in any language were *unique au monde*. His European education had resulted in a very tactile passion for the past and for beauty. When he had his New York residence, now the Pierpont Morgan Library, remodelled in 1906, he furnished it with Istrian marble mantelpieces, sixteenth-century Paduan andirons, original wooden ceilings and other details scavenged from Europe, as well as a tapestry which he bought from Joseph Duveen and which had once belonged to Cardinal Mazarin, that other voracious collector of works of art. Morgan's taste was 'American eclectic' and derived from a lifetime of travel, the highlights of which he now sought to combine in one house, so much so that even his agent, Charles Follent McKim, saw himself called upon to advise restraint: 'While fully recognizing great merit of Chateau D'Arnay chimney piece we should strongly recommend a consistent Italian marble example in the building of Italian Renaissance design.'[3]

While the New York residence was appointed in European splendour most of the collection intended to fill it was still in exile, in London, where it was kept for tax reasons. A visitor to Morgan's house in Princes Gate, the Bishop of Massachusetts, recalled seeing in the upstairs drawing room paintings by Gainsborough, Rembrandt, Hals, Velázquez and Van Dyck, as well as Louis XV furniture, Sèvres porcelain, antiquities, miniatures by Holbein, Nicholas Hilliard and Isaac Oliver and a profusion of jewelled boxes.

The remodelling of the New York mansion, meanwhile, was progressing apace, and Morgan showed not only exacting taste, but also a sense of irony when he decorated his sumptuous East Room with a sixteenth-century Brussels tapestry, *The Triumph of Avarice*. Today, the Pierpont Morgan Library, the collector's legacy, stands almost pathetically squat among the towering rockscapes of Manhattan. Described by the art historian Bernard Berenson as 'a pawnbroker's shop for Croesus', some of its interior rooms have been faithfully preserved. The neo-Renaissance library is a treasury second to none for modern and medieval autographs; it contains some of the greatest treasures on paper of the West, with examples of seemingly every literary and musical figure of any renown, as well as a profusion of incunabula: two Gutenberg bibles, the celebrated *Farnese Hours*, manuscript scores by Mahler, Beethoven, Mozart and Bach, letters and notebooks by Shelley, Johnson, Dickens and Burns, original drawings by Blake, Shakespeare folios, the works of Sir Thomas Browne in early printings, the only surviving manuscript fragment of Milton's *Paradise Lost* – the list seems endless, and endlessly rich.

In Morgan's study, across a vaulted rotunda with historicizing frescos, one impression above all is conveyed: despite the fine quality of the works displayed around the room, on the mantelpiece, on the ledge running round the walls, on the walls themselves and on the desk, despite the fact that there are masterworks by great artists in plenty, fine medieval paintings, stained-glass windows, Italian Renaissance reliefs attributed to Perugino, Botticelli, Cima da Conegliano and Raphael (though later shown to be by a different hand), the famous double portrait of Luther and his wife, Katharina von Bora, exceptional Renaissance bronzes, etc., the overall sense is one of clutter, of stuff, of a room crammed with things, the apotheosis of a Victorian study in which each of the multitude of knick-knacks happens to be worth millions.

Morgan was one of a breed of American collectors that came to dominate the beginning of the twentieth century, men who underwrote the purchases of their agents in Europe with blank cheques and who were positively distrustful if they paid less than a six-figure sum for any major work of art they wanted. This was the age of the moguls, during which Morgan, together with (and competing against) William Randolph Hearst, Andrew Mellon, John D. Rockefeller, Jr., Henry Clay Frick, Andrew Carnegie, Benjamin Altman, Samuel H. Kress and a handful of others, seemed set on denuding Europe of its treasures, amassing more of them than anyone had done since Rudolf II and Napoleon, and sometimes more quickly than either of them. In their young country, the great collectors displayed a ravenous appetite for what was old, in the Land of the Free they craved the paraphernalia of the lives of those whose wealth had been earned by serfs and slaves.

One man more than any other shaped these collections and the taste that informed them, and, by extension, many of the holdings of great American museums and the aesthetic of America in the twentieth century: Joseph Duveen, later Sir Joseph and then Lord Duveen of Millbank.

As a young man, Duveen had founded his career as an art dealer on the spectacular purchase of an entire German collection, assembled by Oskar Hainauer and catalogued by no less an authority than Wilhelm von Bode, the director of the Berlin museums, for the dizzying sum of $2.5 million (some $50 million in today's money) in 1906. It proved an excellent investment. Duveen would continue to sell works from the Hainauer Collection for his entire working life, to H. E. Huntington, Frick and Morgan, among others.

The central premise underlying his meteoric rise to the grandest of art dealers and adviser to some of the most acquisitive collectors the world had seen was simple: there was plenty of money in the United States and plenty of old, valuable art in Europe. All he had to do was to establish a connection between the two. Which meant first turning the taste of American collectors away from lugubrious French and Victorian landscape painting towards the Italian Renaissance, a far more profitable and exciting field.

Duveen's most successful selling ploy was his apparent reluctance to sell anything at all. Whenever wealthy clients came to the shop to browse for statuettes or vases, there would be one painting prominently displayed that would not be for sale, either because it was already promised for someone else, or because Duveen doubted that it would be right for the client, or the client for it, or because the dealer himself could not bring himself to part with it. The onus of proving his worthiness was upon the client, be it Hearst, Rockefeller or even some less bona fide person, and time and again Duveen would find his good heart finally won over in the face of a collector's eloquence. 'Duveen didn't want to sell his stuff, but they always badgered the poor feller till he gave in,' a sympathetic Mrs Hearst was once overheard to say.[4] A collecting novice, a Californian industrialist, found this out to his cost when he came to visit Duveen's gallery. He was kept waiting for half an hour and then admitted with the greatest courtesy. Immediately his appetites were whetted by a Rembrandt portrait prominently displayed on an easel. The price was a $100,000, which in itself did not pose the slightest problem. The problem was Duveen's concern about the appropriateness of the transaction. On hearing that the prospective client did not own any other pictures, he flatly refused to sell. 'I can't possibly sell a Rembrandt to a man who owns no other pictures, the Rembrandt would be lonely,'[5] he opined and would not be swayed. The downcast supplicant had to leave without the Rembrandt. Business life, however, had taught him a few tricks of his own. Over the following years he acquired a series of less celebrated Duveens, building up a collection of sufficient quality to force the dealer to release the portrait that had originally caught his eye.

Duveen remains a legendary presence among art dealers and collectors. Everyone has their favourite anecdote of this man who almost realized his ambition of cornering the American market of old master paintings for himself and who thought nothing of approaching a work one of his clients had rashly purchased from a different dealer and saying, *en passant*, 'I smell fresh paint.' The work, of course, would be sent back and the chastened collector returned to Duveen's fold. This was a strategy he knew to employ to great effect: a remark uttered almost inaudibly could devastate his competitors.

Seemingly cavalier in his *modus operandi*, Duveen was in fact acutely aware of his clients' ambitions and would often work for months before dangling just the right picture in front of a collector in his famously nonchalant way. When an art historian saw fit to chide him for having put too much brilliant varnish on a restored canvas, Duveen remarked that his clients mainly wanted to see themselves reflected when looking at their pictures. There was more at stake in these transactions than simply the possession of a great work of art: canonization, admittance into the great chain of previous owners, into the mystique of provenance, supplied helpfully by the dealer in the form of a scholarly brochure accompanying every painting sold by him. Duveen did not sell pictures: he sold immortality.

In order to keep himself the one and only dealer in the market, he had to make sacrifices: he bought pictures from his clients that he considered too poor for their walls, too appallingly saccharine to hang next to a Raphael, too bland for the dramatic setting. These would go (usually in exchange for something from his gallery) into his own vaults, which in time became a veritable menagerie of the hated, the bad or the dangerous: asked why he had bought a near-contemporary work from a collector, he answered: 'I didn't want that fellow to get used to buying modern pictures, there are too damn many of them.'6 This was one of the more obvious ways in which Duveen tried, successfully for a while, to dominate American collecting habits. Less immediately apparent was his preference for certain genres over others, which, he believed, would not sell in the States: not too much nudity, attractive women (if not overly suggestive) but no nude men, nothing lascivious or even faintly immoral (the sale of a Gainsborough once almost collapsed because the sitter, Mrs Elliot, had run off with her gardener), no too overtly religious scenes, no martyrs wallowing in suffering and, most importantly, no small fry. He could sell the Sistine Chapel several times over, he believed, but works that were too cheap or painted by artists who were too little known were just not worth the trouble. Considering the fact that Duveen was constantly in debt, he should have sold the contents of his copious cellars, and was repeatedly advised to do so. This, however, he could not do; it would swamp the market and allow men of less impeccable taste to lapse back into mediocrity from which his ministrations had rescued them.

Duveen's greatest secret weapon and part of his astounding success was an American in exile, the art historian Bernard Berenson, who had built himself up to be (arguably together with von Bode in Berlin) the greatest and most indisputable authority on Italian art. Berenson's expertise, his merest word, could establish or destroy the authenticity of any work he chose to pronounce upon – and he chose to pronounce regularly, aided by a generous retainer from Duveen, to whom he, in turn, would lend the scholarly respectability and the Italian radiance that the dealer himself, who had never been to university and whose father had been little more than a wealthy draper, could not quite muster. Berenson was everything Duveen was not: he came from Boston and had been to Harvard, was an aesthete, a scholar and a bookman, a former protégé of Isabelle Stewart Gardner. Surrounded by some of the finest works of the Renaissance he lived in Italy in an exquisite villa, the intimate of counts and princesses. His authority had mythical proportions.

Theirs was the most formidable partnership in the art world, though even Berenson's scholarship was not infallible. In one of the most interesting asides in art history, he created a painter, Amico di Sandro, simply to satisfy his need for firm attributions. This Renaissance master was the creator of an increasingly large canon of fine works until his own maker decided that it would be prudent to do away with him after all and reattributed his entire output to other masters, thereby depriving the Italian Renaissance of one of its most enigmatic and short-lived geniuses.

It was attribution that made the partnership between Berenson and Duveen so valuable, and it was attribution that would end it. When Duveen wanted to sell an *Adoration of the Shepherds*, a painting he believed to be by Giorgione, to Andrew Mellon, one of his best customers, he found to his dismay that Berenson insisted it was by Titian, a master who in the seventy years of his career produced so many fine pictures that their value relative to that of a Giorgione was small. Moreover, Mellon already possessed several Titians but no Giorgione. The question of attribution was therefore of greatest importance. Berenson, however, was not to be convinced, not to be reasoned with, not to be out-argued and certainly not to be bullied. He studied the picture and again rejected his collaborator's attribution. Uncertain and dissatisfied without a Berenson authentification, Mellon returned the picture and Duveen considered his friendship with the great scholar to be at an end.

As purveyor of fine paintings to the new aristocracy, Duveen had to accommodate their whims. Huntington once sent back Gainsborough's *Blue Boy* because he did not consider it blue enough. Such artistic criteria presumably inspired Harold Macmillan to call the Americans Romans to Britain's Greeks. If the parallel between the American moguls and the rapacious Romans seems obvious now, they saw themselves rather as Medicis and Gonzagas, princes of the Renaissance, a period whose artistic grandeur and brutal efficiency contributed, together with Duveen's good offices, to making it their favourite. On Saturday afternoons Frick would sit in his palazzo on Park Avenue on a Renaissance throne reading the *Saturday Evening Post* to the majestic chords of his house organ played by a musician employed for this act of worship. The catalogue Morgan commissioned of his collection, a work of several years of scholarship by one George Williamson, resembled an illuminated manuscript, its colourful illustration and gold and silver leaf laid on so thick that the designs of his watch collection could be engraved on to the pages just as they were on the originals. When he died, in 1913, it was lying by his bed.

Those who dealt with this new nobility were well advised to play along, and even the otherwise aloof Berenson was not above encouraging his patroness, Isabella Stewart Gardner, to buy a portrait because it depicted 'the greatest and most fascinating lady of the Renaissance – your worthy precursor and patron saint – Isabella d'Este, Marchioness of Mantua'.[7] The American, who liked to believe that she was descended from Robert the Bruce and took her second name from Mary Stuart, obviously considered this line of thought entirely appropriate and purchased the work.

The prince of all these princes was William Randolph Hearst, who must have felt it positively frivolous to waste his time on little gestures like name changes. A newspaper tycoon who had made a fortune out of making the gutter press and who had had a hand in starting the American–Spanish War in 1898, through deliberate misinformation to increase the circulation of his *Journal*, he was the archetype of the autocratic and ruthless entrepreneur whose self-aggrandizement had become his *raison d'être*. It comes as little surprise, then, that he was the inspiration for Orson Welles's 1941 film, *Citizen Kane*, which the Hearst press understandably attempted to scupper. Welles had looked closely and invented little: from the charisma and the curious sentimentality of a man running an unparalleled media empire to his Quixotic attempts at making his mistress, the actress Marion Davies, into a great star despite her obvious lack of talent; from his need for total control of the people around him to his inability to control himself; and his almost pathological urge to amass and accumulate riches and treasures to demonstrate his power, an urge that could never be satisfied.

There was no 'Rosebud' in Hearst's life that could succinctly and poignantly explain his maniacal gallop through existence to an audience of adoring film students, and yet his career serves as an illustration of the nature and force of an obsession lived out to the full. This came to be expressed most acutely in his San Simeon mansion, a building in what was later called the Bastard-Spanish-Moorish-Romanesque-Gothic-Renaissance-Bull-Market-Damn-the-Expense Style and an extravaganza previously unseen even in the United States. It was, writes his biographer, 'not built from scratch to suit certain living needs, but was a mosaic of Hearst's memories, inspirations and possessions. In his card-index memory he had recollections of decorative schemes and arrangements he had seen in European castles and cathedrals, and which he wished to incorporate in his own palace'.[8] He had already amassed hundreds of crates filled with entire gothic rooms, carved ceilings, choir stalls, panelling, staircases, stained glass, sarcophagi, tapestries and countless other items that would come in handy for a palace that was yet to be erected, a building to supplement the two castles already in his possession, one of which, St Donat's Castle in Glamorganshire, North Wales, he hardly ever visited.

In his San Simeon palace, Hearst himself slept in a bed that had once belonged to Cardinal Richelieu. In the Clarendon building in New York, the elevator leading to his three-floor apartment, crammed full of armour, canvases, tapestries and sculptures, was a converted confession box that had once been witness to whispered sins and intrigues at the Vatican. The bathtub was of Parian marble and had once accommodated President Wilson at the White House. Everything had to be on the most lavish scale. Hearst, the newspaper man, owned an airfield, 10,000 head of cattle, a dairy, a thoroughbred stud farm, a poultry farm, scores of cars, a small army of gardeners and a private zoo in which lions and tigers, polar bears and other creatures were shown off to admiring guests, who became themselves, at least temporarily, part of his enormous collection. Not since Versailles had the world seen a palace so phenomenal and a master so lavishly, so prodigiously wasteful.

Underlying all this was an unquenchable need for possession and control. His newspapers allowed him to control minds and the course of politics (he was instrumental in the election of two presidents), his money gave him control over the world. Even his attempts at making his mistress the greatest diva Hollywood had seen were dominated by his possessive instinct: 'She had beauty and talent. He would supply the instructors, the writers and directors to bring it out, and the publicity to exploit it . . . He was possessive about everything he owned. Miss Davies was his most prized possession, whom he would train, groom, push and publicise until she reached the heights.'[9] It was not to be, and the actress, whom he had plucked from the chorus of a Ziegfeld extravaganza, became the grande dame of his castle instead of enthralling the world on celluloid. This instinct to have and control made him an easy prey for art dealers. He simply could not resist anything that came his way. At auction he would habitually outbid everybody else (as a result his mere presence would boost prices) and he once bought a $40,000 carpet simply because the window display marked it the most expensive in the world. It was shipped off to one of his warehouses never to be seen again. He was well aware of this Achilles' heel. 'I'm afraid I'm like a dipsomaniac with a bottle,' he told *The New York Times*, 'they keep sending me these art catalogues and I can't resist them.'[10] Duveen worked his favourite trick on him by telling an agitated Hearst (who had just quarrelled with Miss Davies) that a Van Dyck he was admiring was in fact for Mrs Duveen and not for sale. This piece of information resulted, after a discussion as protracted as it was passionate, in a transaction of $345,000, enough to comfort a disappointed Mrs Duveen. Typically, Hearst had overpaid wildly in his determination to possess what was threatening to slip from his hand. The painting was later resold for $89,000.

A staff of thirty men worked at Hearst's warehouses on 143rd Street and in the Bronx, where millions of dollars' worth of art and antiques lay crated up, including the entire cloisters of two monasteries, one of them alone stored in 10,700 crates, and tens of thousands of books, many of whom their owner had never seen and would never lay eyes on. Here the possessions were catalogued and photographed and bound for Hearst to ogle in the safety of his home, a record of ownership almost rendering the objects themselves redundant. Two cabinetmakers and an armourer were in full-time employment here.

In the end even Hearst's fabulous wealth – his income was around $15,000,000 (c. $160,000,000 in today's money) a year – could not withstand his obsessive urge to possess and he found himself in 1937 to be $126,000,000 (c. $1.6 billion today) in debt, most of this through spending on works of art and on San Simeon. Now the walls of his castles in the air came crashing down, burying underneath them his power and an entire era. Hearst and his mistress had to leave their apartment at the Clarendon, which had by now spread over five floors of art-packed rooms; he had to sell and auction off many of his objects just to save his company and stay afloat; he had to give up his Hollywood dreams for Miss Davies; and restrict the number of his residences to a mere four. He managed to hold on to much of his empire, to his palace and to great parts of his collections, but his power and his position at the cutting edge of journalism were all but broken. He now faced what he had done his utmost to avoid facing all his life: death itself.

Life went on for another fourteen years, but much of it was a drawn-out form of atrophy; humiliated by a constant need of loans, stung by the release of *Citizen Kane*, weeping, he left his castle for the last time to take refuge from a world he understood less and less in a Beverly Hills villa and a life governed by doctors and nurses. His odd falsetto voice would still be heard over the telephone at his newspaper offices at all hours of the day and night in a feeble attempt to assert control, but the arms of his empire were run by other, younger, men who did little more than show deference when necessary.

Hearst's fear of death had been the great taboo of his career, scrupulously observed by his employees, who had been under orders to keep away from him any discussion of the matter or any inkling of its constant reality. His staff went to extremes to keep him in the illusion of eternal life. When one of the palms at San Simeon died unexpectedly, the gardeners painted its leaves green until it could be replaced during Hearst's absence. He hated attending funerals and would send deputies, solicitors and exorbitant flower wreaths rather than attend the last rites even of close associates. He was sentimental about his childhood memories. During his baronial banquets, which were attended by film stars and other celebrities, the table settings would include, among antique silverware and exquisite porcelain, ketchup in the original bottles to remind him of picnics he had had with his parents. Special guests were honoured by being allowed to sleep in bed linen decorated with his mother's monogram and inherited from her. Now, watched by nurses and kept alive by medicines, the illusion could be upheld no longer and the immortality he had tried to purchase with every item he had ever bought was running through weakening fingers. He died, aged eighty-eight, on 14 August 1951.

Part III

Incantations

And suddenly the memory returns. The taste was that of the little crumb of madeleine which on Sunday mornings at Combray . . . when I went to say good day to her in her bedroom, my aunt Léonie used to give me, dipping it first in her own cup of real or of lime-flower tea . . . But when from a long-distant past nothing subsists, after the people are dead, after the things are broken and scattered, still, alone, more fragile, but with more vitality, more unsubstantial, more persistent, more faithful, the smell and taste of things remain poised a long time, like souls, ready to remind us, waiting and hoping for their moment, amid the ruins of all the rest; and bear unfaltering, in the tiny and almost impalpable drop of their essence, the vast structure of recollection.

Marcel Proust, *À la recherche du temps perdu*[1]

This refutes Gertrude Stein's claim 'a rose is a rose is a rose': that it has become a different object if Napoleon wore it on his uniform. A key is no longer a key if it belonged to the Bastille. A knitting needle is an object with a special aura if Marie Antoinette made it rattle, and a shaving kit will evoke horrible associations if it was once owned by Danton.

Lorenz Tomerius, 'Das Glück, zu finden. Die Lust, zu zeigen'[2]

Why Boiling People is Wrong

When the bones of King *Arthur* were digged up, the old Race might think, they beheld therein some Originals of themselves; Unto these of our Urnes none here can pretend relation, and can only behold the Reliques of those persons, who in their life giving the Laws unto their predecessors, after long obscurity, now lye at their mercies. But remembring the early civility they brought upon these Countreys, and forgetting long passed mischiefs; We mercifully preserve their bones, and pisse not upon their ashes.

Thomas Browne, *Urne Buriall*[1]

The gentlemen at Christie's had obviously taken the greatest trouble to hide both their own embarrassment and to spare their readers. The delicately phrased entry in the sale catalogue of Wednesday 29 October 1969, dealing, among others, with 'The Celebrated Vignali Collection of Napoleon Relics' eventually read:

A small dried-up object, genteely described as a mummified tendon, taken from his body during the post-mortem. (The authenticity of the macabre relic has been confirmed by the publication in the *Revue des Mondes* of a posthumous memoir by St Denis, in which he expressly states that he and Vignali took away small pieces of Napoleon's corpse during the autopsy.)

There was no lot number and no estimate. In the event, the 'mummified tendon', the great man's most private of private parts, did not reach its reserve price and was returned to its owner, an American book dealer.

Mr St Denis, who had been able to authenticate Napoleon's last indignity in his banishment on St Helena, had been his 'personal valet and mameluke' on the island and stood in as his accountant and *chasseur*. The exiled emperor had ordered that a post-mortem should be performed on his body as soon as possible and the procedure was duly undertaken on the afternoon of his death. The billiard table had to double as a mortuary slab. The doctor who had been sent to look after him came into his own. Two years earlier, when Napoleon felt his health failing, he had asked for a priest ('an educated man, under forty, easy to get on with, and not prejudiced against Gallican principles') and a doctor. He had been sent two men of the cloth from his home island of Corsica, one infirm after a stroke and barely able to speak, the other a young man who could hardly read or write. The requested doctor appeared in the shape of a thirty-year-old dissecting-room assistant, one François Antommarchi, who was only too happy to acknowledge that until then he 'had had only corpses to deal with'.[2] Not having been of great help to his ailing patient while he was alive, Antommarchi could now spring into action and demonstrate his expertise in front of the British officers and doctors looking on. After the autopsy, during which Antommarchi had located 'a very extended cancerous ulcer', the emperor was laid out in his green Chasseur's uniform, which had been turned inside out recently because it was so faded. The whole English garrison came to pay their last respects. It was generally agreed that the emperor looked very beautiful with a fine, regular and placid countenance.

It seems likely that Napoleon had not yielded to stomach cancer, but had died a slow and painful death from arsenic-poisoning, administered, it has been suggested, in the emperor's almond milk by the British governor of the island, Hudson Lowe, who was terrified of his prisoner and of the responsibility placed upon his shoulders, and who may have acted on higher orders.[3] A more likely, and less dramatic, explanation is that the real and unwitting murderer was a Swedish chemist by the name of Scheele, who had invented a dye containing copper arsenic, which was used in wallpaper in Napoleon's quarters. When damp, the wallpaper emitted vapours that may well have killed the exile over the months and years of his stay there.

The course of the emperor's physical decline, the remarkable state of preservation of his body when it was finally transferred to the Pantheon in Paris, and the levels of the poison found in various locks of hair that were taken from the corpse all indicate arsenic rather than cancer as the cause of death. For the dignitaries who saw at that time the body of the greatest Frenchman who had ever lived, it seemed little short of a miracle that it had hardly decomposed, a fact reminiscent of stories of saints who, when exhumed, often centuries after their burial, were found to be perfectly preserved and smelling of sweet flowers and incense. Those who wanted to believe simply took it as one more indication that Napoleon had passed into the pantheon of the immortals, the secular saints of the Grande Nation. The Christian idea of the body as being impervious to decay and corruption formed a link to a powerful tradition that seemed both logical and natural. Arsenic may thus have contributed to the myth of the emperor's supernatural powers, a man of providence, an incarnation of the universal spirit itself driving forward history. This was no mere mortal and what had once been his, or had been in contact with him, duly achieved the status of a holy relic to be revered.

The abbé and Mr St Denis, the late emperor's valet, were not left incapacitated by their grief for a fellow Corsican and went about discreetly cementing his legacy by capitalizing on the solid demand for Napoleonic mementoes, in which there was already a robust trade throughout Europe. In his will, Napoleon had left his chaplain the

stately sum of 100,000 francs. The abbé now saw the opportunity of multiplying his benefactor's generosity. During the autopsy, he removed some of Napoleon's beard and body hair, as well as bits of his skin, generously dividing some of these between his friends. The 'mummified tendon' later to reappear at Christie's was part of his spoils, as was one of the death masks made by the good doctor Antommarchi.

Their collection of Napoleon memorabilia stayed in Corsica until the London firm of Maggs Brothers bought the relics from Vignali's collateral descendants. From there they went to a Dr Rosenbach, a New York bookseller, along with the emperor's letters and documents confirming the authenticity of the 'mummified tendon'.

The Christie's experts, having overcome their scruples about this most unusual of lots, had hoped to sell it for up to £30,000. Bidding started at £10. Only one bidder, however, was willing to go as high as £14,000. He was Mr Brian Gimelson of Fort Washington, Pennsylvania, who was particularly interested in relics of Napoleon because his own wife was called Josephine. (*The Times* of 30 October 1969 carried a photograph of Josephine Gimelson holding a pair of the emperor's breeches.) Earlier that year Christie's had successfully sold the dead emperor's hat, and the Hôtel Rameau in Versailles had sold some locks of Napoleon's hair, his spectacles, straw from his coffin, and a willow tree that had been planted near his tomb.

The veneration of and trade in relics sacred and profane had a long pedigree in France and throughout Europe and every collection is, to some extent, a reliquary preserving fragments of a realm beyond our reach. During the Middle Ages this passion blossomed in its purest form.

By an appropriate coincidence, Monsieur St Denis shared his saintly surname with one Abbot Suger, who had documented his passion for collecting holy relics some 800 years before Napoleon was mutilated in the interest of pious greed and the burgeoning cult around his legend.

Suger, born in 1081, was an avid relic hunter and had assembled a treasure for the greater glory of God in the royal Abbey of St Denis, near Paris. Not only was the treasure documented, but he himself also recorded in his autobiography the motives for its creation:

To me, I confess, it always has seemed right that the most expensive things should be used above all for the administration of the holy Eucharist. If golden vessels, vials and mortars were used to collect 'the blood of goats or calves or the red heifer', how much more should gold vases, precious stones and whatever is most valuable among created things be set out with continual reverence and full devotion 'to receive the blood of Jesus Christ' (Heb. 9:1 3f.).[4]

Suger had been dedicated to the abbey at the age of nine, like many younger sons of the minor nobility. He was appointed abbot in 1122 and held the post until his death in 1155.

One of the most important and influential men in France, Suger believed that the glory of God was also the glory of his country and that God should be worshipped as King Solomon had worshipped him: in a sanctuary resplendent with gold, silver and precious stones. He therefore set about renovating the somewhat dilapidated abbey and equipping it with statues, holy vessels and reliquaries made by the best workmen. Suger presided over an astonishing collection of relics and half-relics, the latter being objects of uncertain origin but unquestionable appeal that had found their way into the treasure. Among these were a Greek vase with Bacchic scenes, a Sassanian bowl thought to be the cup of Solomon himself, a Roman stone bathtub that was placed behind the high altar, a unicorn's horn, the teeth of an elephant, and a gryphon's claw, as well as other curiosities. Though these had unpleasantly heathen connotations the sanctity of the other relics could not be doubted, for they included items once belonging to the Saviour Himself: his swaddling clothes, parts of his crown of thorns, nails from the Holy Cross, etc.

Already at this time the somewhat uncritical attitude Suger displayed towards his treasures' provenance did not go unnoticed. He, however, remained firm:

Some of our intimates cautiously suggested that it might have been better for our reputation and that of the church as well if we had chosen to investigate the truth of the inscriptions [i.e., the provenance of relics] in private. Fired by my own faith, I replied that, if the inscriptions were true, I would rather have it discovered publicly than check it secretly and invite the skepticism of those who had not been present. Thus we brought the aforesaid altar into our midst and summoned goldsmiths, who carefully opened the little compartments containing the holy arms, upon which sat the little crystals with their inscriptions. God granting, just as we had hoped, with all looking on, we found everything there.[5]

Among the holy relics held by the abbey was a set of remains described as follows in '. . . un coffre de bahut d'environ deux pieds et demy de long et un pied de large . . . dedans icelluy coffre les ossemens du corps Monsieur St Louis'[6] ('. . . a coffer, about two-and-a-half foot long and one foot broad . . . inside this coffer the bones of the body of Monsieur St Louis'). *Les ossemens du corps Monsieur St Louis* had found their way to France after a long and adventurous journey. The saint had died in Tunis in 1137. As was the medieval custom in cases of eminent and holy men dying while abroad, the flesh was boiled off their bones in a large cauldron of wine and water. The crusaders had practised this technique for some time. Unable to preserve and take back home entire bodies of knights fallen in the holy war in the heat of the Middle East the bones would suffice. They had seen the holy sites, after all, had died for Christ himself, had been martyred in the name of God at the hands of infidels. One obvious problem with this practice was that, once divided from the flesh, the bone of a saintly knight of Christ was impossible to tell apart from that of a commoner, a thief, or even an infidel, a fact used to best effect by relic merchants specialized in supplying Europe with Middle Eastern *venerabilia*.

In the case of Monsieur St Louis there were no such doubts. His soft tissue was buried in Monreale in Sicily, while his bones and heart were transferred, wrapped in scented silk, to St Denis. But his posthumous journeys had not ended. In 1305, the abbey swapped his skull, minus the jawbone, for a box of pious allsorts – a reliquary containing specimens from all the relics held in the Sainte Chapelle – while the jaw was given a special reliquary all of its own. Later abbots were to find themselves equally unable to resist the temptation to exchange interesting relics for parts of the saint's skeleton.

Suger may have been the Middle Ages's most enthusiastic hunter and embellisher of relics but his love of saintly remains was shared by many. Following the access to the Middle East gained by the crusaders, the trade in relics blossomed when body parts of innumerable saints and objects connected to them were venerated, bought and sold, disputed and forged on a staggering scale. Such was the potential value of relics that when St Francis of Assisi, exhausted by fasting and strenuous penances, was nearing his death, he was put under round-the-clock armed guard to prevent the rival city of Perugia from snatching his precious body. To this day Assisi, the second most-visited gravesite in the Catholic world, benefits from a steady stream of pilgrims.

The first great reliquary of Christendom was the Rome of the East, Constantinople, which had in its walls not only the body of St Stephen, but also the headdress of the prophet Elijah and the very tablets of the law received by Moses on Mount Sinai, the manna given to the Israelites in the desert, the trumpet blown by Joshua outside the walls of Jericho, the chains of St Peter, and many other precious and holy objects. Indeed, most items of significance from the life of the Saviour Himself were also here. Along with the column at which Jesus was flagellated, Anthony, Archbishop of Novgorod, tells us in 1200 that he saw slabs from Christ's tomb and the table at which he had celebrated the Last Supper, as well as a chart used to measure the height of Jesus as a growing boy.

The Saviour posed a dilemma to relic lovers. While martyrs generally left behind remains that could be venerated, his own body, having ascended into heaven, was beyond the reach of both the pious and the greedy. The significance of the Holy Cross was therefore all the greater. It had been fortuitously found, along with the nails, the title tablet and the crown of thorns, by Empress Helena, who had sent half of it to Constantinople while leaving the other half at the Church of the Holy Sepulchre in Jerusalem, where it remained, until it vanished when Saladin took the city in 1187. Throughout the Middle Ages, fragments of the True Cross appeared all over Europe. Some have survived to this day.

Sceptics have pointed out time and again that whole forests were felled in order to satisfy the demand for pieces of the cross. To the faithful, however, there was another explanation, which had been supplied by Bishop Nola, who had written in the fifth century that the cross would keep renewing itself whenever pieces were cut away from it.

Where the Holy Cross itself was not available, the nails that fastened the Saviour's body to it were a good substitute. No fewer than twenty-nine places in Europe alone claim to possess a holy nail: Apache, Ancon, Arras, Bamberg, the convent of Indecision in Bavaria, Carpentras, Catana, Colle in Tuscany, Cologne, Compiègne, Krakow, the Escorial, Florence, Livorno, Milan, Monza, the Monastery of St Patrick in Naples, Paris, both Santa Croce and Santa Maria in Campitelli in Rome, Siena, Spoleto, Torcello, Torno on Lake Como, Toul, Trèves, Troyes, Venice (three nails) and Vienna. Most early Christian writers assume that Jesus was nailed to the cross by four spikes, though others, such as Gregory Nazianzen and the fifth-century Greek poet Nonnus, believed that the Saviour had been crucified with his feet crossed and a single nail driven through them. This caused some consternation: it may be true that not all the nails in existence were whole, but the inherent difficulty was still not easily explained away.

Constantinople, that great repository of sacred bric-à-brac, was unperturbed by such quibbles. Empress Helena, who seems to have spent much of her reign locating holy relics, once cast a nail from the Holy Cross into the sea to calm a storm. Another one was fitted to the head of a statue of the Emperor Constantine, while a third was incorporated into his helmet. In an effort to fulfil an ancient prophecy, the emperor had another one fashioned into a part of the bridle for his horse as a bit, after Zechariah 14.20, which reads, cryptically, 'In that day that which is upon the bridle of the horse shall be holy to the Lord.'

Constantine also understood the value of these objects in diplomacy. A fifth nail from the cross was sent to Russia, and is now in Moscow. Yet another one was given to Pope Gregory, who passed it on to the Frankish Princess Theodolina. She used her nail as part of her crown, the famous Iron Crown of Lombardy, which she later donated to the church at Monza in Italy, where it remained from 628 and was used for the coronation of Charlemagne. When Napoleon Bonaparte, neither immune to the allure of relics nor ignorant of their symbolic power, crowned himself King of Italy he used the Iron Crown.

More immediate relics of the Saviour were harder to come by, and the faithful were reduced mainly to venerating nail parings, hairs plucked from his beard, strands of hair, loincloths and tears wept by Christ on various occasions. One such tear, in the Church of the Holy Trinity in Vendôme, could be seen quivering continuously in its crystal vial. It was shed for the last time 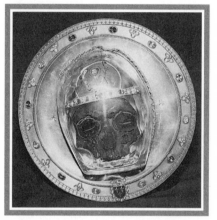 when the relic was destroyed during the French Revolution. During the twelfth century, a supposed tooth of Christ caused a theological dispute when the theologian Guibert de Nogend pointed out that the Lord could not have left teeth behind. The owners of the relic, the monks of Saint-Medard-de-Soisson, however, countered that this was a milk tooth.

In the thirteenth century, the town of Lucques in the Auvergne attracted pilgrims with a crucifix that was said to contain the navel of the infant Jesus. A second holy navel was venerated in the Roman church Santa Maria della Popolo, later to be the scene of the meeting of two artistic geniuses who jointly worked on a commission there, Annibale Carracci and Michelangelo Merisi da Caravaggio. A third holy navel was exhibited at Chalons-sur-Marne. This miraculous multiplication was explained by the original navel having been divided into several relics, but the faithful of Chalons-sur-Marne eventually had to face the reality that their reliquary, when opened, was found to contain nothing but gravel.

The breast milk of the Blessed Virgin Mary was spread throughout Christendom, leading Calvin to point out later that, even if she had been a professional wet-nurse, the Mother of Christ could not have produced so much of it. Sixty-nine churches claimed to own some drops, forty-six of them in France alone. Even Eton College possessed two. Other lesser relics were the stool on which Mary had been sitting during the Annunciation, the bucket and pail that were to be found near by, and a stone on which she rested during the flight to Egypt.

The desperate search for relics of the Saviour reached its apotheosis in a cult that was very popular during the Middle Ages: the veneration of the Holy Prepuce. There was bitter rivalry between no fewer than eight places in France that claimed to have the true foreskin of Christ. One of them, Charroux, even derived its name from the proud possession: *chair rouge* – red flesh. Asked to adjudicate on this delicate matter, Pope Innocent III flatly refused, ruling that only the Saviour Himself was likely to know which one was genuine. As the papal delegate Arnaud-Amaury had said, in very different circumstances, during the Albigensian crusade in 1206: the Lord will recognize his own. His successor, Pope Clement VII, had no such scruples and issued a bull promising indulgences to all those going on a pilgrimage to Charroux to venerate the relic.

The prepuce at Coulombs, near Nogent-le-Roi, was especially renowned for making the infertile fertile again, and was even lent to King Henry V of England when he found it difficult to sire an heir in 1422. As late as 1872 the parish priest of Coulombs would, it is alleged, take the twelfth-century ivory cross containing the relic into the presbytery, where he would allow the women of the parish to kiss the reliquary in holy devotion.

One great centre of relic worship and trade owed its wealth in sacred objects to an erroneous translation. Cologne is the resting place of many relics, among them the Three Kings and those of St Ursula and her 11,000 virgins. Ursula's legend is one of the oldest of Christianity. Famed for her beauty, she was the daughter of a British king, Deonotus, in the early third century AD. When a barbarian king asked for her hand, adding that in case she chose not to accept he would lay waste her father's lands, she consented, provided her new husband would accept her religion, and that her father would first allow her to make a pilgrimage to Rome. Ursula and her retinue of virgins sailed down the Rhine to Basle, where they disembarked their eleven ships and were joined by the bishop of the city. In Rome, Pope Ciriacus welcomed the pilgrims. He felt strangely touched by the princess and had a dream commanding him to return to Cologne together with the virgins. He then resigned from his office and joined the girls, much to the horror of his cardinals, who were so angry with their pope joining a band of young girls that they struck him off the papal register. As the eleven ships sailed into Cologne, they were already expected ashore: the Huns had got word of the huge party of virgins coming their way. An epic bloodbath followed, leaving 11,000 decapitated virgins, enough martyr blood for any Catholic story. Amid all the butchery, the leader of the Huns was so stricken by the beauty of the princess that he offered to marry her. She refused and he shot her with an arrow. One of the virgins miraculously managed to hide from the blood-thirsty men. Disconsolate at the fact that her companions had tasted martyrdom and she had not, she killed herself the morning after the massacre.

Ursula and her maidens were all canonized (apart from the one who committed suicide) and allocated a feast day, the 21st of October. They were buried in a Roman cemetery, which was fortuitously rediscovered almost a thousand years after her death, in 1106. It was not just the virgin saints who were exhumed: apart from the saintly girls the graveyard happily yielded a good number of ancient bishops and other Christian worthies, all still clearly identified. Fifty years later, in 1155, Abbot Gerlach would further substantiate the claim by manufacturing 200 headstones with the virgins' names on them. The legend of Ursula comes to us through a Latin inscription installed in the church dedicated to her by a Roman senator named Clematius, who renovated the sacred building and recorded her legend. Ten lines in Latin relate the tragic story.

The Huns, of course, never reached Cologne, and there never was a pope called Ciriacus in third-century Rome. It is likely that St Ursula is the Christian incarnation of a Teutonic moon goddess named Hörsel, who travelled in a boat and held dominion over the souls of dead maidens, 1,000 of whom formed her retinue. The number of Ursula's companions may originate from a Latin abbreviation used in the original inscription: XI.M.V. It was read to stand for *undecim millia virgines*, though scholars have long argued that it is much more likely to be short for *undecin martyres virgines*, 'eleven virgin martyrs'.

This scholarly dispute, however, does little to discourage the faithful. St Ursula's Church houses a profusion of relics even today; not only the skull of the saint herself on the altar, but also those of many of her sweet maidens, and of others found with them. The so-called Gold Chamber in the church contains a whole congregation of saints, some of which are kept in precious reliquaries and wrapped in embroidered cloths, while others are arranged along walls, protected by wire netting. Some bones are arranged to spell out the name of the saint. For a time, Cologne even became a successful exporter of relics, which it willingly supplied throughout the Christian world until, in 1300, Pope Boniface IX issued the bull *Detestandae feritatis abusum*, which put an end to the worst excesses of the trade.

In the late twelfth century, St Ursula and her virgins did not prove enough for Reinald von Dassel, the Archbishop of Cologne, a man of God gluttonous for saintly bones. He succeeded in securing one of Christianity's greatest prizes: the bones of the Magi who had worshipped the infant Jesus and brought him their well-known gifts.

The Magi themselves have a history at least as peculiar as that of

St Ursula. Early Christian writers found it impossible to agree on either number or names of the holy men who had found their way to the manger. Zarvanades, Gusnaphus, Kagba, Badalima and Bithisaria were touted as likely names until Caspar, Melchior and Balthasar finally emerged from the field and came home by a nose. Over the centuries, this version became accepted as fact, and by the eighth century the Venerable Bede could describe Melchior as 'old and white-haired, hairy with a long beard and long locks' with all the confidence of one who had known him personally. The bones of the holy men reached Cologne (how could it be otherwise?) via Constantinople, where emperor Constantine had brought them after a visit to the Holy Land. The Cologne Dome was erected in their honour, a shrine designed to be worthy of them.

Today, packs of pilgrims beat their path to the golden reliquary in the cathedral, dressed much like tourists everywhere. They capture their spiritual experience and the sartorial inadequacies around them on video. In the nineteenth century, the German poet Heinrich Heine recorded his own visit to their shrine in a poem. Having converted to Christianity for social reasons, he described his own visit to Cologne Cathedral, a huge space dimly lit by oil lamps. He paid his respects to the chapel in which the Magi are housed, and found them not lying in their sarcophagi, but sitting upright and lecturing him on why exactly they ought to be respected: firstly because they were dead, secondly because they were kings, and thirdly because they were saints. Heine remained resolutely unimpressed and gave voice to his hope that the cathedral would eventually be converted into a cavalry stable.

Few people are immune to ancestor worship and the magic of physical closeness across time: holding a Roman coin in one's hand and wondering what it might have bought, visiting historic sites, seeing Mozart's violin, a manuscript by Beethoven, a poem in Shelley's hand, Churchill's slippers, a baseball autographed by Babe Ruth or a letter written by a great man and dealing with matters that are small and intimate. These objects seem to contain the past, are mute witnesses to history, bearing within them the immediacy of touch preserved over years and centuries.

Ancestor cult is one of the very oldest forms of religious observance and evidence of it dates back to the earliest finds of human cultural activity. Even the mightiest regimes and ideologies have been powerless to eradicate it while others, such as Stalin's USSR, found it expedient to encourage it. No amount of atheist rationalism, though, has been able to expunge it altogether; when the Red Guards smashed China's great heritage during the Cultural Revolution, even the zealous mobs of youngsters driving the destruction did not dare lay a finger on the tombs of the Ming emperors, which still stand today as they were hundreds of years ago, protected by an avenue of mythical beasts in stone, untouched by the hammers of ideology, staring at the visitors, exactly as they did centuries ago.

Many religions venerate relics, and they are important in some Buddhist traditions, but nothing can equal Christian fervour in this respect. Being an important part of Christian worship, relics were treated very seriously by theologians. Scholastic writers classified relics into *reliquiae insignes*, those that included either the entire corpse or at least head, arms or legs, and *reliquiae non insignes*, lesser relics. The division was carried further when the faithful came to distinguish between *notabiles*, large and significant body parts, and *exiguae*, such as fingers and teeth. Even today, the relics of the Catholic Church are officially classified as being first class, i.e., *insignes*, second class, *exiguae*, and third class, i.e., objects merely touched by or belonging to a saint.

To the mind of the believer, relics are imbued with talismanic qualities. It is a curious fact that they who want to be closest to the life of those they venerate often find themselves involved in the most gruesome aspects of decay and death. Relics, however, are both dead and alive – parts of dead bodies or inanimate objects, but alive with the aura, the spirit of something greater, and more holy, than we are. They may appear to be shrivelled, desiccated body parts and bones, or objects such as chains, nails or clothes, but at the same time they are a link to a world beyond, carriers of a living force, emissaries from a world capable of overturning the laws of our own.

Relics touch on a curious dialectic of collecting: whatever we collect we have to kill; literally in the case of butterflies or beetles, metaphorically in the case of other objects, which are removed from their usual surroundings, functions and circulation, and placed in an artificial environment, bereft of their former usefulness, turned into objects of a different order, dead to the world. No stamp collector will plunder his albums for his correspondence, even if some of his stamps might still be valid. No collector of teacups scours markets and antique shops simply for cups from which to drink his tea. Even the occasional use of objects in a collection, musical instruments, books or vintage cars, is incidental, and not what the collection is about.

At the same time these objects have taken on a new life, as part of an organism, as part of the collector's mirror image, entities that place their own demands on his life and that create their own rules, exude their own power. Like relics they are dead and yet very much alive in the mind of the believer, the collector, the devotee. In being so, they form a bridge between our limited world and an infinitely richer one, that of history or art, of charisma or of holiness – a world of ultimate authenticity and thus a profoundly romantic utopia. Through them, the collector can live on after his own life has come to an end; and the collection becomes a bulwark against mortality.

The double nature of the relic, dead matter and living promise, is illustrated in a secular setting in one of the most affecting museums in Europe, the Museo Belliniano in Catania, Sicily, a city of a softly decaying, continuous past.

Outside the museum dedicated to the opera composer who was born here is the Piazza San Francesco. The Baroque church opposite has a fluorescent *Ave Maria* above the door and a St Francis with fluorescent halo. Inside, a mummified corpse of a saint is decked out in festive clothes while a gory display of St Lucy's eyes and St Agatha's breasts all painted in vivid colours keep alive the memory of martyrdom. The museum itself is situated in an old apartment house and can be reached only through a courtyard with washing flapping in the breeze. Mementoes of Bellini's short life are crowded together, seemingly untouched for decades, a secular pendant to the church across the square. No exhibition designer or education consultant has ever been allowed to disturb its timeless peace. In the alcove in which he was born (a plaque on its back wall reads *In questo alcove vene alla luce Bellini*, 'Bellini saw the light of the world in this alcove') is his piano, unrestored, as if he had been the last person to touch it, the keys discoloured with age. The chair in front of it in the form of a shell with dolphin legs has been allowed to rot away like its owner, like its owner's city. That is its charm.

In a niche of the museum is the coffin in which Bellini's corpse was transferred from Milan to Catania, forty-one years after his death in 1835. The purple velvet is bleached and torn, a tin laurel wreath is lying on the lid, and a gilt lyre. A death mask taken from the corpse, so many years afterwards, is displayed here – the nose was all but gone. On the walls of the niche, contemporary photos in tasteful gilt frames show a corpse as it appeared after the exhumation and the opening of the coffin, in an advanced state of mummification, more pharaoh than romantic hero. On the opposite wall is the dead composer in the 'official version' of a century in love with genius: Bellini as youthful genius with translucent skin and visionary gaze, still covered by his shroud but already embraced by adoring angels carrying him to the pantheon of opera, to immortality. Death and transfiguration.

The secular religion of romanticism uses the same language as the official religion of the Catholic Church, as indeed does every collection. In undergoing this transformation, the objects thus sanctified remind us of the very beginnings of our civilization: of fetishes and totems, of headhunters, of the scalps triumphantly displayed by Indian warriors, and to the ancestor cult which is at the beginning of every religious understanding of the world. Just as cannibals who would consume the flesh of their enemy during ritual meals ingested part of his prowess and *élan vital*, relics, both secular and sacred, allow us to tap into a power and into a realm otherwise closed to us.

In Melanesian cultures *Mana*, the mysterious life force pervading every aspect of the living world, is believed especially to reside in the

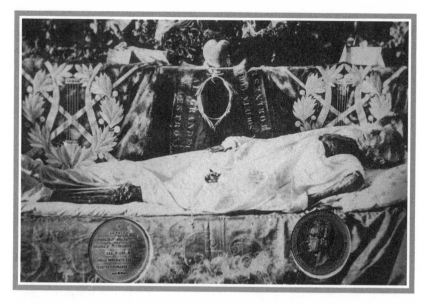

skulls of ancestors and of enemies killed in battle. Such skulls are often kept in spirit houses, together with ritual objects.[7] *Mana*, 'holiness', that powerful presence where there is an absence, has lost little of its force in our rational world. Let him or her who is unmoved by the history contained in a small object that has survived for centuries cast the first stone.

Collecting relics is a kind of collecting that is very much alive in a time in which pop and film memorabilia are the single biggest growth area in the international art market. In the minds of those devoted to them, many historical figures that are collected, among them Diana, Princess of Wales, the Kennedys and Elvis Presley, have stepped across the boundary that divides mere mortals from secular saints, and their remembrance from religious worship.

There are hybrids between reliquaries and collections. The virgins, kings and assorted minor saints in Cologne have important elements of a collection in their arrangement and classification, and in the way in which they form and define a space and a class of things. The same phenomenon can be observed in catacombs and ossaries often found in Catholic countries, in Palermo, Rome, Vienna and Paris, for instance, in which the decayed bodies of the dead (not relics, as these were ordinary mortals), are put on display, used as parts of works of art (such as the skulls in the *danse macabre* frieze in Wolhusen in Switzerland, which are let into the walls to form the heads of the painted figures) or arranged into elaborate displays of geometric patterns and allegorical tableaux made of skulls and bones. They speak at the same time of the inevitability of death and of the transience of human life, and, by virtue of the fact that they are all the bones of believers, all to be rescued and restored on the Day of Judgement, of eternal life. Like relics, they thus become instruments of salvation.

Such instruments are not always so dramatic. By surrounding ourselves with objects we hope to immerse ourselves in what is represented by them, with what they represent to us who are unwilling to accept that it will always remain elusive and cannot be locked into things. Instead of shooting the messenger we stuff him, believing him to be the message.

A different, more meaningful, more ordered world can speak out of things as humble as old shoes or bottles, out of autographs or first editions, which, in their pleasing arrangement, in their structure and variety, tell of beauty, of security; and every object we so crave is in fact an attribute of what we are craving for. Even the sanitized miniature world of a train set with its polished engines and little station houses, its evergreen trees and its tiny rosy-cheeked passengers can thus become a utopia that holds a powerful attraction above the world outside, and the control over the timetables of an old Märklin set stands in stark contrast to the powerlessness we cannot help but feel when faced with time itself. It embodies the simpler passions and the smaller world of childhood, even though the very need for it testifies to the complexities, the innumerable failures and compromises of adulthood.

Too many shamans have ruled over our ancestors for us to recognize that the paraphernalia of a kind of happiness do not contain that happiness within them, that they are expressions of a state, not its agents. The man who finds himself a job, a wife, a house with a garden with apple trees in it, a child, a family car and a big, bounding dog, and then discovers that all this does not amount to the happiness he had dreamed of and had identified with these things, falls victim to it just as much as another who cannot resurrect a glorious past out of a

collection of uniforms from the Napoleonic Wars. Conquest is followed by disillusionment and the necessity for further conquests. We were wrong, a voice within us says, it was not this one after all, while we already identify everything we find wanting in our life in an object as yet outside our magic circle. This must be it. The most important object of a collection is the next one. Possession may be able to shore us up against having to face the world without all defence but only the next conquest will finally bring with it contentment. While the hands still grasp one thing, and while the mind still determines its place in the order of our chattels, the hungry eyes are already far ahead.

A curse seems to overshadow this pursuit of life through the material world. Medusa, the beautiful maiden famous for her lovely tresses, was made into a monster with serpents for hair as a punishment for violating the Temple of Minerva. From then on, she suffered terrible loneliness as nothing living could abide her sight without being turned into stone. Surrounded by a sculpture garden of death, and craving the fulfilment she had known but was never to experience again, she fell into a mad rage searching for lovers and killing them instantly with her approach. Those who, like her, seek transcendence through things alone are condemned to suffer the same fate.

Three Flying Ducks

For years he didn't know why he was chasing down exhausted objects.
All that frantic passion for a baseball and he finally understood it was
Eleanor on his mind, it was some terror working deep beneath the skin
that made him gather up things, amass possessions and effects against
the dark shape of some unshoulderable loss. Memorabilia. What he
remembered, what lived in the old smoked leather of the catcher's mitt
in the basement was the touch of his Eleanor, those were his wife's eyes
in the oval photographs of men with handlebar moustaches. The state
of loss, in fact, the facticity in its lonely length.

Don DeLillo, *Underworld*[1]

They are part of the repertoire of small escapes, part of the canon of
suburbia: the three ceramic ducks, their glazed wings shining in the
lamp light, flying away in an ascending line on the living-room walls
of countless homes, one bird smaller than the next to suggest distance
and perspective, flying across thousands of wallpaper patterns, plain
or textured, flowery or rhomboid, winging their way into a better
world, towards a little freedom, an assumed, unspoiled nature somewhere beyond these walls.

Their journey is as reassuring as the annual hoarse cries of their
live, feathered cousins flying overhead on their transatlantic quest for
survival, and they are not alone in evoking that other world into which
one can dream oneself for a few stolen seconds: the foxhunt prints, the
jolly friar catching the reflection of a sinking sun in a wine glass in his

cellar, the stag at bay standing amid primordial woods, the porcelain cats and chubby children and dogs at play, the peasant girl leaning seductively against a haystack. These evocations of an innocent life may be contrasted with objects that conjure up different worlds: stately homes and royalty and commemoration mugs and tea towels, a fictitious rococo flourish in the form of a toilet-roll doll, a vision of carefree bohemia in an oil painting of a Parisian street café brought back from that little stand in Montmartre.

These things are kitsch, tat, not to be admitted by the rules of good taste, which have been unbending and rigid ever since they were changed for the last time by the previous generation. It is easy to despise them and the fact that they are derivative, mere gestures in the direction of art, mass-produced and without originality, too cute and too cuddly and too much imitations of imitations of real art to have any value. But it is the very fact that these gestures can be acquired for a few pounds from a mail-order catalogue which makes them interesting, for this is the consequence of mass production and the beginning of the possibility of collecting in the age of technical reproduction, with all that brings with it. Only with mass production came the idea of the complete set, the full series, the vocabulary of a mentality that until then could not express itself through accumulating things according to arbitrary principles. Before this moment, collectors of art, of natural objects, of shells or coins or scientific instruments or portraits, of antiquities and of books had no way of hoping to achieve completeness. There was no complete set of Greek sculpture, no full series of exotic flowers, no last single bird of paradise to get to finish a collection, no final Raphael drawing to round things off. Collecting was by its very nature open-ended and there were always other pieces, other examples, that could be found and added. Mass production changed all this. Even if infinitely varying Barbie dolls seem to have been produced, even if the little coloured tin tops that sit on champagne corks seem to proliferate without control, we know that their number must be finite, that there were only so many patterns of Meissen produced during the nineteenth century, only so many football cards printed featuring Manchester United players, only so many stamps issued by the newly independent former British colonies. Even if one or more of them should prove elusive for an entire collecting life, in principle the collection can be completed, can achieve its logical destiny – and can consequently cause its creator the greatest trouble as his goal is achieved but his urge to continue far from satisfied.

A creature of mass-production, kitsch allows us to regain a moment of self-possession, the illusion of individuality; by indulging and inviting sentiment in the safety of a storyline, a picture frame or a song, it becomes an effective substitute for feeling at first hand and without a scripted ending. Nothing is safe from kitsch. Even the highest art, especially the highest art, can be kitschified in the twinkle of a heavy-lidded eye and many a great work of art is great because its proximity with kitsch is truly frightening. Who would not see it in Michelangelo's *Pietà*, in Mahler's Fifth Symphony or in *Romeo and Juliet*? This may well be retrospective, for kitsch as we know it, the word at least, was born in Munich around 1870 when certain art dealers spoke about flogging their factory artworks, of *verkitschen*, not only to the culture-hungry burghers of an emerging empire, but also to American tourists who wanted German art on the cheap and would often ask non-English-speaking dealers for a 'sketch'. Kitsch is essentially domestic and domesticates whatever it paints gold with its merciless Midas touch. Even in death and mourning there is a vague sense of titillation, of voyeurism and voluptuousness, as can be witnessed on any nineteenth-century tombstone with its grieving, bare-breasted graces and charming putti. Nothing is beyond its power to domesticate. Its visions of freedom are attractive precisely because there is no risk of it actually becoming real, because they occur in an ideal world, close and wonderful enough to be dreamed of, far enough away not to be actively pursued. Its cosiness, eroticism and exoticism never quite goes away and, under the guise of art and of convention, it gets away with murder.

In our sophisticated times it has become fashionable to collect kitsch, to show superiority by smiling at the naïvety of other periods and classes, half implicated and all the more exonerated for having mastered its appeal. It has, however, one power that is stronger than any other: just as it turns love into a vision too lovely to be spoiled by messy reality, it succeeds in the singular feat of killing death. When St Paul asked in his Letter to the Ephesians (15.55) 'Death, where is thy sting?' he did not realize that kitsch could draw its thorn just as effectively as salvation. Kitsch is the death of death, for even the grim reaper becomes a homely figure. Alpine ranges are reduced for tourists to the size of paperweights and divine mysteries are transformed into plastercasts of the Sacred Heart, or into a blond Jesus on the cross, opening and closing his eyes in graceful death pangs as the picture is tilted left and right. Suffering is sweet; agony and ecstasy are revealed to be kinky cousins. Death itself is either drowned in the excess and wide-eyed innocence of the sentimental novel, or simply not allowed his turn at all. And they lived happily ever after.

One way of making the world one's oyster is to reduce the world to oyster size. This is what kitsch does, as everything beyond human comprehension zooms down to postcard format. If collecting is an art (it can be), then kitsch is not confined to assemblies of garden gnomes, Cinderella dolls or memorabilia of that most tragic of female heroines, the misunderstood Habsburg Empress Elisabeth, Sissi to her friends, the proto-Diana of the nineteenth century, whose legend was blessed even with an early violent death.

Mass-produced objects are the most common face of collecting today, though hardly the most spectacular: the mantelpiece populated by ceramic pigs, the cabinet with Sheffield plate, the album with old city views, the shelf with wineglasses or hat-pins or fluffy animals, the box with old football stubs, theatre programmes or train tickets from around the world; little shrines all of them to different pasts, escapes from the present, assertions of individuality, of longing and of hope. Often they are salvage operations, rescue missions designed to save from extinction something that others would not stoop to pick up or hesitate to throw away. A man collects milk bottles 'because I saw that people were throwing them away'. Now he has thousands of them, classified according to origin and age, a British geography in milk bottles and a garden shed transformed.

Robert Opie, one of the best-known of the devotees of the everyday, collects food packaging and household ephemera. In his house in Ealing, west London, and in a museum in Gloucester, Opie has an estimated 500,000 items of packaging and household goods-related packaging, advertising, matchboxes, etc. He describes his own childhood as an apprenticeship during which he learned from his parents, renowned collectors of children's books and childhood lore. He went through the usual stages of stamp and coin collecting until, he describes, he found himself one day eating a packet of Munchies.

I suddenly looked at the pack and thought, 'If I throw this away I will never, ever, see it again, and yet there is a whole wealth of history.' The sudden realization came to me that this was something I should be saving, and I thought what an enormous part of social history I was about to throw away. That packet was going to be priced at seven pence, it would soon be priced at eight pence, or whatever it was. Yet I was about to throw it away, damage it. I knew I should be saving these things. The next packet was a McVitie's one. From that time on I have saved every packet that I've consumed the contents of.[2]

Opie admits that not in his wildest dreams could he have conceived that his 'Munchies moment' would mushroom into a large house filled with household ephemera, plus a warehouse and two museum spaces, several exhibitions, a series of books and a steady business selling nostalgic images and renting out objects to period film productions. In doing all this, he sees himself as a pioneer.

It's rather like climbing Everest: since time immemorial someone's been trying to get to the top, but who is the pioneer? Is it the man who actually got to the summit first, or is it the man who made it to Base One? It's the same with packaging . . . I see myself in relation to all those other people who have done these crazy sort of things. Unless you do these crazy things you don't start to understand. Sending a man to the moon may have been perceived as the most stupid thing imaginable, but think of all the benefits of that technological leap.

The lady walking along the Rotterdam street was horrified when a small, middle-aged man she had never seen before approached her and started talking about her high-heeled boots. She started abusing him roundly, calling him a pervert, a dirty old man. It took him a long time to explain to her that it was not her he was interested in, but her boots alone, fine examples of craftsmanship and design, a valuable addition to his collection. He was Arnold de Wit. Eventually she relented, and promised him the pair of boots as soon as she would no longer have any use for them. The de Wit shoe collection in Rotterdam is usually added to not as a consequence of desperately misconstruable approaches on the open street, but at antique fairs. The main corpus of the former cobbler's treasures is formed by miniature footwear made of porcelain, leather, metal, and so forth, everything, in fact, that is small: model shoes, baby shoes, Chinese shoes for bound feet, shoe matchboxes, shoe inkwells and pincushions, and Victorian ladies' boots. Despite this clear priority, he finds it difficult to ignore a pair of masterworks being ground thin on the pavement when he sees them. Shoes are no ordinary items of apparel, he explains. Many people have an almost ritualistic relationship with their footwear. Buying it and caring for it is more than just a necessity, it is a form of devotion. The objects in his collection allow their owner to walk into other people's lives. There is the pair of first Communion shoes worn by one M. G. Jonckbloedt on 26 April 1896, that pretty pair of wedding shoes that belonged to a Mrs de Bont and worn on 12 July 1894; there are all the aspirations and hopes and moments of beauty bound up in children's shoes and porcelain shoes, going-out shoes and evening shoes. Given that none of his children shows any promise in keeping the collection going his greatest wish is to see his shoes go to a museum, to be preserved for the nation. 'I could make myself rich,' he admits, 'by turning my collection over to an American, but I cannot do it, I am too much of a collector for this.'[3]

While Opie collects inedible food (given the fact that the boxes promising nourishment are usually empty), others collect unwearable shoes, medals that were not awarded to them, doorknobs and keys without doors to be opened by them, orange wrappers without oranges inside, numberplates which no longer identify any cars, dolls without girls to play with them, holy water fonts that no longer dispense holy water, thimbles that have stopped shielding against pinpricks and hat-pins without hats to pin to elaborate coiffures. Their uselessness *vis-à-vis* their previous existence, in which they had a purpose in the context of things, stands out and unifies them into collected objects, taken out of circulation and pinned up like butterflies, regarded now as specimens, as 'examples of', as links to another realm of history, of authenticity, of beauty. Collected objects lose their utilitarian value (there are exceptions, of course) and gain another one, are imbued with meaning and qualities of representation beyond their original station.

Whether and to what extent they also retain their symbolic value (the nourishment of food, the fetish value of shoes, the poignancy of baby clothes, the glory of combat and distinction represented by medals, the liberating key, etc.) is a question that is tempting but impossible to answer. How significant is it that someone who was locked up in a Stalinist labour camp for five years starts collecting keys, that a woman surrounds herself with dolls, recordings of matinée idols or Princess Diana memorabilia or teapots, or that a man collects Princess Diana memorabilia or, indeed, model railway sets, erotic art or weapons? (And what, inversely, does it indicate that one hardly ever finds a man collecting dolls or embroidery samplers, a woman devoting her life to machine tools and steam engines?) In the case of Wolf Stein, the Amsterdam book collector who had been first in hiding and then in a concentration camp until he was seventeen and who invited me into his house, the connection was immediate and clear: 'I didn't have much of a formal education in my youth and I always hope I may make up for it if I read all these.' Other collectors can only themselves answer this question, especially if their area of interest is less symbolically obvious and concerns itself with high art, or postcards, typewriters or ethnographic objects. What is certain is only that the collected objects have a value for the individual collector that only other collectors can understand.

The question of value is intriguing in itself. As often as not the objects collected are the cast-offs of society, overtaken by technological advance, used and disposable, outmoded, disregarded, unfashionable. There may be an avid (and, indeed, carefully fuelled) market in Swatch watches and Beanie Babies, but that marketing is based itself on the consumer understanding that the current series will one day no longer be produced, will become unavailable. When the Pokémon craze filled children's rooms of this world with costly and ugly dolls and swapping cards, the producers of these toys, cursed by parents everywhere, showed great insight in choosing their slogan: *Gotta catch 'em all!* For grown-ups there is a similar market: the collector's edition, items produced explicitly for collectors and not for use, watches, in other words, that are never intended to show the time to someone needing to know, teddy bears that will be kept away from the messy paws of children, and heritage teacups not at any time intended for any tea. This is the apotheosis of consumption; the utilitarian object that is intended not to have a use, but to be placed on a shelf, skipping the phase of circulation and utilization altogether. While these can be bought at predetermined prices, other items have value only in certain circles, among a group of initiates whose rules and knowledge are deeply arcane and shared by only a few.

What, then, makes a collected object valuable – why is someone prepared to pay a small fortune for a stamp that is no longer valid, for an empty matchbox that missed the rubbish bin only because its last user had a poor aim, for a bottle that has not contained any wine for decades? All these are useless, have lost their value as objects that do anything in and of themselves. Their value can lie only, if not in their usefulness, then in their significance; they mean something, stand for something, carry associations that make them valuable in the eye of the collector. As carriers of significance their uselessness is an asset.[4] Like the bound feet of Chinese women and the long fingernails of the Mandarins, the very fact that they are not suited for any practical purpose enhances their value as being purely representational. It is not what they are but what they stand for, the promise they contain. In this sense, every collected object is not just a relic from the world in which it had a practical application, but a holy relic, just as the arm of Theresa of Avila is not valued for its muscle tissue and bone content or its ability, now lost, to carry things and to be formed into one half of a pair of folded hands; it is not as an arm that it is venerated but as an object imbued with saintliness, with otherworldliness, as a key to heaven, to a world infinitely richer than our everyday existence. The objects in a collection connect us with something far away.

Relics form a bridge with heaven and immortality; other objects bridge space (the *exotica* in the *Wunderkammer*, such as ostrich eggs or coconuts), bridge time (historical artefacts and ensembles of them), our distance from nature (birds' eggs, for example) or from genius (the work of great artists), etc. At the same time a collection establishes authority over the chosen area, for it is the collector to whom it falls to classify, to include or exclude, to chose. Every object in a collection has to have a significance to be admitted into the fold. A stone may be desirable in a mineralogical collection because of its rare composition, in a regional collection because it is typical of its origin, a handful of gravel as an example of what gravel looks like. A church may be interested in a stone because it belonged to its original foundations, or because it was thrown at St Stephen, the first Christian martyr. It may also be thought valuable, as by one anonymous collector, because the Empress Elisabeth, Sissi, of Austria had stumbled over it. The collector in question was not interested in the stone as stone and would have bought a rake if that had been the imperial obstacle. In much the same way, the other collectors seek a special significance in the object, and it is only this meaning it carries that transfers value to it. It is this moment of transcendence, of the possession of transcendence, that makes every collected object, be it a matchbox or a martyr's fingernail, valuable. Every collected item is, to some extent, a totem.

It was mass production that allowed a broad range of people to indulge their fancy by filling the world with a multitude of cheap things. This was the moment of the democratization of collecting. Whereas the fashion for *naturalia* and *artificialia* required connections and money in order to obtain exotic specimens of birds, stones or plants, or to buy works of art, to commission artists with original work and grave-robbers with excavations, mass-produced objects could be collected by the very kind of people for whom they had been made: ordinary people.

The charm of the endlessly produced consumer article has its flip side, of course. The gained availability goes hand in hand with a loss of authenticity, and the hunger for the real, the unique and the rare becomes ever stronger. Collectors search for limited editions, for rare misprints, first editions, and objects with interesting faults precisely because they re-establish this uniqueness, while others turn their back on the mass market altogether and collect things that are not and cannot be mass produced: antiquities and old masters, seashells, butterflies. Nothing, in fact, is more important than regaining this authenticity and through this hunger for the original there will always be a market supplying fakes, things made to appear like something they are not (though these, incidentally, are collected too). Collector and forger live in uneasy proximity.

The three ducks are still suspended in their eternal flight towards freedom and the beauty of nature. They do not really form a collection (though there are those who collect them), nor are they part of a larger collection in the strict sense of the word; and yet they belong here as much as they belong on the walls of so many living rooms. Not only are they potential collections, they embody many of the traits that can be found in larger collections; they belong to the strange class of objects that bind their possessors intellectually and emotionally to another world. They are not alone. Next to them, a little lower, on the mantelpiece, is a pair of dancing dolls, a Spaniard in a torero outfit and a woman with flamenco dress and castanets. Their skin is pink moulded plastic and their costumes made from polyester glued on to the bodies. Lips and eyes are painted in red, white and black. The woman holds her castanets aloft and seems to be twirling round while looking at her partner seductively, her emerald green dress in spectacular ruffles; the man stands in the proud pose of the bullfighter, red cape and sword in hand as if to deliver the *coup de grâce* to her, comically elegant with his high trousers and tiny jacket. They were purchased in Barcelona, in Seville or in Madrid, or in one of thousands of other locations throughout Spain, during a holiday some years ago. Now they are that holiday, solitary representatives of ten days of a different life, a brief sojourn in another world.

Anglers and Utopias

Sojourns in another world, a world that is inhabited only by the imagination of the collector and at the same time also forms part of another realm, be it memory or imagination, beauty or genius, are the promise of every collector's cabinet, of the enclosed space in which he takes refuge and where he himself is demiurge and ultimate arbiter, deciding over admission and expulsion, over order and arrangement, over value and beauty. It is not incidental that this paragraph uses male pronouns only, for there is a marked difference between female and male collectors. Although overall slightly more women describe themselves as collectors,[1] the majority of those whose lives are taken over by their collections, who live for it and are dominated by its demands, are men. It seems fruitless to launch into generalizations here, but a few observations may serve to sketch out this phenomenon.

If for the last 3,000 years women had dominated Western societies and had relegated men to the position of useful if brutish servants and occasional lovers, our world might be very much more happy, more harmonious and more medieval. The single-minded pursuit of one *idée fixe* to the exclusion of everything else, and the accompanying phenomena of isolation, fierce competition, the overpowering will to win, an atrophying of empathy, seem to be associated with the male psyche. It takes a certain mind-set to devote one's entire life to the development of a modified watch movement that is slightly more accurate or can withstand a little more shaking. This tunnel-vision mentality has spurned the technical inventions as well as wars (indeed, many inventions useful to us are a byproduct of warfare). Both great innovations and encyclopaedic collections take a mind prepared to live in seclusion and just keep chipping away at the impossibility of the task. The male of the species seems not yet to have emerged entirely out of the proverbial garden shed, the only place in which some men seem to be comfortable and truly to be themselves, left to whatever hobby they have taken up as an excuse for being alone. One of the founding fathers of the American space programme, Werner von Braun, had gained his rocket-building expertise in Nazi Germany designing the V1 and V2 missiles used to bomb London. In pursuing his obsession with rocket flight he was oblivious to (or simply uninterested in) whether he was in the American desert researching to put a man on the moon in the name of freedom and democracy, or whether he was working for Hitler and exploiting slave labourers killed by the thousand. It takes this mind-set, its voluntary seclusion and single-minded pursuit of one goal and one goal only, to keep on going oblivious of the consequences. Men seem to be more comfortable with, or more in need of, the hunt, and with the business of conquest and possession, with the loneliness of this task and with submission to its demands, with social and intellectual hierarchies. Military metaphors come to mind when describing such arrangements: an army of things, objects regimented on the shelves, all lined up like soldiers. The mirror image of this obsession is the painstaking identification and strict classification of objects into hierarchies and systems. The characteristics of emotional paucity and the language of collecting overlap in many ways: holding on to one's feelings, bottling up, being retentive, not letting go.

The whole phenomenon of retreat into a world of predictable patterns and away from an environment of social complexity and competing claims for attention and for love brings to mind autism, and, indeed, the majority of those suffering from this condition are boys and men. While the autistic spectrum reaches from mild eccentricity to severe disability, one clinical condition in particular, Asperger's Syndrome, the least severe of the autistic disorders, serves to illustrate this point. This syndrome is characterized by a whole range of symptoms: a resistance to change, relying on repeating patterns, stilted speech, immersion into arcane topics, such as transport timetables, which assume great importance, and collecting series of objects worthless to others.[2] While the most severe form of autism shows only a slight male bias in the distribution of cases, at the highest ability levels, at the most 'normal' and functional end of the spectrum, the ratio can be as high as fifteen to one.[3] This, of course, is not to say that collecting is inherently autistic any more than that it is inherently male, or that collectors cannot be rounded human beings with thriving personal relationships, but the similarity is arresting and can be transferred to other predominantly male activities. How many woman anglers can one count sitting by the river alone on any given day?

'I used to be a fisherman from years back,' says Alex Shear, the Noah of American life. 'I lived on the rivers.' He is not, to his mind, a collector. 'I don't like the term "collector",' he explains. 'I'm a cultural anthropologist, some kind of picker. The guy who is doing a dig in Pompeii, is he known as a collector? Obviously not.' To Shear, the entire United States are a Pompeii under whose lava of lost identities and corporate lifestyle one can unearth the true, the innocent America of the 1950s, the time of his own childhood. His monumental task of rescuing this civilization has led him to accumulate not one but a multitude of collections, all numbered and categorized, roughly, in chapters of his own devising.

'My job is to be the steward of innocence,' Shear states simply. 'My pieces are pure, they have nothing to say. There has to be a place that is as close to pure as possible and away from the cerebral manipulations and the politicizing. I have America's only known lifestyle archive.'

This archive of the American Soul contains everything that post-war wealth in the United States produced, imagined and feared: oversized jars of mustard and fallout shelters, hundreds of Barbie dolls and Flamingo-brand bobby pins, wooden templates for cast-iron manhole covers, Pop Brand radios and elaborate hair-drying contraptions, 'Glo-Glo' boots and food blenders, rows of suitcases with salesmen's samples from colourful telephones to miniature swimming pools, fairground bumper cars and homely toasters, advertisements for washing machines ('Just Like Electric Mummy') and bathing caps (one labelled 'Aqua Original Exclusive Mermaid Millinery Creation').

More than most other collectors his passion has its roots very immediately in his own biography. A highly successful product designer who would scour flea markets for ideas and trends, Shear found his ideas plagiarized and had to go to court over copyright infringements, an experience that was both cathartic and traumatic and formed his idea of the country he was living in more strongly than any other experience. The deceit and unfairness, he calls it rape, which he witnessed caused him to re-evaluate his life. Before long, he says,

I was buying substitutions for people in terms of character and integrity. During my case I threw out all my address books because my friends abandoned me and believed these huge companies. I traded all this stuff in for people. You have a major crisis in life, you find yourself in court like a Kafka novel. I started thinking about this and this was very very disturbing and when the fog lifted I had all these objects and I wanted to somehow build my world with character. This stuff was so pure and beautiful with the honesty and the integrity, everything I didn't see in humans. I built my perfect world. I started with a beautiful dream, I went through meditation. I was seeking truth. I was not satisfied, so I kept going east. I'm like a patriot but I don't wave flags, I just buy stuff.

The 'stuff' Shear has bought already, more than 100,000 objects to date, fills several warehouses. It is a search for innocence through the innocence of pure consumerism and a rescue mission with eschatological urgency. 'We have so much here, and because we're so teenage in our culture we don't take ourselves seriously. This is what I'm trying to preserve: the ages of innocence. Human character gets lost and values become less important. I go and seek those inanimate objects that have the characters we all used to have, like honesty, integrity.'

He is quick to acknowledge the direct connection his obsession has with his own life. Son of a toy wholesaler and fad-spotter who would fill his warehouse with whatever he thought might become the next hot thing, from Betty Boop dolls to Hula Hoops, from yo-yos to Flexible Flyer sleds, Alex and his twin brother were allowed to play with these toys only if they replaced them afterwards, undamaged and in their original packaging.

The warehouse was a lending library – I never had a sense of ownership. When I saw those toys again, in the flea markets, I wanted to own them. I had an intense nostalgia experience, and I basically began buying back my father's warehouse. I had my dad's entire listing of accounts in my head, and I bought them all back. It was very exciting, and I knew that something was going on, not consciously, but I knew something was going on. There was something about that process of going out looking for the missing pieces. I revisited my father thousands of times through this stuff.

Even as a child, he says, he could communicate with his father only through the things in the warehouse.

Being a twin, too, was an experience he found difficult to deal with.

When society sees you as a unit, you have a job that's bigger than you. I dislike being 'alike' so much that that's why I always climb up the back side of the mountain – there's too much traffic on the front. I used to answer to my brother's name, because I didn't know who I was. Will Alex Shear please stand up? I always used to fantasize that a guy in a fifties Argyle sweater would stand up, and the sweater would be empty. It was in the fields that I started to find myself, and I believe that in those fields are many of the answers to this life. Is my collection autobiographical? You'd better believe it. A lot of my life is in the stuff.

Shear's stocktaking of an American life, though, was only one aspect of his attempt to possess the American Dream, through the familiar household items of the nation's supposed Golden Age. Part of this project, he explains, is to define the cracks in the veneer, the obscure chapters that were never supposed to happen and are therefore all the more revealing:

I buy failures. I have a terrific collection of them. During the Gulf War I collected cases of Norman Schwartzkopf and Colin Powell dolls that were made in China. Cases! They have Asian eyes. I have African-American Barbies with tattoos on. Well, the families went wild and they had lots of recalls, very expensive for Mattel. I'm still looking for Asian Barbies. That would make my day. I have cases of Coca-Cola plastic cans that have all shrunk. Why is this important? Well, Coke doesn't make mistakes. This is important for kids. This is why this has to be catalogued.

The paradoxes that shape a great nation are close to his heart: failures in the land that worships success, purity in the great melting-pot, innocence amid the reality of corporate America. To Shear, they are not contradictions: somewhere amid the 1,200 categories and subcollections (one is tempted to think of Rudolf II's Mannerist project) is the essence of America, the spirit that has been lost is preserved in their integrity. It took Shear a decision to end an unloved job as an accountant and then as an executive at Macey's to find his true vocation:

Then I realized that the thing I love is stuff, and that it speaks to me, and it's the soul of America – these things that came out of the home of the average Joe and Jane – and there is something quintessentially American about them, and they somehow have to be saved, because I have never seen anything like them in the Smithsonian or anywhere else, and when I look at these things they begin to make sense to me as the embodiment of American can-do, American innovativeness, Yankee ingenuity, build-a-better-mousetrap – a latter-day extension of the pioneer spirit, the cowboy spirit, the reckless exciting desire to go over the next mountain.

Having made a fortune out of his product designs he was able to indulge his passion and to allow his art, as he considers it, to mirror his life: when his marriage deteriorated he began collecting plastic brides and grooms, during the court trauma he discovered militaria and dressed in khakis.

He had always been particular about controlling his environment: 'When I was a teenager,' Shear says, 'I was obsessed with my hair. I had a flat-top crew cut, and it had to be perfectly flat, like the deck of an aircraft carrier. If it was off by two degrees, I would start to sweat in horror, and I would tilt my head two degrees to compensate. I used to go around town looking for barbers with steady hands.' Now, finally, after his divorce, the court case, and his decision to devote himself entirely to his project of rescuing the American spirit from flea markets and jumble sales, his life was in his own hands.

'Two of every sort shall come to thee, to keep them alive.' This was Noah's task. His spiritual descendants still follow in his footsteps, adhering to the gospel that things cannot be allowed to go to waste, to perish, to be forgotten, to vanish altogether. Incantations are not sung in churches alone: anyone can build a little temple, or an altar in a corner of the room. Even, and especially, the humble and the insignificant are often extended the hand of rescue. Saving the world, or a world, preserving history or genius, saintliness or innocence, touching something beyond our random existences is a labour of love, a constant ritual, is one face of the desire to be authentic, to be human.

A Theatre of Memories

The work is of wood, marked with many images, and full of little boxes; there are various orders and grades in it. He gives a place to each individual figure and ornament, and he showed me such a mass of papers that, though I always thought that Cicero was the fountain of richest eloquence, scarcely would I have thought that one author could contain so much or that so many volumes could be pieced together out of his writings. I wrote to you before the name of the author who is called Julius Camillus. He stammers badly and speaks Latin with difficulty, excusing himself with the pretext that through continually using his pen he has nearly lost the use of speech . . . He calls this theatre of his by many names, saying now that it is a built or constructed mind . . . and now that it is a windowed one. He pretends that all things that the human mind can conceive and which we cannot see with the corporeal eye, after being collected together by diligent meditation may be expressed by certain corporeal signs in such a way that the beholder may at once perceive with his eyes everything that is otherwise hidden in the depths of the human mind. And it is because of this corporeal looking that he calls it a theatre.

Erasmus, *Epistolae*[1]

Viglius Zuichemus, who was writing this so breathlessly to his great correspondent Erasmus of Rotterdam in 1532, had just been shown one of the most famous edifices of the Renaissance, a structure talked about by intellectuals in France, Italy and beyond: Giulio Camillo's Theatre of Memory.

The structure itself did not survive for much more than a few decades and only fragmentary descriptions of it are preserved. With so suspiciously few sources to go on, and in view of its creator's reputation for being a charlatan, some scholars even believe that it may never have existed, though honourable witnesses like Viglius seem to vouch for the fact that it was indeed more than a scholar's outrageous fantasy.

Camillo was clearly a man obsessed. Little is known about the precise circumstances of his life, but he seems to have given up a professorship in Bologna in order to devote himself entirely to his *idée fixe*, the theatre, the culmination, or so he thought, of two thousand years' worth of theories about memory, rhetoric, occult knowledge and the proper method of thought. His reputation had preceded him. 'They say that this man has constructed a certain Amphitheatre, a work of wonderful skill, into which whoever is admitted as spectator will be able to discourse on any subject no less fluently than Cicero,'[2] Viglius had reported to Erasmus some weeks earlier, and had continued to give a rough idea of the workings of this wondrous machine: 'It is said that this Architect has drawn up in certain places whatever about anything is found in Cicero . . . Certain orders or grades of figures are disposed . . . with stupendous labour and divine skill.'

The scholar, Camillo, was working on his greatest work, a kind of grand unified theory of memory and companion encyclopaedia to the theatre itself, which, he hoped, would revolutionize the way people thought about the world and how they utilized their thought in discourse. The King of France, Francis I, was intrigued by this idea and sent for the Italian magus, promising him the grand sum of 1,500 ducats if he brought his theatre to Paris with him and assembled it there without showing it to anyone but the king himself. Camillo set off on the laborious journey from Bologna to Paris, made more difficult by the fact that he was cursed with a terrible stammer and spoke little Latin and French probably not at all; his great treasure packed and crated up and brought to the coast by ox cart, from there to a French harbour by cog and the entire breadth of France by cart again, an agonizing period during which his life's work, his theatre, manuscripts, drawings, ornaments, symbols, utensils and books were in danger of being damaged, lost, spoiled by rain, stolen by vagrants or robbed by outlaws every step of the way.

He did finally reach the French court and settled there around 1534 after another trip to Italy to pick up some things left behind. Now he set about constructing, or reconstructing, the great theatre for his new and powerful patron, the king himself, all under the ever-watchful eye of a court starving for gossip and of scholars eager to find out about this miraculous engine of the mind.[3] What we know about the building that took shape in some courtyard of the royal court is gleaned from Camillo's own description in his *Idea del Theatro*, a mere shadow of the *magnum opus* he hoped to write but never did, a little book which appeared after his death.

The historian Frances Yates has attempted to reconstruct the interior of the building. The first thing Francis I would have realized was that it was he who was standing on stage and looking into the auditorium, instead of taking his customary place among the audience. The panorama presented to him was a seven-tier amphitheatre divided into seven segments, each fronted by one of the seven pillars of wisdom that were supposed to have stood in Solomon's temple. The galleries, however, which surrounded the stage in a semi-circle, were not peopled by expensively clad courtiers and ladies in low-cut dresses out for an evening's dinner and entertainment, but by symbols, trapdoors and inscriptions, all of which formed a metaphorical order of the world.

Each of the seven segments was allocated to one of the seven planets (from left to right: Moon, Mercury, Venus, Sun, Mars, Jupiter and Saturn), while the ascending tiers had a symbolic system all of their own. The first tier, that closest to the stage, was given over to the Planet, the second was called the Banquet, signifying the first and simplest stage of Creation. From there the order ascended to the Cave, Gorgon and her Sisters, Pasiphe and the Bull, the Sandals of Mercury and, finally, Prometheus, all decorated with the appropriate allegories and symbolism and supplemented with trapdoors behind which the inquiring mind would find the appropriate glosses on Cicero's writings, prepared by Camillo himself.

The star of this theatre was the human mind, or, more precisely, memory. The structure was nothing more or less than a mnemonic system, Camillo would have explained to the astounded monarch, allowing him to visualize everything on earth and put it into its appropriate place in the symbolic order of the world, to be retrieved at the appropriate moment during a debate or long oration, the most elaborate memory aid ever constructed. If the king, for instance, wanted to discourse about himself as a patron of the arts and sciences, he would find them on the highest realm, given over to human activities, Prometheus. Here, in the Saturnian segment to his right, he would see right under the wooden roof a figure of Cybele looking down on him, the allegory of the arts of the Saturnian, earth-related matters: geometry, geography and agriculture. If his mind was inclined to loftier things, he could look right ahead at the Apollonian segment dedicated to the sun, where the Promethean tier showed, among other figures, Apollo and the Muses, signifying the art of poetry. Everything, every emotion, every activity, was localized in this contraption that was, in effect, a collection of possibilities as well as a gigantic memory aid.

Francis would have found his troubled campaigns against the Habsburg Emperor Charles V in the column of Mars, where he could see the Planet's influence asserting itself throughout Creation: as a pure principle on the lower rung, allied only with its cabbalistic principle of Sephira; then, on the Banquet level, as earthly volcanic power and spiritual Purgatory; as mixed element representing vigour but also discord on the level of the Cave; then as intellectual influence on the fourth level, Gorgon and her Sisters, where it stood for hasty and rash decisions; as human nature in Pasiphe and the Bull, arrogance and pride; ascending to the Sandals of Mercury, where it became a human action, striking fire and being cruel; to the highest level, Prometheus, the human arts and the art of the smith, of the military and of the butcher.

The king, wishing to remind himself of victorious battles, could have chosen the two fighting Serpents on this level as symbols of the arts of combat, though the terrifying Furies close to them would have brought to his mind the flip side of glory on the battlefield, which he had also experienced at first hand: prisons, tortures and punishment. The Serpents and the Furies, therefore, could have summed up his martial career, while the items in the compartment of the Apollonian Prometheus would have reminded him of his goals: the Clock and the Lion for good government, Apollo as Shepherd, the pastoral art. From the Serpents to the Clock and Lion and from the Furies to the divine Shepherd, Francis could have given a speech on the virtues of a ruler there and then, aided by the images in front of him, which he had thus associated with events and aspirations of his own life.

It is not certain that Francis I ever saw the theatre, as it is not certain that it was ever finished. We do know that Giulio Camillo left France after a while; the king had obviously grown bored with the Italian stammerer and had extended the hand of patronage to another artist and philosopher. Camillo had received only 500 ducats, a third of the promised sum, and had been forced, after the money had been used up paying for building material, copyists and artists, to admit to himself that he would not be able to finish his work there. He seems to have left it behind in Paris, possibly altogether despairing of ever scraping together the funds to realize his ambition. There is an uncertain sighting of the theatre at court in the 1550s, but when a scholar investigated its existence half a century later he could find no trace of it anywhere.

Camillo's elaborate Theatre of Memory stands in a long tradition of thinking on the art of memory, on its power, conception and shape. Legend has it that the art was born when the pre-Socratic poet, Simonides of Ceos, survived a disaster during which all the guests at a banquet had been killed by a collapsing ceiling and were so badly disfigured that even their relatives could not identify them. Remembering the places at which they had sat at table, Simonides was able to put names to the corpses and to help the mourners. It occurred to him that this feat of memory had been possible only because he had associated each banquet guest with a locality, and he began to experiment with similarly localizing abstract ideas. He could, for instance, place imaginary objects with symbolic qualities in a house he envisioned or along a path, and then pick them up one by one, spinning on the thread of thought aided by these symbols without the need of written notes.

The account of Simonides and his momentous discovery is relayed by Cicero, the most famous exponent of the art of memory in antiquity. Another Roman writer, Quintilian, illustrates the method. To use it to best effect, he writes, the orator should choose

. . . a spacious house divided into a number of rooms. Everything of note therein is diligently imprinted on the mind, in order that thought may be able to run through all the parts without let or hindrance. The first task is to secure that there shall be no difficulty in running through these, for that memory must be most firmly fixed which helps another memory. Then what has been written down or thought of, is noted by a sign to remind of it. This sign may be drawn from a whole 'thing', as navigation or warfare, or from some 'word'; for what is slipping from memory is recovered by the admonition of a single 'word' . . . These signs are then arranged as follows. The first notion is placed, as it were, in the forecourt; the second, let us say in the atrium, the remainder are placed in order all round the impluvium and committed not only to bedrooms and parlors but even to statues and the like. This done, when it is required to revive the memory, one begins from the first place to run through all, demanding what has been entrusted to them of which one will be reminded by the image . . . What I have spoken of as being done in a house can also be done in public buildings, or on a long journey, or in going through a city with pictures. Or we can imagine such places for ourselves. We require, therefore places, either real or imaginary, and images and simulacra which must be invented. Images are as words by which we note the things we have to learn, so that as Cicero says, 'we use places as wax and images as letters'.[4]

These places for memorization and with them the theory of artificial memory were developed further during the Middle Ages and the Renaissance. Albertus Magnus and Thomas Aquinas both analysed and propagated this method as a useful way of learning by heart legal, devotional and philosophical texts. Ramon Lull, the thirteenth-century Spanish mystic and philosopher, whose Hermetic thought so influenced alchemists all over Europe and especially in Rudolf's Prague, introduced a more dynamic system of memory based on divine attributes, a neo-Platonist reinterpretation of the art in which the human intellect was encouraged to imitate the divine. In the Renaissance a whole flood of treatises and larger works dealt with the art of memory and its applications in philosophy, in the cabbala as understood by Christian scholars, in natural magic and in alchemy. Giordano Bruno even transformed the art into a fully-fledged occult system of knowledge, a process of initiation into the mysteries of God's own creative power.[5]

The English Hermetic philosopher Robert Fludd had developed a theatre of memory of his own accord, which he outlined in his 1619

work *Utrisque Cosmi, Maioris
scilicet et Minoris, metaphysica,
physica, atque technica Historia* (a
title that to modern ears sounds
inescapably Borghesian).

Fludd's theatre, possibly inspired
by stories about Camillo he had
picked up while in France and mod-
elled on Shakespeare's Globe (the
engraving in his work is ambiva-
lently labelled *Theatrum Orbi* –
'World' or 'Globe Theatre'),[6] fused
the mystical ideas of Bruno with
an arrangement similar to that of
Camillo's legendary but long destroyed construction. To Fludd,
however, the mystical number of
memory and of universal order appears to have been five, not seven,
and the theatre was divided into fives. Later other writers, such as
John Willis, followed Fludd and drafted theatres of memories of their
own.[7]

The dramatization of memory and the cultivation of imaginary
museums seems to have taken hold of a small but significant part of
English culture in the seventeenth century. Francis Bacon, himself
much exercised by the nature of memory, designed an ideal collection
all of his own, a perfect island in the middle of nowhere, a utopia. The
imaginary travellers he sent on a voyage in his *The New Atlantis* reach
an isle inhabited by a race of wise people whose governor, the Father
of Solomon's House, a wonderfully oriental potentate-cum-initiate in
richly decorated robes, explains the purpose and organization of his
great and sophisticated civilization. 'The end of our foundation,' he
relates, 'is the knowledge of causes, and secret motions of things; and
the enlarging of the bounds of human empire, to the effecting of all
things possible.' He proceeds to describe the foundation in its various
parts. There are automatons, designed to further

. . . the knowledge of the Causes and secret motions of things and the enlarging of the bounds of Human Empire, to be effecting of all things possible . . . We have divers curious clocks, and other like motions of return, and perpetual motions. We imitate also motions of living creatures, but images of men, beasts, birds, fishes, and serpents. We have also a great number of other various motions, strange for equality, fineness and subtlety.[8]

It is a great and wonderful display that the New Atlantians have put on for their entertainment and edification. There are 'houses of deceits of the senses' with optical and other illusions, and

. . . two very long and fair galleries: in one of these we place patterns and samples of all manner of the more rare and excellent inventions: in the other we place the statues of all principal inventors. There we have the statue of your Columbus, that discovered the West Indies: also the inventor of ships: your monk that was the inventor of ordnance and of gunpowder: the inventor of music: the inventor of letters: the inventor of printing: the inventor of observations of astronomy: the inventor of works in metal: the inventor of glass: the inventor of silk of the worm: the inventor of wine: the inventor of corn and bread: the inventor of sugars: and all these, by more certain tradition than you have.[9]

Apart from these galleries devoted to the founders of wisdom, there are 'parks and enclosures of all sorts of beasts and birds which we use not only for view or rareness, but likewise for dissections and trials', health chambers, orchards and gardens, furnaces and laboratories, perspective houses, treasuries, and engine houses 'where are prepared engines and instruments for all sorts of motions'.[10]

What the travellers are shown on this mysterious island is, in fact, an alchemist's perfect chamber of miracles, complete with galleries, laboratories, menageries and botanical gardens, an otherworldly version of Rudolf's laird in Hradčany Castle. Bacon attached great importance to such 'goodly large cabinet[s], wherein whatsoever the hand of man by exquisite art of engine hath made is rare in stuff, form, or motion; whatsoever singularity chance and the shuffle of things hath produced; whatsoever nature hath wrought in things that want life and may be kept; shall be sorted and included'.[11] They were instruments of knowledge, covering not only

... nature, free and at large (when she is left to her own and does her work her own way), – such as that of the heavenly bodies, meteors, earth and sea, minerals, plants, animals, – but much more of nature under constraint and vexed; that is to say, when by art and the hand of man she is forced out of her natural state, and squeezed and moulded. Therefore I set down at length all experiments of the mechanical arts, of the operative part of the liberal arts, of the many crafts which are not yet grown into arts properly so called ... seeing that the nature of things betrays itself more readily under the vexations of art than in its natural freedom.[12]

Imaginary collections are as important as real ones: both place on their stage memories as contained in objects; both seek to lock out death by building fortresses of remembrance and permanence. Little more than a century after Bacon's earnest exposition of the perfect *Wunderkammer* the auctioneer Thomas Ballerd, 'bookseller at the rising-sun in little-Britain', prepared a sale catalogue which sought to attract the attention of connoisseurs with

... many very Valuable and Uncommon Books, in most Faculties and Languages, Chiefly in PHYSIC, CHURURGERY, CHYMISTRY, DIVINITY, PHILOLOGY, HISTORY, and other Polite Parts of Learning. Most of the Classics: Not. Varior. Old Elzevier's and other Choice Editions, well Bound, and very Fair. Also BOOKS of SCULPTURE & PAINTING, with Choice Manuscripts. WHICH Will begin to be sold by AUCTION, at the Black-boy Coffee-house in Ave-Mary-Lane, near Ludgate, on MONDAY the 8th Day of January, 17 10/11, beginning every Evening at Four of the Clock, till the Sale is finish'd.[13]

He was auctioning off the collection and library of the late Sir Thomas Browne (1605–82), who had, in his early career, made use of the mnemonic systems that were so fashionable until the middle of the seventeenth century. In the middle of his career, however, Browne saw a new problem that was transforming attitudes to knowledge and to memory, and with it attitudes to the nature and ideal of collecting: in a world that seemed to be constantly expanding it was no longer possible to possess a mind of truly universal scope, to encompass all that was to be known in one head, one library or in one cabinet. Specialization was required. 'Knowledge is made by oblivion, and to purchase a clear and warrantable body of Truth, we must forget and part with much we know.'[14]

The *ars memoria* as a tool for understanding the world and its hidden harmonies had to admit defeat in the face of what Louis MacNiece would later call the world's tendency for being 'incorrigibly plural'. Browne found that memory alone was not enough to stem the tide of forgetting:

Memory slips away, age, time, events pass mostly into oblivion; commentaries therefore must be made ready in good time to obviate so great an evil. Not to rearrange the thoughts of writers in commonplace books, which will be doing again what has been done, but from a fresh reading of books to set down an abstract in free style, to include all that is difficult and worthy of note; whatever the author himself, the memory of like things, or natural genius supplies.[15]

His consolation against thoughts of mortality and his impending role as food for worms was a warm adherence to the minutiae of life, a love of particulars, as he himself explained:

I hope I may expect your candour, if not pardon, if I bee sometimes so particular in circumstances while I discours of things wherin I take so much delight, for even Julius Scaliger who doth not use to bee tedious, being a notable huntsman himself when hee writes of doggs could not refrayne from setting down the names of some of his owne and that his beloved bich Urania pissed with one legge up.[16]

As an amateur scholar who really loved scholarship but disdained grand systems, Browne had the wit and the luxury to write an account that has become one of the great collection catalogues of the seventeenth century, the *Musaeum Clausum or Bibliotheca Abscondita*, the detailed list of a collection published by him for the information of his fellow scholars. It addressed itself to the reader with all the learnedness to be expected of one of the seventeenth century's finest minds:

Sir,

With many thanks I return that noble Catalogue of Books, Rarities and Singularities of Art and Nature, which you were pleased to communicate unto me. There are many Collections of this kind in Europe. And, besides the printed accounts of the Museum Aldrovandi, Calceolarianum Voscardi, Vormianum; the Casa Abhellita at Loretto, and Threasor of S. Dennis, the Repository of the Duke of Tuscany, that of the Duke of Saxony, and that noble one of the Emperour at Vienna, and many more are of singular note. Of what in this kind I have by me I shall maide no repetition, and you having already had a view thereof, I am bold to present you with the List of a Collection, which I may justly say you have not seen before.

The Title is, as above, Musaeum Clausum, or Bibliotheca Abscondita: containing some remarkable Books, Antiquities, Pictures and Rarities of several kinds, scarce or never seen by any man now living.

He who knows where all this Treasure now is, is a great Apollo. I'm sure I am not He. However, I am,

Sir, Yours, &c.

Thomas Browne

The following catalogue then lists in great detail a number of items so wonderful that they deserve to be described, at least in part, in Browne's own words:

Draughts of three passionate Looks; of Thyestes when he was told at the Table that he had eaten a piece of his own Son; of Bajazet when he went into the Iron Cage; of OEdipus when he first came to know that he had killed his Father, and married his own Mother.

A fair English Lady drawn Al Negro, or in the ethiopian hue excelling the original White and Red Beauty, with this Subscription, *Sed quondam volo nocte Nioriorem.*

Mummia Tholosana; or, The complete Head and Body of Father Crispin, buried long ago in the Vault of the Cordeliers at Tholouse, where the Skins of the dead so drie and parch up without corruption that their persons may be known very long after, with this Inscription, *Ecce iterum Crispinus.*

King Mithridates his *Oneirocritica. Aristotle de Precationibus. Democritus de his quz fiunt apad Orcum, Oceani circumnavigatio.* A defence of Arnoldus de Villa Nova, whom the learned Postellus conceived to be the author of *De Tribe Impostoribus*. A learned explanation of the receit to make a divell . . . A Tragedy of Thyestes, and another of Medea, writ by Diogenes the Cynick. King Alfred upon Aristotle de Plantis. Seneca's Epistles to S. Paul. King Solomon de Umbris Idzarurn, which Chicus Asculanus, in his Comment upon Johannes de Sacrobosco, would make us believe he saw in the Library of the Duke of Bavaria.

Ars honest petandi in societate by M. Ortuinum (the art of farting decently in public, by Hardouin de Graetz).

Imitations Johann Fischart's *Catalogus Catalogarum* (1590)

Joh. Faust Magia Naturalis, Fledermaeuse zu machen in 16mo in: Catalogus Etlicher sehr alter Buecher welche Neulin in Irrland oaf einem alten eroberten Schlosse in einer Bibliothec gefunden worden 4to frankfort 1650[17]

This collection stands out among the great cabinets of rarities, as it contains works that could not be found anywhere else but here: the art of farting decently in public might have been of limited use in polite society; scholars, however, would have given anything for some of the books. Original works by King Alfred, the correspondence between a Roman stoic and Saint Paul himself, even King Solomon and Doctor Faust feature in this roll call of all that was unattainable, a great wish list of literature. It may therefore come as little surprise that none of these works existed outside of this catalogue. Browne, however, epitomized the spirit of the cabinet of rarities and its attractions, very similar to Tradescant's Ark, which he might have visited and of which he possessed the catalogue, the *Musaeum Tradescantianum*, the first and ill-fated cooperation between John Tradescant and the devious Elias Ashmole.

Browne had a fine collection of books on cabinets of curiosities himself, with a clear emphasis on those dealing with natural history. The sale of his library included volumes such as Francesco Calceolari's *Musaeum Calceolarium* (1622), several works by Ulisse Aldrovandi (their beautiful names are worth reciting for sheer pleasure: *Musaeum metallicum; Serpentum et draconum historiae; De quadrupedibus digitatis viviparis et oviparis*, etc.) and Athanasius Kircher's famous works inspired by his Vatican collection, such as the *Obeliscus Pamphilius; Oedipus Aegyptiacus; Mundus Subterraneus;* and *China Illustrata.*

Browne was well versed in collecting literature. He had even taken the trouble to write an entire book himself refuting what he believed to be 'vulgar errors' about creatures and natural phenomena such as could be found in the cabinets of the time. He was also, however, intrigued by the sheer beauty of strangeness that seemed to rule these collections, and the minds that amassed them. Apart from the farce in the rather Mozartian scatology of some of the imaginary books this collection is one of high drama, a fictional realization of every collector's dream. There is the strangeness of foreign lands in the subcollection of leaning towers and the drawing of the moonlight market, tragedy and terror in the face of Oedipus frozen at the moment of his deepest despair (a device foreshadowing the career of the Viennese sculptor Franz Xaver Messerschmidt who would depict himself in states of emotional extremes some 200 years later), terror of a different kind in the accounts of torture, the wonderfully brazen idea of an English woman drawn 'al negro', a real mummy with a beautiful story to boot, and the conflagration of nature and religion so beloved of Mannerism in the cross fashioned from a frog skull. No cabinet could have been conceived more perfectly.

While Browne amused himself by holding up his contemporaries' obsessions to ridicule he himself was by no means immune to this folly. After a visit to his house, John Evelyn, who had also written about Sir Hans Sloane, noted: 'Next morning I went to see Sir Th: Browne [. . .] whose whole house & Garden being a Paradise & Cabinet of rarities, & that of the best collection, especialy medails, books, Plants, natural things, did exceedingly refresh me.'[18]

Browne's humour as expressed in his *Musaeum Clausum* (in which we may also find shades of genuinely wishful thinking) hid a more sombre, melancholic side of a man constantly preoccupied with mortality, with remembrance and with memory. His *Urne Buriall,* or, to give it its full title

HYDRIOTAPHIA
URNE – BURIALL
OR,
A Discourse on the Sepulchrall
Urnes lately found in
NORFOLK
Together with
The Garden of CYRUS
OR THE
Quincunciall, Lozenge, or
Net-work Plantations of the An
cients, Artificially, Naturally,
Mystically Considered
With Sundry Observations

is a work of darkness and forebodings of oblivion, all the more valuable for being one of the few discursive sources in which a man who had dedicated his life to collecting and reflection deals with the reality that nevertheless is perhaps the single greatest presence in every collection: death. From the very first line this ostensibly archaeological work declares its hand:

When the Funerall pyre was out, and the last valediction was over, men took a lasting adieu of their interred Friends, little expecting the curiosity of future ages should comment upon their ashes, and having no old experience of the duration of their Reliques, held no opinion of such after considerations.[19]

Brown would have had a soulmate in Ecclesiastes, whose cry 'vanity of vanities' reverberates throughout his thinking: 'If we begin to die when we live, and long life be but a prolongation of death; our life is a sad composition; We live with death, and die not in a moment.' A human life, a universe to the one who is living it, is as nothing when compared to eternity, to the sweeping tides of history. Every human mind, though, is its own trap, and 'the long habit of living indisposeth us for dying'.[20]

It is this fear of 'the necessity of oblivion', of death as the ultimate stranger whom one cannot know without being taken by him, that fosters a need to collect, to create permanence, to treat the graveyard earth, a vast field of past urn burials, as a repository of treasures and miracles: 'Time hath endlesse rarities, and shows of all varieties; which reveals old things in heaven, makes new discoveries in earth, and even earth it self a discovery. That great Antiquity *America* lay buried for a thousand years; and a large part of the earth is still in the Urne unto us.'[21] Permanence and immortality, though, recede in the same measure as they are being sought, and the urge to accumulate proves its own undoing: 'Avarice makes us the sport of death.' What we collect, therefore, is both instrument of our survival beyond the grave and the very reminder of our inexorable end:

Beside, to preserve the living, and make the dead to live, to keep men out of their Urnes, and discourse of humane fragments in them, is not impertinent unto our profession; whose study is life and death, who daily behold examples of mortality, and of all men least need artificial *mementos*, or coffins by our bed side, to minde us of our graves.[22]

In fact, the very shape of the urns found in Norfolk illustrates that

in collecting things we are 'making our last bed like our first; nor much unlike the Urnes of our Nativity, while we lay in the nether part of the Earth, and inward vault of our Microcosme'.[23]

Concluding his meditation on the last things that the urns have inspired in him, Browne declares the vessels themselves to be spectacular failures, reminding us of nothing more than death and decay and not of those who sought to gain eternity through them:

Had they made as good provision for their names, as they have done for their Reliques, they had not so grossly erred in the art of perpetuation. But to subsist in bones, and be but Pyramidally extant, is a fallacy in duration. Vain ashes, which in the oblivion of names, persons, times, and sexes, have found unto themselves, a fruitlesse continuation, and only arise unto late posterity, as Emblemes of mortall vanities; Antidotes against pride, vain-glory, and madding vices. Pagan vain-glories which thought the world might last for ever, had encouragement for ambition, and finding no *Atropos* unto the immortality of their Names, were never dampt with the necessity of oblivion.[24]

The boundless optimism of the Renaissance cabinet, of the scholar searching for celestial harmonies and for truth through symbolic representation of universal principles, had made way for scepticism, certain only of the last uncertainties. Browne would still quote the authors of antiquity against the 'vulgar errors' he attacked, but the world had moved on into territories 'never known by the ancients'. Europe and the European mind increasingly had nothing to rely on but itself.

Every collection is a theatre of memories, a dramatization and a *mise-en-scène* of personal and collective pasts, of a remembered child-hood and of remembrance after death. It guarantees the presence of these memories through the objects evoking them. It is more even than a symbolic presence: a transubstantiation. The world beyond what we can touch is with us in and through them, and through communion with them it is possible to commune with it and become part of it.

Giulio Camillo was the only person to try to collect the world in its entirety through allegorical representation: every element, every human quality and activity, every realm of the physical and metaphys-ical worlds had a place in his theatre, was localized and put into context. He who possessed this theatre possessed the world in its entirety as a metaphor, as mythological representation in hundreds of allegorical images. Others created individual collections of the mind: ideal and grotesque, sacramental and satirical.[25] The writings of Jorge Luis Borges are informed by the same mischievous sensibility, but the art of memory as an instrument of understanding the world and conquering the spirit has long since died or been relegated to the fairground with mnemonic conjuring tricks of people appearing on television and parading their ability to memorize sequences of playing cards or random numbers. How are the mighty fallen!

While the palaces of memory of old have fallen into disrepair and been replaced by computers and circus tents, the idea of the imaginary collection lives on, not least in literature, and in the mind of every collector aspiring to the ideal object to round off an ensemble. It lives on in other forms as well, in collections that very obviously encase memories or a conception of the past, in local museums devoted to the lives of people from decades or centuries ago, or in the private shrines erected to remember the dead; rooms furnished to remember what would otherwise be irrevocably lost.

Can one be a collector without actually collecting or amassing anything, but by giving away? Many collectors were also great patrons and patronage has always been the other face of collecting, be it through commissioning artists or through endowments, but it is only after meeting Alberto Vilar, the grandest patron of opera in perhaps any century, that I really began to entertain this notion.

For someone who is the benefactor to end all benefactors, Alberto Vilar is at first sight remarkably unremarkable: a man of average height, slender, with neat, greying hair and oval glasses, dressed in pinstripe trousers and open shirt and a cardigan with colourful leather appliqué (red and bright green), more a vision of your average American middle manager home from work than a purveyor of generosity on a scale unprecedented since the Medici.

By his own estimation, Vilar, who became a financier rather than a musician at the insistence of his father, and who has made his fortune by investing heavily in firms like Microsoft and Cisco Systems since the early 1980s, has given $150 million to opera houses and other arts institutions over the last ten years or so. Today one can go to see an opera in New York, San Francisco, Boston, Milan, Bayreuth, Vienna, London and St Petersburg and the likelihood is that the hall in which one sits, the surtitles one watches, the air conditioning, the training of one of the singers one sees, or sometimes the entire production have been paid for in full by Alberto Vilar. 'This season the Met will put on six of my operas at $2 million a piece and I'm proud of every one of those operas,' he says with obvious satisfaction.[26]

Vilar does not just like being acknowledged, he thinks it is imperative, and to his eyes the appreciation of the public is strangely skewed:

There's much superficial recognition of the singers, as if the whole art form depended on them. Not that they're not important but I say, guess what: the singers wouldn't exist without the philanthropy. I have many friends who are professional singers and 100 per cent of my friends like me, they like what I do. There's no opera program in the world that doesn't have pictures of the singers, and some have pictures of the intendant, the director, the conductor, pictures of pictures, but never of the sponsor. Let me crack the code of philanthropy for you: You Must Appreciate. Human beings like to hear the word Thank You. When you give $50 million the least people can do is to say Thank You. I just find it strange that you are walking around that house and nobody knows you.

Vilar indulges his taste for grand opera, ideally Puccini's *Turandot* staged by Franco Zeffirelli, by underwriting the productions. This gives him a good deal of power and considerable influence on the policy even of big opera houses. He denies this but obliges with an anecdote illustrating it:

Bayreuth commissioned Jürgen Flimm to do a *Ring*. Well, he went a little bit overboard and most people said so. It turns out that the Met was going to do a production of *Fidelio*, which is one of my favourite operas, and guess who was going to do it? Jürgen Flimm. So I called up Joe [Volpe, Chief Executive of the Met] and said 'Joe, are we going to do this crazy thing that we had in Bayreuth?' and he said: 'No, Alberto, we are controlling this.' So I underwrote the production. It was OK. I don't say to the Met you will put on him or her, I just say yes or no, I simply say 'I wouldn't be comfortable with this production, or, this production is too modern for me.'

Is it possible that Vilar collects by giving? That he gains the esteem and the culture that would not usually be accorded to a financier, and collects entire opera productions (without taking them home), just as Pierpont Morgan collected incunabula?[27] His New York apartment is a shrine to opera and to music and many of its features are imitations of ornaments from great opera houses and concert halls around the world. His generosity has given him power and control in a world that is notoriously difficult to control and to influence. He has bought more than recognition. He has managed, more subtly than a politician and more effectively than a great artist, to make the world of opera his world, simply by purchasing it, and he now spends much of his time travelling around the world to visit 'his' productions and to enjoy the paraphernalia: a production in Milan, the next in St Petersburg, board meetings at the Metropolitan Opera, and evenings with celebrated artists, all results of his willingness to part with what he himself terms his 'hard-earned cash'. Is this not a kind of collection?

Part IV

The Tower of Fools

And the whole earth was of one language, and of one speech. And it came to pass, as they journeyed from the east, that they found a plain in the land of Shin'ar; and they dwelt there. And they said to one another, Come, let us make bricks, and burn them thoroughly. And they had brick for stone, and mud had they for mortar. And they said, Come, let us build us a city and a tower, whose top may reach to heaven, and let us make us a name, lest we be scattered abroad upon the face of the whole earth.

Genesis 11.1–4

A Veritable Vello-Maniac

[He will] pursue a volume in an active or seductive way; he will use
intrigue and stealth; he will hazard his fortune and he will journey
around the world, or even marry for the gain of a coveted book.

The psychiatrist Dr Norman S. Weiner on the bibliophile[1]

For him that stealeth, or borroweth, and returneth not, this book from
its owner, let it change into a serpent in his hand and rend him. Let him
be struck with palsy, and all his members blasted. Let him languish in
pain crying aloud for mercy, and let there be no surcease to his agony
till he sing in dissolution. Let bookworms gnaw his entrails and when
at last he goeth to his final punishment, let the flames of Hell consume
him for ever.

Curse on book thieves from the library
of the Monastery of San Pedro, Barcelona

The heavy leather binding is embossed carefully, if not quite symmetri-
cally. An ornate lozenge with a swirling pattern forms the centrepiece,
surrounded by rectangular borders. On the right-hand side, brass
hinges that were once nailed to the lid have left their traces. In the top
centre an inscription: PAROCHIE KERK VAN LOENEN; and at
the bottom: 1807. One has to open it with care; the binding is broken,
too heavy for the old paper and hemp that used to hold it together.
The spine of the book flaps open and reveals its anatomy, arteries of

string and membranes of leather and of paper. A dry smell rises from it, a tantalizing intimation of the secrets this book holds. There is an inscription in the inside of the lid: L. K., which probably stands for 'Loenen Kerk', the church to which the bible used to belong. The frontispiece opposite shows a portal in the austere way of the Dutch Baroque. The panel reads:

BIBLIA

DAT IS

De gantsche H. Schrifture
Vervattende alle de Canonycke

Boecken des Ouden en des Nieuwen

TESTAMENTS

The bible was printed in Amsterdam, in 1761, by Losel, Onder de Linden. My mother gave it to us as a wedding gift. It is a relic of my great-grandfather's collection, which overshadowed my childhood with its mystery and wonder. Its connection with our family does not span centuries of pious Calvinist Dutchmen, and the inscriptions are witness to a somewhat confused history: Dutch and German, and now English, and who knows what else.

My great-grandfather bought this bible, along with many others. Bibles, and with them a stubborn and eclectic desire for the Truth, were his great passion. He possessed and read them in many languages and old editions, some with precious bindings and others in more unassuming garb. I have another one of these, a well-thumbed pocket bible replete with his personal annotations and with newspaper clippings: 'The Advice of a Psychiatrist' lies on top, a collection of useful platitudes or words of wisdom; 'Search for peace first and foremost' is underlined. 'God's word in 1392 languages' is the next clipping, then a little drawing in ballpoint on a newspaper margin, two people in a doorway, with an illegible caption. They are followed by many others: 'Old Hebrew text found', 'New editions', 'Historical psalms', 'A key to understanding the Bible', etc. Then there are the scribblings in the margins, underlinings in coloured pencil and notes in ballpoint. Some passages are highlighted in red or blue; words and sentences in the heavy, ceremonial Dutch, which always seems at once frightening and ridiculous to me. This is one of the red passages, all of which seem to deal with human relationships: 'En Hij zeide: Neem nu uwen zoon, uwen eenige, dien gij liefhebt, Izak, en ga heen naar het land Moria, en offer hem aldaar tot een brandoffer, op eenen van de bergen, dien Ik u zeggen zal'. ('And He said: take thy son, thy only one, whom thou lovest, Isaac, and go to the land Moria, and make a burned offering of him there, on one of the mountains, which I shall show thee.') It sounds more distant and yet more immediate in an older version, in massive, Gothic letters and with tiny cross-references in the margins:

> *Ende Hy seyde; Neemt nu uwen sone*
> *uwen eenigen*
> *dien gy lief hebt*
> *Isaac*
> *ende gaet henen na het lant Morija;*
> *ende offert hem aldaer tot een brand-offer*
> *op een van de bergen*
> *dien ik u seggen zal.*

These two bibles in my study establish my fraudulent family history. One might think my great-grandfather a terrible bible-basher, a Calvinist bigot with a head full of Old Testament verses and bowdler-ized science. He was, in fact, a Calvinist, but in no way a bigot. He was too many things to be that: translator, tea taster, stockbroker, biscuit manufacturer, bad flautist, clandestine antiques dealer and spurious feeder of swans, member of the Dutch resistance, Russian scholar and great collector. One thing that Willem Eldert Blom was not, however, was my real great-grandfather. I have adopted him in the same way that my mother did before me when she moved into his house as a girl of eight just after the war, the daughter by a previous marriage of his son's new wife, a German girl in Holland, a little enemy. While the local children and her teachers, some of whom had been tortured by the Gestapo, took their revenge against the Third Reich out on an eight-year-old with bullying, dog shit and segregation, Willem read her stories, translated *prima vista* from Greek, Latin, French and English, in his book-lined front room. When he died, aged ninety-four, a few books of his library found their way into our house. Everything wonderful seemed to stem from him, be connected with him and with that country in which I spent my school holidays, that wonderfully unGerman country of contented people who lived by canals and beaches swept by savage winter storms, of large, curtainless windows and long bicycle rides hard on the heels of my much faster cousins, of windmill biscuits and cheese and different smells all conspiratorially connected to that language which I learned almost as fast as my mother had done, and with the same intent: not to be noticed, not to be different, to belong. He was my great-grandfather all right, if perhaps not by the reckoning of those who think along blood lines so much more pettily than he did. A child who had not met his father, far less his grandfather or great-grandfather, I fervently made him my own, and with him the family legends that surrounded him. He was that mythical patriarch, Abraham, or Moses maybe, and his was the Promised Land.

So much is bound up with objects and their history, so many feelings, hopes and delusions we need to preserve in order to preserve ourselves. Books have the most powerful and subtle connotations, for they are never only objects, they have a voice with which they speak across time and across lives, a voice contingent only in part on their material nature and expressed forcefully in their text. They are at once relics of a different era and personalities forever in the prime of their life, talking as objects and as books, from their own time and from that of the reader's. In the case of our family bible there is half a century between the printing and the binding it is housed in; they already talk different languages. The text is both 250 years old, and millennia. It speaks to a secular mind as powerfully as it does to a religious one, but in radically altered ways.

Book collecting has many faces. It is perhaps the richest, most ambiguous form of collecting. There are those who treat books simply as objects and who open them only to check place and date of printing, the edition, the quality of the paper and the typeface of the print. They may collect first editions, or all titles published by a particular publisher or written by a certain author, or books printed in Würzburg or Oxford in the sixteenth century, or books bound by a particular Paris workshop, or bound in morocco leather, or books with Expressionist bindings, or blue books, small books, tall books, or rare uncut copies. 'Most of these will never be opened,' comments an employee at Henry

Sotheran, the famous London antiquarian bookseller, pointing to the glow of leather bindings and gold lettering on the surrounding walls. 'They are collected, not read.' In the eighteenth century, many book collectors bought two copies of each book; one for the collection, one to be read.

Nowhere has collecting more different faces than among those who invest their capital, temporal and financial, in books. Consider Willem Blom's search for Truth in uncounted bibles; the elegant historico-philosophical hand library of the dethroned Crown Prince Ernst Moritz von Sachsen-Altenburg. Wolf Stein attempted to regain his lost childhood through books that had long since taken over his house and his life. Another Jewish refugee I encountered, the former Berlin bookseller Ernst Laske in Tel Aviv, kept pre-Hitlerian Germany alive in his flat: the brash, modern Levantine state outside his doors, inside all *deutsches Bildungsbürgertum*. A woman friend in Vienna owned many thousand novels and never married – her emotional life played itself out vicariously through the characters of the books she read and reread. Show me your library and I'll tell you who you are.

The lives of bibliomaniacs are rarely ever quaint and can be, *in extremis*, utterly alarming – none perhaps more so than that of Sir Thomas Phillipps (1792–1872), whose stated ambition was 'to have one copy of every book in the world'. His is a story of obsession that ended in complete and devastating failure and earned its protagonist nothing more than a handful of monographs and bemused footnotes instead of the grand library that was intended to be his monument in perpetuity.

The illegitimate son of a wealthy cloth dealer, Sir Thomas had the means to devote himself exclusively to his passion for everything that was printed or written by hand. Corresponding with book dealers in London and beyond, he amassed books and manuscripts in his country estate of Thirlestaine House, Cheltenham. He was eager to share his delight in his possessions with other devotees, and to show off his treasures to them. Not all visitors, though, appreciated his way of life, which had moulded itself, and *par force* that of his family, entirely around his passion. Sir Frederick Madden was dismayed and slightly hysterical about the state of his host's residence:

I never saw such a state of things! Every room filled with heaps of papers, MSS., books, charters, packages, & other things, lying in heaps under your feet; piled up on tables, beds, chairs, ladders, &c, &c. and in every room, piles of huge boxes, to the ceiling, containing the more valuable volumes! It was quite sickening! I asked him why he did not clear away the piles of papers &c. from the floor, so as to allow a path to be kept, but he only laughed and said I was not used to it as he was! His own bedroom is much more filled up with books & boxes than when I last saw it, and how it is possible for any lady to sleep or dress herself in such a room, I am at a loss to imagine! In a small room adjoining this are kept all the Meermann MSS. In boxes piled one above the other. These boxes, however, throughout the house, are so constructed, that the lids fall down in front, and the MSS. stand in a row, as if on shelves.[2]

Sir Thomas seemed oblivious to these complaints, and to his visitor's melancholy state of mind. He ploughed on amiably enough, but without taking any notice of Madden's discomfort, expressed again in a diary entry: '17th Rain again all day. The windows of the house are never opened, and the close confined air & smell of papers & MSS. is almost unbearable. It is a complete literary charnel-house.'[3] The host was by no means indifferent to visitors as such. Many scholars came to visit him and were surprised by his kindness and solicitude. Even the meals took on a decidedly bookish quality. A visitor from France relates:

At the end of a day, when we felt that we should have been making our apologies, we were invited by the baronet to an entertainment which he described as 'a dessert of manuscripts'. At the hour when an English table is spread with wine, fruit and rare dishes, we found displayed before out eyes a choice treat of the most precious manuscripts of Middlehill, and we were able, at will, to pass them from one to the other until all hours of the night.[4]

It was no accident of design that Thirlestaine House was a repository of books first and a human habitation second; it had, in fact, been chosen for the books. When his previous residence proved too small to accommodate his treasures, Phillipps had had to face up to the terrible realization that he would have to move his entire library to another place. The circumstances of his family's existence had become quite insupportable, as even he had to admit when he was forced to write to an acquaintance, a Mr Curzon:

I do not see why you cannot come to Middle Hill with Mrs Curson [sic] except that there is hardly room for you!!! You who have travelled and lodged in Greek monasteries might know how to put up with the inconveniences of Middle Hill but I should fear Mrs Curzon would feel wretched among them. We have no room to dine in except the Housekeeper's Room . . . Our Drawing Room & Sitting Room is Lady Phillipps's Boudoir!! If Mrs Curzon could put up with all this we should be most happy to see her with you.[5]

A small tenant farmer was entrusted with organizing and conducting the move. For eight months, from July 1863 to March 1864, a total of 230 horses transported 103 wagon loads of books between the two houses, only for Sir Thomas to write to a friend: 'I have filled four Rooms here & have about 200 Boxes more, ready to come, besides 50 or 60 cases of books & 3 large Book Cases.'[6] At his new residence, a large building with a wide central gallery and two spacious wings, Sir Thomas took to travelling the interior of the 349-foot-long gallery on horseback while supervising the unpacking of his books and the hanging of his pictures. As if this were not enough, a constant stream of new acquisitions kept complicating matters during the move, among them 48 bound volumes of French State Papers, more than 220 bound volumes of Italian letters, 45 folio volumes of Milanese genealogies from the archives of a patrician family, and a collection of the manuscripts of an eighteenth-century Arabic scholar.

Phillipps's self-professed motive for this maniacal devotion to the written word was to salvage what otherwise would be irrevocably lost: 'In amassing my collection, I commenced with purchasing everything that lay within my reach, to which I was instigated by reading various accounts of the destruction of valuable manuscripts.'[7] How many books and manuscripts he ultimately possessed has never been established. His own catalogue, which was printed privately in 1827, contained 23,837 entries. According to Phillipps's own estimate twenty-three years later, he possessed some 20,000 manuscripts and 30,000 books. At his usual accession rate of 40 books per week – he was thought to spend some £4,000 annually on the collection – the total holdings would have grown to about 77,000 items in total, many of them very rare.

It was his great ambition to leave his collection to the nation, as Sir Hans Sloane had done before him, and be assured of immortality for himself and for it. His own insistence on total control of the collection and the failure of his correspondent Benjamin Disraeli, then Chancellor of the Exchequer, to make a reasonable offer on behalf of the government meant that when Phillipps died in 1872 nothing was settled and the collection, still not fully catalogued, only partly unpacked and in a state of total disarray, was committed to auction, or rather auctions, for as I write the sales from the Phillipps Collection are still ongoing at Sotheby's, 168 years after Sir Thomas's death. He himself had been acutely aware of the importance of financial value regarding items that were, in fact, priceless:

As I advanced, the ardour of the pursuit increased until at last I became a perfect vello-maniac, and I gave any price that was asked. Nor do I regret it, for my object was not only to secure good manuscripts for myself but also to raise the public estimation of them, so that their value might be more generally known, and consequently more manuscripts preserved. For nothing tends to the preservation of anything so much as making it bear a high price.[8]

In 1946, both Harvard University and the British Library failed to raise the £110,000 asked for the *Bibliotheca Phillippica*, the latter for a second time. Considering that several sales of medieval and Renaissance manuscripts and rare old editions later the American

Lew David Feldman offered $10 million, sight unseen, for the as yet uncatalogued remainder, this failure weighs all the more heavily.

The *Bibliotheca Phillippica* is no longer extant, and in a way it never really existed. The sheer accumulation of books does not constitute a library. It is also their organization, the ordering mind inhabiting and ruling them. Many of Phillipps's books and manuscripts never left the crates they were delivered in and most of the others were stacked and almost impossible to access. What remains of this great collection is catalogues, hearsay, footnotes and auction prices.

The passion for books can turn those possessed by it into criminals. Nicholas Basbanes relates the case of Stephen Blumberg, who stole some 24,000 rare books from public libraries and stored them in his house in Ottumwa, Iowa. Altogether 268 libraries lost books to him. He had no interest in selling his treasures, he explained when he was caught and tried, he just felt that he had to have them.[9] At his trial, Blumberg's plea for what Basbanes calls his 'criminal bibliomania' was insanity.

One of the few documented murders connected with collecting, later to inspire one of the first works of Gustave Flaubert, is recorded in Spain, in the 1830s. The villain of the story is one Don Vincente, a librarian in a monastery near Tarragona, which was robbed of much of its gold and precious books by a gang of daring thieves. Soon after Don Vincente left the order and reappeared as a rare-book dealer in Barcelona, who became known for his unwillingness to sell anything of value and for the fact that he bought far more than he allowed to leave his shop. In 1836, a great treasure came up for auction, the *Furs e Ordinations de Valencia (Edicts and Ordinances for Valencia)*, believed to be the only surviving copy of a book printed by Lambert Palmart, Spain's first printer, in 1482. To his uncontainable fury Don Vincente found himself outbid by a syndicate of rival dealers led by one Augustino Patxot. Three days later Patxot's shop was burned down and he was found inside, murdered. A whole wave of murders swept Barcelona and surroundings, the victims all men of learning, scholars and book lovers. Don Vincente soon became prime suspect in this case and, when his apartment was searched, the *Furs e Ordinations de Valencia* was found on the top shelf of his library. Other books that had belonged to recent murder victims were also discovered. When asked whether he felt remorse for what he had done, Don Vincente simply replied, 'Every man must die sooner or later, but good books must be conserved.' His defence lawyer faced an uphill battle, but he had a secret weapon with which he hoped to get his client off. When the prosecutor pointed out that the copy of the *Furs e Ordinations* must be the one stolen from the murder victim as it was unique the lawyer leaped to his feet and showed the court proof that a second copy survived in Paris, and that it was therefore possible for yet another one to exist. Don Vincente, far from being grateful for this lifeline thrown to him by his attorney, was devastated and lost control of himself altogether. 'My copy is not unique!' he was heard shouting in rage and disbelief, a sentence he was heard to repeat over and over until the day of his execution.

When the great thirteenth-century Jewish philosopher Maimonides searched for a title for his *magnum opus* he found perhaps the archetypal name for all of literature: *More Nebuchim* (*A Guide for the Perplexed*). Like a child that needs to hear the same story over and over again to grasp the shape of things, the structure with which to see the world, all reading and every story reassures that there is form, that events have a beginning and an end, that catharsis follows catastrophe, that good wins over evil, that the bedlam of our daily lives can be cast into a mould of meaning, of recognizable convention: I met so-and-so yesterday, and I said, and he said, and I said . . .

We need to rehearse this in the face of a chaotic world, again and again, for reading and storytelling are consolations for the perplexed. Collecting is an aspect of this process. The collector, like the reader, seeks to convince himself that there is structure, that things can be ordered and understood, even if they seem to obey alien rules, or no rules at all. The library, a space where books are ordered and classified and not just jumbled in heaps of unconnected titles, becomes a story in its own right; within it, at least, things have their place in the scheme of things, on their shelf.

For the German philosopher and bibliophile Walter Benjamin, this principle was all important.[10] Benjamin was perhaps the most poetic and exact chronicler of and observing participant in the passionate relations between people and things that consitute collecting. In his essay 'Ich packe meine Bibliothek aus' ('Unpacking my Library'), he describes the sensual power and the philosophical complexities of his collection to which he devoted much of his life.

I am unpacking my library. Yes. It is not yet in its shelves, the faint boredom of order is not yet manifest. I am not yet able to take parade by walking past them in front of a friendly audience. They don't have to fear all this. Please follow me into the disorder of opened boxes, in the air filled with wood dust and on to the floor covered with torn packing paper, among the piles of volumes which have seen the light of day after three years of captivity.[11]

Invited to follow the collector into the chaos of the world before the third day of Creation, the reader is soon treated to the spectacle of Benjamin's spirit hovering over the waters and surveying the curious passion that led to this wonderful moment of confusion and delight: 'Every passion borders on chaos, that of the collector on the chaos of memory.'[12] Order, the writer concludes, is nothing but 'a state of suspense above the abyss'.[13]

The dialectic of the relic and the taxidermic specimen, awakened to a new life only through suffering death in the world of its origin, holds for a library as well:

It is the deepest enchantment of the collector to include individual pieces in his circle of power in which it petrifies as the last shudder, the shudder of being acquired, is still running over it. Everything that was ever remembered, thought, and conscious, becomes the foundation, frame, plinth, and lock of his possession. The period, landscape, craft, and owners from which it originated – in the eye of the collector they all fuse into a magical encyclopaedia which has at its core the fate of every one of his objects.[14]

Death and transfiguration in the collection ('for the true collector the acquisition of an old book is also its rebirth'[15]) work a curious alchemy, as it is not only the collection that lives for the collector, but also he himself who lives through and in it. Subject and object merge in an image of harmlessness exemplified by the nineteenth-century domestic idylls of that most sentimental of all painters of interiors, Carl Spitzweg:

Happiness of the collector, of the private individual! Behind nobody has less been suspected and nobody has been more snug than he, who was able to continue his disreputable life behind the Spitzweg mask. For his mind is inhabited by ghosts . . . which ensure that he has the most intimate relation to his possessions possible: not that his possessions would live in him, it is he who lives through and within them.[16]

With seismographic accuracy Benjamin traces the components of a collector's mind. In the figure of the great collector the urge to conserve fuses with exhibitionism and vanity and with the fixation on one goal to the exclusion of all distracting influences.[17] Looking at lithographs by Daumier that depict art lovers and collectors, Benjamin notes their similarity to 'those gold diggers, necromancers and misers which can be found on the paintings of old masters'.[18] Like the alchemists of old, who wanted to create gold through understanding the divine harmonies resonating underneath the bewildering multiplicity of the physical world, the collector 'has taken up arms against dispersal. The great collector is touched to the core by the confusion and the dispersal in which the things are found in this world'.[19]

There is in these words the echo of a poet writing 700 years earlier: Petrarch (1304–74), an inveterate bibliophile and hunter for manuscripts in danger of the destruction of oblivion. Conversing with one of his heroes from antiquity, Cicero, Petrarch poured out his grief to the great orator:

You have heard what I think of your life and your genius. Are you hoping to hear of your books also; what fate has befallen them, how they are esteemed by the masses and among scholars? They still are in existence, glorious volumes, but we of today are too feeble a folk to read them, or even to be acquainted with their mere titles. Your fame extends far and wide; your name is mighty, and fills the ears of men; and yet those who really know you are very few, be it because the times are unfavourable, or because men's minds are slow and dull, or, as I am the more inclined to believe, because the love of money forces our thoughts in other directions. Consequently right in our own day, unless I am much mistaken, some of your books have disappeared, I fear beyond recovery. It is a great grief to me, a great disgrace to this generation, a great wrong done to posterity. The shame of failing to cultivate our own talents, thereby depriving the future of the fruits that they might have yielded, is not enough for us; we must waste and spoil, through our cruel and insufferable neglect, the fruits of your labours too, and of those of your fellows as well, for the fate that I lament in the case of your own books has befallen the works of many another illustrious man.[20]

In some mysterious way we know that the Tower of Babel must have been a library. Its base was a common language just as its ruination was the loss of mutual understanding between its builders, God's punishment for their presumption, the true beginning of division in the world. Breughel's huge snail's house of a tower growing out of the

rock must have been filled, we imagine, with an indeterminable number of tablets in indecipherable cuneiform – each a fragment of hidden knowledge of the true order of the world, ruined by those who did not understand its nature.

Jorge Luis Borges, in his customary way of taking the plausible to fantastical extremes, constructed his own Library of Babel, an inescapable universe in which the books, all uniform and housed in hexagonal room after hexagonal room, contain every possible combination of letters, forming every work of nonsense and of sense that can and might be written: 'This much is already known: for every sensible line of straightforward statement, there are leagues of senseless cacophonies, verbal jumbles and incoherences.'[21] Vast armies of scholars scour this labyrinth of meaninglessness in the pursuit of some scraps of meaning, something to hold on to in the chaos of randomness and chance. Their quest, he writes, is essentially quixotic and will drive them mad if it does not kill them, but the rewards, hypothetical as they are, are enormous, for among the garbled pages of nonsense and endless repetition of the same twenty-five symbols is all possible knowledge: 'the minutely detailed history of the future, the archangels' autobiographies, the faithful catalogue of the Library, thousands and thousands of false catalogues, the demonstration of the fallacy of those catalogues, the demonstration of the fallacy of the true catalogue, the Gnostic gospel of Basilides, the commentary on that gospel . . . the true story of your death . . .'[22]

This elegant parable of learning and collecting allows all of us to feel that we inhabit some small corner of that eternal library and that it is yet possible to find order in chaos, to find the book that encapsulates all others. The Mannerist scholar-magi of Rudolf II's day surrounded themselves with diversity in order to be granted the vision to see the one Platonic idea underlying all of it, the ultimate truth and the alphabet of creation. Like their collections, every attempt to organize the world (or some small fragment of it) is a testament of defiant optimism, of the hope that order has not yet surrendered to chaos, justice to injustice, meaning to chance, entirely. Every library becomes a compendium, a book of spells to ward off the evil eye.

The subtle dialectic of order suspended over a sea of chaos that Benjamin diagnosed in every collection seems especially true of libraries. The different sizes, colours, textures and typefaces of spines and covers populating shelves and tables always introduce an intimation of disorder and disintegration into the most ordered shelf (those ordering books according to colour and size transfer this anarchy to their content). The mind controlling this near-chaos, aided, perhaps, by a catalogue, is the master of the universe. It is also that most dangerous thing, a contented hermit. Surrounded by imaginary realms and people, by periods and riches that open themselves only to the reader's eye, the book lover craves no company and no approbation from outside. Nothing is needed for his happiness but solitude in which to immerse and forget himself, to emerge into other worlds and new self-possession.

Sometimes the worlds in which the reader emerges can be unexpected. One of the most remarkable book collections to be assembled exists, appropriately enough, on paper only. It was brought together in 2000 by Russell Ash and Brian Lake, two London book dealers. Their small publication *Bizarre Books* is the result of decades of loving devotion. Among the many (and invariably genuine) literary gems detailed in their catalogue are indispensable titles such as: William Harper's *An Historical Curiosity, by a Birmingham Resident. One Hundred and Forty-one Ways of Spelling Birmingham*; the *Handbook for the Limbless*, published by the Disabled Society in 1922; *Erections on Allotments*, published by the Allotment Society; and many other valuable publications, proof, if proof were needed, that while everything can be collected every last question will, given enough time, have a book devoted to itself. Borges would approve. Among the other titles in this catalogue are: *Warfare in the Enemy's Rear*; *Truncheons: Their Romance and Reality*; *Who's Who in Barbed Wire*; *The History of the Concrete Roof Tile*; *The Romance of Concrete*; *Leadership Secrets of Attila the Hun*; *How to Avoid Huge Ships*; *The Darjeeling Disaster – Its Bright Side*; *Railway Literature 1556–1830*; *Swine Judging for Beginners*; *The Earthworms of Ontario*; *Cameos of Vegetarian Literature*; *A Holiday with a Hegelian*; and *The Joy of Cataloguing*.

Quod erat demonstrandum.

Leporello and His Master

No day passed when there wasn't a quarrel in the house, on account of his coffee, his milk, or a plate of macaroni that he'd asked for. The cook had forgotten his polenta; the head groom had given him a bad coachman . . . dogs had barked in the night; the Count had invited so may guests that *he* had to eat at a little side table. A hunting horn had shattered his ears with piercing discords. A priest had bored him in trying to convert him. The Count had not greeted him first, before the rest. The soup had been served him too hot, maliciously. A servant had made him wait for a drink. He had not been presented to an important gentleman . . . The Count had lent a book without telling him. A groom had not raised his hat in passing. He had spoken German and no one had understood him.

He is angry – they laugh. He shows some of his own Italian poetry – they laugh. He gesticulates in declaiming Italian – they laugh. On entering a room he bows as Marcel the famous dancing master taught him sixty years back – they laugh. At every ball he most gravely dances the minuet – they laugh. He puts on his white plumed hat, his suit of embroidered silk, his black velvet waistcoat, his garters with the strass buckles, his silk stockings – they laugh.

Prince Charles de Ligne,
Mélanges militaire, littéraires et sentimentaires[1]

There was no doubt – the Chevalier de Seignalt was getting old. The once-famous *galant* who had spent his life tearing through Europe making and losing fortunes and having love affairs wherever he went had become a cantankerous old man whose remaining social activities exhausted themselves in warring with the servants. There was precious little else to do. His patron, Count Waldstein, was away most of the time and the Castle of Duchow, in which he had accepted a position, was situated in the furthest reaches of already remote Bohemia.

In this new and last of many incarnations de Seignalt, who was called Neuhaus by his German acquaintances and Casanova by the others, cast himself, only half willingly, as a man of letters, a librarian and a writer. For days on end he would scribble away furiously, writing insulting letters to employees, philosophical and mathematical ones to other correspondents (he believed he had found a formula for squaring the circle and was, as ever, trying to sell his secret), stage plays, an unsuccessful novel and a manuscript that was to see the light of day twenty years after his death, in German and French, the latter in a heavily edited and corrupted version. The title of the twelve-part manuscript was *Histoire de ma Vie, jusqu'à l'an 1797*. After publication it rapidly reached fame and considerable notoriety and was widely believed to have been written by Stendal. Casanova himself, many thought, was nothing more than a literary construct.

In his *Histoire* Casanova, who was real enough of course, had created his masterwork, the greatest feat of his career. Writing it was the one way in which he could not only gain the fame and respect that had eluded him during his life, but also immortalize the collection for whose acquisition he was to become so famous: a collection of women all over Europe, women charmed, seduced and conquered by the chevalier.[2]

The story he recounted bore witness to a driven life that had made him familiar with all European capitals and at home in none. In Venice, his home city, he had been imprisoned in the famous lead chambers, cells that were heated by the sun until many of their inmates lost their mind. He had managed to escape and tried to make his luck elsewhere with nothing but his charisma and wit to count on. In Paris he had organized a lottery and made a great deal of money, lost all of it again on extravagant living and an ill-conceived venture at silk manufacture, won and lost huge sums at gambling tables throughout Europe, advised aristocrats in the secret arts of the cabbala (of which he had little more knowledge than they), at one time extracting fifty pounds of precious metals and jewels from one Mme d'Urfé on behalf of Selenis, the Spirit of the Moon. He tried and failed to repeat his success with setting up a lottery first in London and then, within a year, at the courts of Brunswick, Prussia, Moscow, Warsaw, Dresden and Madrid, leaving behind him a trail of female (and occasionally male) conquests. Now age and penury had confined him to the deepest provinces.

One of the projects undertaken by Casanova in his chilly study while waiting for another cup of cocoa or glass of wine and cursing the tardy servant, has survived in the archives, along with the rest of his papers: it contains notes for and redrafts of the second act of an opera called *Don Giovanni*. While the extent of Casanova's involvement in the writing of it is uncertain, it seems likely that he did indeed serve at least as an adviser to the man who was to take the credit for the libretto, Lorenzo da Ponte, whom Casanova had known for many years and who could hardly have wished for a more competent or experienced consultant.

In the opera da Ponte, or perhaps Casanova himself, gives the role of archivist and bookkeeper to another figure, Leporello, the manservant, who describes in his 'catalogue aria' the extent of his master's expertise in the art of womanizing:

Madamina, il catalogo è questo	Little Madam, the catalogue is right here
Delle belle che amò il padron mio;	Of the beauties my patron has loved;
Un catalogo egli è che ho fatt'io.	A catalogue of my own devising.
Osservate, leggete con me.	Come here, read it with me.
In Italia seicento e quaranta,	In Italy six hundred and forty,
In Almagna duecento e trentuna,	In Germany two hundred and thirty-one,
Cento in Francia, in Turchia novantuna,	A hundred in France, ninety-one in Turkey,
Ma in Ispagna son già mille e tre!	But in Spain there are a thousand and three!

'Ma in Ispagna son già mille e tre!' Every collector needs his Leporello to exhort posterity 'Osservate, leggete con me', 'Observe, read with me', witness this accomplishment. A 'leporello' is not just the name of a comical manservant, but also of an accordion-folded book, popular in the eighteenth and nineteenth centuries for pictorial works such as costume and landscape prints, the ideal record keeper and faithful companion.

Without his catalogue, every major collector has to fear the dispersal of his collection and his own descent into obscurity. A catalogue is not an appendage to a large collection, it is its apogee. While paintings, books, gold snuffboxes and other precious things might eventually pass back into the world through necessity, greed or ignorance, and carry with them no visible record of their previous ownership (unless, of course, collectors honour the Chinese custom of putting collectors' stamps on items of calligraphy and other graphic work), a catalogue will in one way guarantee the survival of the collection as ensemble, as organism and as personality. Wherever it stands, in a library or in a second-hand bookshop, given pride of place on a shelf or buried under a pile of cheap thrillers, it will always go on proclaiming, with the delicate voice of its carefully set print on cream wove paper, *mille e tre, mille e tre!*

Lacking such a travel companion as Leporello to recount his exploits, the ageing Casanova had to assume the role of the talkative subordinate for himself. He had good reason, though, to insist on immortalizing his achievements. He had assembled a collection that was remarkable because of its sheer size, entertainment value, and because of the sacrifices he had made for it. Unfortunately, however, it was highly ephemeral and without due documentation nothing would remain of it.

Casanova's travelling itinerary, the precondition for these conquests, is in itself worthy of the attentions of a Leporello. It is all the more remarkable if one takes into account the travelling conditions of the time. Stagecoaches travelled about thirty to forty miles per day, arduous, bone-rattling ten-hour journeys throught dust or mud, stifling heat or chilly winds, passengers thrown together with five other travellers in the cabin, another two or three on the roof, and in the basket at the back 'chickens, eggs, vegetables and wealthy peasants'.[3] Travelling was never easy and always expensive, including nights in coaching inns, bribes to coachmen, food, wine and other expenses. Needless to say, the Chevalier de Seignalt managed to squeeze in (probably literally) a few furtive encounters *en route.*

Whatever Casanova's role in creating the most classical account of Don Giovanni, the two figures have often been afterwards conflated or confused and they are used almost interchangeably to describe a compulsive womanizer. In them both, the ecstatic moment of possession, which so many collectors seek, is to be taken literally, though the traffic also goes both ways: 'I have twenty thousand records and that means that twenty thousand women can't betray me,' a distinguished, and at the time of talking slightly inebriated, collector once told me.[4] Casanova attempted to marry conquest with safety from betrayal by casting himself in the role of the betrayer; others seek to do the same by choosing to invest their feelings in objects instead of people.

The dialectic of conquest and possession, both words endowed with great erotic charge, typifies every collector's response to his or her objects. The art critic Brian Sewell told me about two American collectors of old master drawings. One of them would travel to London, choose one or more drawings at a Bond Street gallery and have them wrapped in brown paper for transport back to New York. His chauffeur-driven car would wait for him in front of the gallery. When he died, all the drawings he had purchased in London were found, still in their brown-paper wrappings. The enjoyment was purely in the possession, in the fact that they were his. He no longer needed to look at them. The second collector would make the same journey from Manhattan to London, go to Bond Street, be courted by the dealers, buy drawings and have them packed in brown-paper wrappings. 'You should have seen the orgiastic sweat on his forehead as he raped that paper as soon as he had climbed into his limousine,' Sewell added.

Like a lover a collector will jealously guard his possessions, and like a lover he will talk and think about them in erotic, narcissistic terms: the object of desire. It is beautiful because it can be touched, for love without touch is a poor substitute. It is, as Paul Valéry wrote about art itself, 'the substitution of sensation for hypothesis, of marvellous presence for prodigious memory; it is an infinite library as well as an immense museum: Venus transformed into a document'.[5] The retreat into this narcissistic universe, the more graceful aspect of what may also be called an autistic streak, makes the collector, like a lover, believe that the world and the desired are there just for him: 'The passion for an object leads to its being construed as God's special handiwork: the collector of porcelain eggs will imagine that God never made a more beautiful or rarer form, and that He created it purely for the delight of porcelain egg collectors . . .'[6] Enter Mr Utz.

That collecting is to a large degree erotically driven has caused the French historian Jacques Attali to call every collector a Don Juan[7] and collecting has received a fair share of attention from psychoanalysts.[8] It is all the more remarkable that another passionate collector and the founder of psychoanalysis, Sigmund Freud, had hardly anything to say on the subject. Despite or perhaps because of the fact that he was himself victim to this passion, he was uncharacteristically silent about it and its psychological significance. His last house, though, at Maresfield Gardens in Hampstead, London, is eloquent in its own right, filled as it is not only with books, but also, and especially, with antiquities, which populate cabinets and cases, mantelpieces and tables, including his desk. 'The core of paranoia,' he had written in 1908, 'is the detachment of the libido from objects. A reverse course is taken by the collector who directs his surplus libido on to an inanimate object: a love of things.'[9] Things are famously less fickle in their love than people:

When an old maid keeps a dog or an old bachelor collects snuffboxes, the former is finding a substitute for her need for a companion in marriage and the latter for his need for – a multitude of conquests. Every collector is a substitute for a Don Juan Tenerio, and so too is the mountaineer, the sportsman, and such people. These are erotic equivalents.[10]

The parallel with the pet dog has not eluded other writers. 'For the collector,' Maurice Rheims writes, 'the object is a sort of docile dog which receives caresses and returns them in its own way; or rather, reflects them like a mirror constructed in such a way as to throw back images not of the real but of the desirable.'[11] Dogs, much like hat-pins or toy cars, do not run off because their affection is exhausted. It is quite safe to invest one's love in them. Loved in the way their owners want to be, and indulged with as they themselves want to indulge, they are both object and fulfilment of desire.

In protecting the possession of these erotic equivalents, jealous collectors can go to extraordinary lengths. An unnamed European collector who prided himself on possessing the only copy of a work immediately flew to New York when he found another copy in the catalogue of a book dealer there. He bought the copy for a considerable sum, took it to a commissioner for oaths and burned it in front of him in order to have his act verified. Then he returned home satisfied and safe in the knowledge that he was once again the owner of the only known copy of his treasured book.

In Greek legend, King Tantalos was cursed with never being able to reach the delicious fruit hanging on branches just in front of him that would retract as soon as he reached out to them. Collectors suffer the reverse curse. They reach the objects of their longing only to find that those objects are nothing but symbols of what they craved for, that it was the longing itself, and the ecstatic moment of acquisition, that fooled them – for a moment only – into believing that in *this* object lay the key to satisfying their hunger. The enchantment wears off as soon as we touch what we desired. It is just not confirmed collectors who suffer this fate. This is what sends us all into shops, trying to buy contentment, beauty, completeness, only to find that, once the intoxication of the moment is gone, we need another dose of it, that it is the elation of the moment that makes us happy, not the addition to our wardrobe. Like beautiful princesses turning into old hags, a coach and horses being transformed into a pumpkin with toads in harness, and a proud castle imploding into a muddy hovel, we find that our desires alight for a while on objects only to take flight when we finally believe we have caught up with them. What we hold in our hands crumbles, while our longing, temporarily assuming the shape of this thing or that, remains dancing in front of us, enticingly, maddeningly. Like Casanova we are left chasing after it, trying to satisfy immaterial passions with matter, with moments of fulfilment, proving like him that we still can conquer, that it is not too late, while Leporello stands by, bemusedly reciting the catalogue of our follies.

Mr Soane is Not at Home

I hid myself behind the tapestry and heard him say, 'All this must be left behind [*Il faut quitter tout celà*].' He stopped at every step, for he was very weak, and turned first to one side, then the other, and casting a glance on the object that caught his eye, he said from the depth of his heart, 'All this must be left behind.' And turning around, he finished, 'And also that. What a trouble I suffered to acquire these things! Can I abandon them without regret? I will never see them again where I am going.'

Louis-Henri de Loménie,
Comte de Brienne, on seeing the ageing Cardinal
Mazarin walk through his famous collection on a final visit to his palais[1]

It seems curious for a man who made his living out of designing buildings for the living to be obsessed with ruins and with tombs, but death and decay were clearly never far from Sir John Soane's mind. In his imagination the buildings whose classical elegance still grace London and the English countryside grew into sprawling organisms of columns and pilasters, and crumbled into picturesque ghosts of their former selves. A sheet by his pupil and draughtsman Joseph Gandy seems to have emerged straight from the master's head.

A huge hall is inhabited by mounting rockeries of architectural models, paintings, cross-sections and ornaments on a gigantic scale. The Bank of England, Soane's most significant commission, is bathed in mysterious light. It shines like an enormous Hellenic temple. A flight of steps leads up to it, past a monument, the draped tomb of the

architect's late wife. Dozens of façades, mausoleums, country houses, bridges, scale models and gold-framed artists' impressions make up the furniture of this survey of an artist's life's achievements. In the foreground a tiny, solitary figure is labouring away at a large table, busily drawing and redrawing the plans of the Old Lady of Threadneedle Street into all eternity.

He looks grey and careworn, insignificant amid the heaped architectural glories surrounding him. He is almost small enough to inhabit them. He alone, the only living being in the room (apart, perhaps, from a few unseen mice), is transitory, nothing but a visitor here – and yet the compass he holds is the instrument by which his inspiration has shaped everything that now makes him look so dwarfed.

It is no accident that this vision reminds one of Piranesi's *Roman Ruins*, for both Soane and Gandy were admirers of this genius of utopian architecture. Not only the *Ruins* spring to mind, but also Piranesi's fantastical *Carceri* – the prisons are present behind the looming grandeur of Soane's amassed oeuvre.

'He is full of matter: extravagant 'tis true, often absurd, but from his overflowings you may gather information,'[2] Soane had written of the legendary Italian printer and archaeologist who tried to preserve the glories of Rome by etching them into copper as visions of an imagined past. As a scholar of the Royal Academy, Soane had set off for Italy in 1778 and had met Piranesi there, briefly, just before the master's death. While accusing him of extravagance and absurdity,

Soane would later buy and study his works avidly. It is the sense of the utopian, of the grandeur and ruin of a bygone era, that fed Soane's own preoccupation with beauty and decay and with the structures that were monuments to both – tombs and mausoleums.

Giovanni Battista Piranesi collected Rome's great past on a fittingly large scale: confronted with decay and architectural vandalism he recorded everything he regarded as memorable in his famous series of etchings. In doing so, he created a world of his own invention, playing with dramatic perspectives and apocalyptic shafts of light and rearranging not only the scale, but also the position of the objects he so admired into a Rome that nobody had ever seen before, turning the eternal city into an internal one. The imaginary prisons, taking his fascination with the grand beyond what had been, or could be, built by human hands, were the culmination of this project. These are prisons without cells, where gigantic vaults, columns and arches reach into infinity, the offspring of an inflamed mind compelled to construct ever-new edifices that serve no purpose. The prisoners who are seen at work are also the architects of their own misery, apparently building ever-more fantastical structures from which they will never be able to escape. The whole enterprise is reminiscent of the deep, internal reaches of a forgotten part of the Tower of Babel, in which, long after the collapse and abandonment of the sacrilegious structure as a whole, a tribe of ant-like workers continues to build away into a void, for no one and no reason. Prisons, rather than palaces or churches, enabled Piranesi to explore the architecture of a city's and an artist's soul, the hidden, inner spaces in which utopian designs bear down on desperately insignificant inmates, and suspended passages and floating staircases lead to more and more unimagined levels of beauty, loneliness and darkness, the template of the great never-worlds created by late pupils such as Borges and Escher.

Soane found much in these etchings that resonated with his own preoccupations. While building and redesigning mansions and country houses, overseeing the construction of the Bank of England and the Dulwich Picture Gallery and conceiving designs for the Houses of Parliament (some of which were eventually erected but burned down soon afterwards), he also made his house a shrine to classicism, to art, and to his own inevitable end. It is still there, at 13 Lincoln's Inn Fields, in the middle of London, arranged just as he left it to the nation in his will, which was enshrined in law by an Act of Parliament in 1833. It must have required great delicacy and infinite care to live in this *Gesamtkunstwerk* of a house in which every inch in almost every room was made part of the great scheme of things. In every passage fragments of sculpture, stucco and plaster casts are arranged along the walls and on the ceiling. Only the drawing room on the first floor escapes the crowd of the august if fragmentary ancestors that have invaded the remainder of the house. Mirrors, niches and unexpected windows open up surprising views and break up the claustrophobia of so much being crammed into so little space. The pictures in the gallery hang in specially constructed frames one behind the other, not a hand's breadth of space is wasted. One visitor described the narrow routes and sudden opening of Soane's house as a Cretan labyrinth:

... curious narrow staircases, landing places, balconies, spring doors, and little rooms filled with fragments to the very ceiling. It was the finest fun imaginable to see the people come in to the library after wandering about below, amidst tombs and capitals, and shafts, and noiseless heads, with a sort of expression of delighted relief at finding themselves again among the living and with coffee and cake ... smirking up to Soane *lui faisant*

leurs compliments with a twisting chuckle of features as if grateful for their escape.[3]

The house draws its visitors in, further and deeper into the mysteries that are so carefully arranged here. In the Monk's Parlour the theme is set. A tiny room, almost overwhelmed by the gigantic stucco ornaments on its ceiling, and by the leering gargoyles on the walls, many of them genuine Gothic remains from the works on the Palace of Westminster in 1823, it has at its centre a simple and elegant round table in mahogany. On it a single item, a skull. The Gothic theme is an unusual choice for an architect who made his name as the apostle of the Greek revival, but Soane the collector could hardly bear seeing these precious fragments go to waste. More than that: amid the riot of motifs and salvaged demons a theme emerges in this architectural realization of a human mind. Contemplation, monastic retreat, *memento mori*. The fragments not only reminded Soane of his unhappy and ultimately doomed involvement with rebuilding the very heart of the empire, but their organization was also his own staging of mortality. In the Monk's Yard, next to the Parlour, was the grave of Fanny, the much-loved dog of Soane's wife, Elizabeth. He had designed this with great if mischievous consideration, delighting in the fact that the dog's tomb was underneath the emphatically modern and prosaic new central-heating system. Tombs, though, were no laughing matter to him. The mausoleum he designed at the Dulwich Picture Gallery was an expression of some of his feelings on the matter: 'a dull, religious light shews the Mausoleum in the full pride of funeral grandeur, displaying its sarcophagi, enriched with the mortal remains of departed worth, and calling back so powerfully the recollections of past times, that we almost believe we are conversing with our departed friends who now sleep in their silent tombs'.[4]

This silent conversation reached its climax in Soane's careful yet flamboyant *mise-en-scène* of the dramatic three-floor-high drop of empty space around which is assembled the most fantastical display of his museum house. Here, amid a cornucopia of busts, friezes, vases and parts of columns, pilasters, capitals and scrolls, is a bust of the man himself, perching on the balustrade of the plunge from the light-flooded dome down to the crypt. He looks on in classical poise as underneath him the spectacle of death unfolds. The central piece had been a symbol for death and for the afterlife already for three millennia by the time Soane was able to buy it in 1825, his biggest scoop as a collector. The Belzoni sarcophagus is a translucent vessel of alabaster, created to take the body of Pharaoh Sethi I into another world. When the sarcophagus reached London in a shipment of Egyptian antiquities excavated by the Italian Giovanni Belzoni, Soane was quick to take advantage of the short-sightedness of the trustees of the British Museum, who bought part of the collection but baulked at spending another £3,000 for the huge casket. An ardent admirer of Napoleon, Soane was inspired by the French fashion for all things Egyptian and leaped at this extraordinary opportunity. When it finally reached his house and was safely installed in the crypt, he held a three-day welcoming party for his treasure for which he sent out almost 900 invitations and ordered 100 additional candles and candelabra to illuminate the heart of his collection for his guests.

Sethi's great sarcophagus in the crypt of 13 Lincoln's Inn Fields was not the only tomb in the house. The model room, dedicated to minia-ture versions of the glories of ancient Greece and Rome, contained, among other treasures, a three-dimensional rendering of the ruined city of Pompeii and, in Soane's own words, 'the Mausoleum of Mau-solos; the Temples of Antoninus and Faustina, at Rome; and of Venus, at Baalbec; a Tomb at Palmyra; and the Temple of Fortuna Virilis, in Rome'.[5] In the crypt, next to the sarcophagus itself, he arranged models of four Etruscan tombs, complete with gifts for use in the next world, wall painting and stucco animals, and miniature skeletons lying in state amid items of pottery. In depicting monuments as fragments, both as ruins and in their pristine, reconstructed state, Soane's collection suspends time; just as he imagined his own buildings in their ruined state and had them drawn as such by his apprentice Gandy; and just as he described a visit by his own ghost to a ruined museum in 1830, a passage written during a phase of acute depression in 1812 (although he was, in fact, alive and well in 1830 and his house and collection stands intact to this day). His continued preoccupation with ruins stayed with him. In the same year, 1812, his *magnum opus*, the Bank of England, was depicted by Gandy in a virtuosic cut-away watercolour which made the whole complex look much like the remains of Pompeii, with trees encroaching on the bare wall, the half-collapsed arches and column stumps of the once-proud structure. Only a building with a chance of becoming a picturesque ruin was worth erecting at all.

The slender façade of 13 Lincoln's Inn Fields betrays little of the ambitious programme realized behind it, an understandable phenom-enon in a city where an empire was ruled from a terraced house a few miles away in Downing Street. Soane, needless to say, designed and built his own tomb literally as well as metaphorically, but he is not interred in his collection. It is surprising how many collectors do choose their life's work as their literal final resting place. Their mind having been given form in what they hope will be imperishable matter, it seems only a small step for their body to join it in perpetuity. Soane himself built a mausoleum for Francis Bourgeois and his friends, Mr and Mrs Noel, into bequest at the Dulwich Picture Gallery, which was itself built to house Bourgeois's collection. In the Folger Shakespeare Library in Washington, DC, a small stone plaque off the main reading room marks the place where the ashes of Henry Clay and Emily Jordan Folger, its founders, are deposited 'for eternity', as the text proclaims. The ageing Henry E. Huntington, the ravenous book and art collector and founder of the eponymous library in California, contemplating the transformation of his collection into a permanent institution, spent much of the planning time designing a mausoleum in the grounds.

Sir Arthur Gilbert, collector of spectacular silver and *objets d'art*, took a different route. Gilbert, originally a London dressmaker who made a fortune from American real estate, set about buying for himself items that would have graced the treasury of any prince: gold snuff-boxes, important silverware and a large number of micro-mosaics were assembled, catalogued and shown off in his Beverly Hills man-sion. When Gilbert sought to establish a new, permanent home for his accumulated treasures, and after the breakdown of negotiations with an American museum unwilling to fulfil his wishes, his choice eventually fell on London's Somerset House, next to the Courtauld Institute, where the collection is displayed today. The sheer dazzle of these objects is astonishing, as diamonds, gold, highly polished silver and aggressively bright colours temporarily disorientate visitors. When his exhibition was designed, Sir Arthur insisted that his Beverly Hills office be recreated as part of the display, including the original Louis XV furniture, pink walls, family photographs and portraits, and a wax figure of the man himself, sitting at his desk in tennis shorts, smiling stiffly, telephone in hand. Forever united with his treasures, the collector is seemingly still at work, making business calls, or bidding for some exquisite piece in a far-away auction.

Arthur Gilbert's insistence on a personal, waxen presence in his collection may seem bizarre, but it is by no means unique. Peter the Great is still present in his *Kunstkamera* as a wax replica dressed in the emperor's own clothes, complete with his legendary battered hat; and the founder of America's first museum, Charles Peale (unable to embalm his family and incorporate it into his display), also took care to be present in his museum in the same way. Many others, while not choosing to be buried or sculpted in wax as pieces of their own collections, have nevertheless been unable to resist the more orthodox route of self-inclusion by oil portrait or bronze or marble bust.

If these metaphorical internments transform collections into their creators' tombs, the tombs of antiquity that stand as models in Soane's house seem to obey the same principles: small worlds, only one or a handful of rooms planned and built around those whose continuing existence and well-being they are supposed to guarantee. Every collector becomes a pharaoh. Thomas Browne may not have believed in their efficacy but despite his doubting interjections tombs came into fashion among the middle classes in the nineteenth century, an era, incidentally, that also saw the rise of the private collection. Now tombs became family graves, designed to lend a semblance of eternity and of old and aristocratic history, complete with stained-glass windows and concocted family mottoes and coats of arms, to a breed of unwilling revolutionaries who had toppled the aristocracy from its perch.

*

This is the shadow looming over every cabinet: The End. Collections have always had overtones of burial and interment. Graves are filled with objects symbolic of future use, shoring up the deceased against irrevocable loss, allowing him a symbolic afterlife with all the comforts of the here and now. The greater a collection, the more precious its contents, the more it must be reminiscent of a mausoleum, left behind by a ruler determined not to be forgotten, not to have his memory squabbled over and his most immediate self disintegrate to dust. Here it is, material and incontestable, for all to see and touch; his memory, his ideal self, the expression of his wealth, his judgement, patronage, beliefs and substance. And yet, we are reminded of Browne's scepticism towards such provisions for eternity:

Had they made as good provision for their names, as they have done for their Reliques, they had not so grossly erred in the art of perpetuation. But to subsist in bones, and be but Pyramidally extant, is a fallacy in duration. Vain ashes, which in the oblivion of names, persons, times, and sexes, have found unto themselves, a fruitlesse continuation, and only arise unto late posterity, as Emblemes of mortall vanities; Antidotes against pride, vain-glory, and madding vices.[6]

Every collection is a constant reminder of the very reality it has been created to stave off. The greater the value of a collection, the greater the risk of loss that it represents; the greater the will to live on, the more glaring the admission of mortality and oblivion. Objects in rows and cases, arranged along the wall or piled up on the floor, are anticipated headstones and memorials, every one of them the grave of a past desire, or of the illusion of having conquered it momentarily, of peace at last.

It is rarely possible to maintain a major collection intact; lack of interest on the part of the heirs, inheritance taxes, and the absence of a unifying will mitigate against this. Some collections are translated into trusts or given to museums, others are sold with only catalogues as witnesses to their former glories. In more modest circumstances, the pieces that were the life and the passion of a collector for many years may end up in jumble sales or rubbish skips. Death is not that sentimental.

After the Black Death, four-teenth-century artists depicted life as a *danse macabre*, a fleeting and futile dance in which skeletons would lead and drag all levels of society to their graves, beginning with (relish this, they say) pope and emperor whose power was null and void. The first of these pictorial sequences appeared in Paris in 1424 and soon *danses macabres* were known all over Europe, usually including verses illustrating the impotence of the formerly so mighty, so pious or so industrious people whose time has come.

In the Parisian *danse* a dead man is taking a bourgeois to his grave, and the dialogue between the corpse and his stricken victim anticipates Cardinal Mazarin's own little gigue with the reaper:

Le Mort

Fol est qui damaser se blesse

On ne scet pour qui on amasse

The Dead Man

He is a fool who injures himself by amassing things

And no one knows why people cannot help but do it

Le Bourgeois

Grant mal me fait: il si tort laissier
Rentes: maisons: cens: nouritures
Mais poures: riches: abaissier
Fu faiz mort: telle est ta nature.
Sage nest pas la creature
Damer trop les biens'q demeure
Au monde: et sot siens de droiture.

Cenir q'plus ont euiz meuret.[7]

The Bourgeois

It pains me to leave so early
The rents and houses, interest and food
But you humiliate poor and rich:
You kill, this is your nature.
And human nature is not wise
In loving too much what must remain
In this world and which belong to it by right.
Those who own more find dying harder.

This dance of death has obvious parallels with Dionysian rituals in which the god of ecstasy and representative of the shadow side of the human soul (lust, intoxication and ritual madness) leads his followers on in frenzied Bacchanalia. Dionysus, Bacchus to the Romans, had the power to seduce and to intoxicate, a power he used freely, usually with happy consequences, but sometimes leaving in his wake savagery and death. His revellers were known to tear animals to pieces and eat them raw. Dionysus was the god of transformation, of masks, changing and revealing what is otherwise hidden, at once both alluring and threatening.

In its Christian garb it is Death, not Dionysus, who sweeps the unwilling revellers along in his merry dance. Among the figures in this inexorable *danse macabre*, next to the Emperor, the Priest, the Doctor,

the Monk, the Knight, the Merchant, the Farmer, the Soldier, etc., all shown with their attributes, is usually one female character: the Maiden (sometimes, unsurprisingly, a whore joins in as well). The contretemps between Death and the Maiden survived the late medieval fashion for *danses macabres* and was revived by the Romantics and beyond.

The *vanitas* tableaux of Death and the Maiden have a durable erotic charge. They still seem to embody much about the nature of collecting in the face of the inevitable.

The promise of love, which the Maiden represents, holds in it all the ambitions and hopes that seem to reverberate through collections over the centuries: beauty, individuality, distinction, possession, status, conquest, display, narcissism – pursuit and fulfilment. Death, hovering in the background, his hourglass raised, waiting impatiently, is the absolute denial and antithesis of all these qualities. The conquest is all his. In death all people are the same, will become the same. There is no distinction and no beauty in the grave, nor are there possessions, rank or even self-delusion. There is neither pursuit nor fulfilment, only an eternity of dust and ashes. While the Maiden pleads with Death throughout the ages the spectator finds himself part of the picture, as a third person in the frame, standing between the two other figures, close to one at first and not knowing how close to the other, but undeniably edging closer with every passing moment. With him is the collector who has wed himself to his possessions: To have and to hold, as *The Book of Common Prayer* Marriage Vow has it, from this day forward, for better for worse, for richer for poorer, in sickness and in health, to love and to cherish, till Death us do part.

Epilogue: Plastic Cups and Mausoleums

Vienna, 1997. I was sitting in the *Bräunerhof*, a café that I had loved and lived in when I had been studying in the city some years earlier, touched that the waiters still knew me, that everything looked as if I had never gone away. Only one new waiter, who had been working in the café for several years, made me realize that some time had passed since the period of my regular visits there. I had occupied the place that I fancied my own, my usual corner, which allowed me to see everything without being too conspicuous myself. In front of me was the coffee I always took, served on a little stainless steel tray with a glass of water, which was, as always, standing in the little puddle created when the waiter slammed the tray on to the marble surface of the table. A newspaper lay next to it. Nothing could be more delicious.

A man sat down opposite me. I had never seen him before and never since, just as if he were a ghost come to give me a message. I do not know his name, though in my notes I have a first name, Heiner, which he might have used, though it might also have been a substitute for the name he did use, dashed off in the rush of writing that followed his departure in order not to arrest the flow.

Those who are inclined to take the mysterious visitor as a fiction may be excused. I can only assure them that our encounter really did take place, one day in 1997, and that this is the most accurate reconstruction my notes would yield.

Do you mind if I sit down here?

Do you see this light? Look at these lamps, these imperfect smoked-glass moons, light for conversation, not for reading. Can you see anything there? I have quite a good spot, but you? This is no light for reading, this is undifferentiated, inhuman chatting light. I feel that as a loss of culture. But I am disturbing you. It won't be long. I will go soon. But I will drink a glass of wine first; I am an alcoholic and, apart from that, I have done something beautiful today and want to celebrate. I came here to have a sandwich and a glass of wine, but sandwiches are out. The kitchen is closed, the waiter says. Still, I want to celebrate. Today I have given away a large part of my library; wonderful books, precious books, sensual books. You are surprised, I can see that. I am sixty-two and have ten years left until I have reached the average life expectancy for Austrian men. It is time to start making my exit while I still can. It is a wonderful feeling of relief. All my life I have collected books, not as a hobby, but as a passion, something, therefore, that creates pain. Never collect, dear sir [he spoke very formally], never!

Waiter! Another glass of wine, please.

I am going, but I noticed you straight away, the very moment I came in here. You are a sensitive chap, in the old sense of the word, not in the modern one. Today, everybody is sensitive, and the world is dissolving into one large puddle of emotion. I saw that. But back to the light. I am new to this café, you must know. I have declared my old one out of bounds, a wonderful, malicious old-men's café, but they have betrayed me there. Over the summer months they cancelled all the most interesting newspapers, just to save a few thousand schillings. But instead of saying Heiner [sic], we haven't got any readers at the moment, they betrayed me by not saying anything and by stuttering stupidly when I confronted them, me, their eldest regular. I took the consequence and left. That Mafia!

Now look at this café: pictures everywhere, all over the walls. It is all done very stylishly, a silhouette of somebody famous here, but I ask you. Pictures like this are barbarous, the very act of hanging pictures is. A single picture, perhaps, but squashing them all together, that is inhuman. You have to excuse me, but look at the place, the wooden chairs, the marble tables between them like ice blocks, the terrible smoked-glass moons, the mirrors which seem to elongate the room into infinity; and then pictures: that is, strictly speaking, a crime. Look at the ceiling for a moment. Coloured by nothing but nicotine. Now *that* is beautiful.

My girlfriend, my lover, who lives across the hall, has no eye for things like that. She has other qualities. She cannot understand what I see in my collection, either. Getting rid of it is an escape. Every collection is kitsch. That is inevitable. Kitsch is everything that is superfluous. Kitsch is the desperate need to die *gemütlich*. I myself have been a slave of my collection for decades. What is it that people collect? Here I have an important sentence for you: *collecting is filling the void.* You must excuse this overly exact phrase, that is the pedant in me. My beloved wife, whom I can't stand, calls me a pedant, too.

I am getting on your nerves, I know. You want to read your paper. I will go in a moment, when the waiter has brought me my glass of wine, which he doesn't want to give me, because he doesn't know yet that I am a harmless drunk. I have seen, by the way, that, when I waved to him and ordered my wine, you winced a little, ashamed to sit at one table together with a drunk. Very understandable. But that is tangential. No parentheses any more.

I have read something, just recently, about an entymological collection in Berlin. Insects! I can imagine it, all these legs. You can have subspecies of flies called after you, for a few thousand schillings. Most people want butterflies, though. But cast your mind back to those cabinets in Berlin. Everything has to be crammed full together, pierced and killed. Order. End. I salute philatelists, though. They have everything in one book, *flap!*, off to the shelf, that's it. From an anal perspective they are the worst, of course. But still. I salute them.

[At this point, the little man got up from his chair in a brief, ceremonial bow. He sat down again.]

The waiter isn't bringing my wine. So there are these people with their cabinets and catalogues afraid that death might get at them. I myself collect plastic cups. When the Queen of Sheba visited King Solomon she brought him gold, frankincense and myrrh, and a long box made of black ebony. She opened a little door in the box and took out a neat stack of plastic cups. Not a collection! An accumulation. Solomon was delighted. He put one of the cups into the royal treasure chamber, at eye height, so that he could look at it. It was light as a feather, opaque and translucent at once, and he could drink from it. I have innumerable plastic cups, but it is not collecting as such. My daughter, Stephanie, has in her kitchen, on top of the cupboard, as the only ornament, a single, lonely plastic cup, which is gathering dust. I am very proud of this. *That* is beauty. I put it there.

We must all learn to see the beauty of these things, of the ordinary: the café, the ashtray. Even the best cafés now have these glass things with some sort of beer ad on it. And then this delicious thing, a sugar bowl, providing sweetness for all.

[The waiter brought him another glass of wine. He emptied it in a single draft and paused for a moment, saying nothing, then:]

This is the lucid moment. I am perfectly lucid. If you have collecting in your guts, you're done for. You yourself collect nothing and say nothing. Not even your eyebrow is moving. I am going soon. Then you have your peace. You are sitting there and are yourself already a victim of this passion. Everyone coming though the entrance door is observed by you and admitted to your collection. You are curious like a pubescent twelve-year-old and knowing like a two-hundred-year-old elephant. That is another pedantic sentence, but it describes you, hungering for another impression like a tiger for his meat. Don't get me wrong, please, I don't want to insult you. Forgive me. I even admire that, I know how dangerous this passion can be, the passion to fill the void. I won't ask you about that void. Not even I am that indiscreet. I myself have decided that I want the void. *Tabula rasa*, you know what I mean. That's why I went for plastic cups. An anti-collection, the first in the world, perhaps. Every cup is the same as every other, equally useful, equally beautiful. All utterly the same. There is no point going on collecting and no point stopping. You can buy them cheaply and at any time, an unlimited supply. Delicious for the sheer perverseness of it all. I can fill all my shelves with plastic cups in neat rows of identical boredom. A fitting farewell indeed. If you die you only have your shroud, everything else goes to the vultures. I have read my poets, too.

What was I saying? Short loss of concentration – stream of consciousness broken. I beg your pardon.

Stephanie does not approve of my domestic arrangements. Neither does my wife. It is my lover across the hall who gets on her nerves, although we no longer see each other regularly. We wanted to pack it in, but she has a shower and I don't so I continue to shower at her place. If I think about it I really do live like an animal. My wife has the shower in our flat. I love her, hate her deeply. We live separate lives, sleep in separate beds, which is painful to me. I may no longer be young, but I am still a man, though not an attractive one, I do admit to that. I have a cool ten kilos too much on my hips, hardly ideal because I can't see my prick. You look shocked. Excuse my crudeness. These things matter less when you get older.

The waiter is punishing me because I am drinking too fast. I will shame him by accepting it. Ageing. I am something of a wrinkle scientist. You will have beautiful wrinkles one day, so-called pain wrinkles, though I am worried about your upper lip. You are camouflaging yourself behind your conservative get-up. I'm just about to leave now. Just one more glass. *Waiter!* We won't see each other again, but we have said it all, anyway. I will kiss you on both cheeks by way of goodbye, whether you want it or not.

[The waiter brought another glass of wine.]

There: the last sentence is approaching – ah . . . damn, now I have lost my impetus –

[The little man got up, kissed me on both cheeks ceremonially, paid the waiter, and left. I have never seen him again.]

Notes

I A Parliament of Monsters

The Dragon and the Tartar Lamb

1 Aldrovandi, Ulisse, *Serpentum et draconum historiae*, p. 402.

2 Obviously Aldrovandi thought the visit important enough, or was flattered enough, to record it nevertheless. Bibliotheca Universitaria, Bologna, *Aldrovandi*, MS 35, cc. 203.

3 Quoted in M. Hodgen, *Early Anthropology in the Sixteenth and Seventeeth Centuries*, Philadelphia, PA, 1964, p. 119.

4 It is understandably difficult to ascertain the structure and particularly the function of early collections as well as the mentality that brought them into being. For a broad-brush treatment of this subject, see: Taylor; and Rheims.

5 The great orator Cicero made his name as a young Roman lawyer by prosecuting one of the greediest collectors history has seen: Caius Tullius Verres, the Quaestor (Governor) of Sicily, who had ransacked the island and its temples for works of art. Cicero's speeches are preserved in his *Orationes contra Verres*. Verres was sentenced and fled the reach of the Roman jurisdiction. See: L. H. G. Greenwood, *The Verrine Orations: An Introduction*, New York, 1928, pp. 9–22. For more general treatments of Roman collecting, see also Bonnaffé, *Les collectionneurs de l'ancienne Rome*; and Fabbrini.

6 On medieval treasuries and their development in general, see: Minges. We know of relatively few medieval collectors; the greatest of them was certainly Jean, duc de Berry, who assembled and commissioned works of art, books, and gems. Minges points out that the medieval French *estude* preceded the Italian *studiolo*. See: Guiffrey; and D. Thornton, *The Scholar in his Study. Ownership and Experience in Renaissance Italy*, New Haven, CT, 1997.

7 For the most meticulous investigation of the *studiolo* and its cultural significance, see: Liebenwein.

8 Quoted in Hibbert, p. 91.

9 For more on the Medici and their collections, see: Berti.

10 Umberto Eco, *Art and Beauty in the Middle Ages*, London, 1986, p. 95.

11 Jean de Léry, *Historie d'un voyage fait en la terre du Bresil, autrement dit Amerique*, La Rochelle, 1578. This crucial moment in European intellectual history and its importance for the history of collecting is summed up very well in Greenblatt, *Marvelous Possessions*. For a more general treatment, see: Kupperman.

12 Francesco Stelluri, *Persio tradotto*, Rome, 1630, quoted in Giuseppe Gabrieli, *Contributi alla storia della Accademia dei Lincei*, Rome, 1989, vol. I, p. 354.

13 Quoted in Clara Sue Kidwell, 'The Accademia dei Lincei and the "Apiarium": A Case Study of the Activities of a Seventeenth-Century Scientific Society', Ph.D. dissertation, University of Oklahoma, 1970, p. 307.

14 It seems significant that the Jesuit Athanasius Kircher, though working in the Vatican, was one of the very few exponents of this neo-Platonist tendency in Italy. Kircher was, of course, a German.

15 Here quoted in David Murray, *Museums: Their History and Their Use*, Glasgow, 1904, vol. I, pp. 19–20.

16 Bernhard of Clairvaux, *Apologia ad Guillelmum*, in *Patrologiae Cursus Completus*, ed. J. P. Mingne, 221 vols, Paris, 1884–94, vol. 182, pp. 91ff. For an English translation of relevant passages, see: Cecilia Davis-Weyer, *Early Medieval Art, 300–1150: Sources and Documents*, Englewood Cliffs, NJ, 1971, pp. 168–70.

17 In *Saturn und die Melancholie* Raymond Klibansky and Fritz Saxl have given an elegant exposition of the Church's opposition to curiosity and its polemic against it. Intelligence, it was felt, should be concentrated on a contemplation of divine mysteries, not on fruitless chases for temporal frivolity. It may be speculated that this, in addition to the lack of expendable income and of mass-produced goods among the majority of Europe's people, was one reason why the passion for collecting gripped Europe only at the time of the Renaissance. If it is true that collecting is partly motivated by an awareness of mortality and a desire to overcome it, then the Christian world view, in which death was by no means the final step into darkness, would have obviated such an occupation.

18 Michel de Montaigne, 'On Cannibals', in *Essays*, trans. J. M. Cohen, London, 1958, pp. 105–6. See also: 'Upon Some Verses of Virgil', in

Montaigne, *Essays*, trans. Charles Cotton, ed. C. C. Hazlitt, Chicago, IL, 1955, p. 257.

19 Pomian, *Collectors and Curiosities*, p. 17.

20 On this question see: Ariès.

21 Robert Herrick, 'To the Virgins To Make Much of Time', in Helen Gardner, ed., *The New Oxford Book of English Verse*, Oxford, 1972, p. 243.

22 The most influential of these, Quiccheberg's *Inscriptiones vel tituli*, appeared in 1565. Quiccheberg, whose name appears in Aldrovandi's guest book, distinguished between five orders of objects: *artificialia, naturalia*, works of craftsmanship, mechanical objects and *diversa*. Worm, in contrast to this, ordered the objects in his collection according to their materials. For other important works describing collections and discussing their order, see: Calceolari; Johnson; Major; Rumphius; Tradescant; and Worm.

23 These objects were often brought back in less than dignified circumstances. An advertisement in the *Amsterdamse Courant*, 11 October 1695, promises a reward to the finder of a stolen seaman's chest, which contained, next to dirty washing, also porcelain, ornamental vases, birds' nests, an 'Indian' bow with arrows, an ivory box with silver ornaments, a Japanese writing box, a tea table and several different exotic fabrics. See: J. van der Waals, *De prentschat von Michiel Hinloopen*, The Hague and Amsterdam, 1988, pp. 220–30.

24 '. . . sonderling-heden oft rariteyten ende wtgelesen sinnelickheden van Indiaensche ende ander wtheemsche zee-horens, schelpen, eerd ende zeege-wassen, mineralen ende oock vreemde gedierten; mitsgaders eenighe con-stichlyck ghemaecte hanswerken ende schilderyen'. *Catalogus oft Register van de sonderling-heden oft rariteyten ente wtgelesen sinnelickheden . . .* , Leiden, 1628.

25 Examples of such tiny cabinets, made for Miss Sara Rothé, survive in the Haags Gemeentemuseum in The Hague. One of them contains a miniature collection of manuscripts, sea urchins and shells, another has drawers just big enough to contain one coin each.

26 The majority of these collections were established after 1650, but already around 1585 individual cabinets are known. For an analysis of this phenom-enon, see: Jaap van der Veen, 'Die klain Vertrek bevat en Weereld vol gewoel', in Bergvelt and Kistemaker. For a general analysis of this period see: Schama.

27 This particularly Dutch combination of Calvinist principle and trading wealth has been described by Schama as well as by Geert Mak in his *Amsterdam: Biography of a City*, London, 1999.

28 Quoted in F. W. T. Hunger, 'Bernadus Paludanus (Berent ten Broecke), 1550–1633. Zijn verzamelingen aen zijn werk', in C. P. Burger, Jr., and F. W. T. Hunger, eds, *Itinerario. Voyage ofte Schipvaert van Jan Huygen van Linschoten naer Oost ofte Portugaels Indien, 1579–1592*, The Hague, 1934, vol. 3, pp. 249–68, here p. 260.
29 S. C. Snellen van Vollenhove, 'Jan Swammerdam's Catalogus', in *De Nederlandsche Spectator*, 1866, p. 126.

A Melancholy Ailment

1 Published in 1661. Quoted here in the Garnier Flammarion edition, Paris, 1970: 'Vous vous étonnez comme cette matière, brouillée pêle-mêle, au gré du hasard, peut avoir constitué un homme, vu qu'il y avait tant de choses nécessaires à la construction de son être, mais vous ne savez pas que cet millions de fois cette manière, s'acheminant au dessein d'un homme, s'est arrêtée à former tantôt une comète, pour le trop ou le trop peu de certaines figures qu'il fallait ou ne fallait pas à designer un homme? Si bien que ce n'est pas merveille qu'entre une infinie quantité de matière qui change et se remue incessamment, elle ait recontreé à faire le peu d'animaux, le végétaux, de minérvaux que nous voyons; non plus que ce n'est pas merveille qu'en cent coups de dés il arrive un rafle. Aussie bien est-il impossible que de ce remuement il ne se fasse quelque chose, et cette chose sera toujours admirée d'un étourdi qui ne saura pas combien peu s'en est fallu qu'elle n'ait pas été faite' (trans. Patrick Creagh).
2 The extent to which there was indeed a prevalence of clinical schizophrenia in the Habsburg family has often been debated. In his *Rudolf II*, pp. 48–9, Evans voices scepticism about some of the more radical analyses of the family history, which ascribed schizophrenia not only to Rudolf and Philip II, but also to Joanna the Mad, Don Carlos, the Duke of Cleves and Philip III. See: H. Luxemberger: 'Psychiatrisch-erbbiologisches Gutachten über Don Julio d'Austria', in *MVGDB* 70, 1932, pp. 41–54. Rumour at the Prague court had it that Rudolf had been ill with syphilis since 1579, but despite references to his 'dissipation' such allegations are impossible to prove.
3 C. Douais, ed., *Dépêches de M. de Fourquevaux, amassadeur du rui Charles IX en Espagne, 1565–72*, 3 vols., Paris, 1896–1904, here vol. I, p. 106.
4 Some rarities had found their way into Europe already during the Middle Ages, of course. They were often kept in the treasures of aristocratic families

or in churches. A church near Halberstadt in Germany displayed the ribs of a whale, while Santa Maria delle Grazie near Mantua sported a stuffed crocodile and a church in Ensisheim, Alsace, a meteorite, several rhinoceros horns and ostrich eggs. Objects that did not fit into the picture of God's creation could thus at least be neutralized by their sacred surroundings and bound in to a larger narrative of miracles and the unlimited powers of the Creator.

5 *Iter Germanicum: Relatio epistolica Danielis Eremitae Belgae de Legatione Magni Hetruriae Ducis ad Rudolphum II* . . . , Vienna, 1637, p. 299.

6 Marie Casaubon, *True and Faithful Relation of What Passed Between Doctor Dee . . . And Some Spirit* . . . , London, 1659, p. 231.

7 The foundations of this early form of science had been laid by Marsilio Ficino (1433–99), who had served another great collector, Cosimo de' Medici, and by the Swiss physician and alchemist Paracelsus (1493–1541), who in ordinary life went by the delectable name Philippus Aureolus Theophrastus Bombastus von Hohenheim. It is therefore not surprising to find among the physicians at Rudolf's court neo-Platonists such as Michael Maier and Robert Fludd, whose *Utriusque Cosmi majoris scilicet et minoris metaphysica atque technica historia in duo volumina secundum cosmi differentiam divisa* (1617–19) detailed the history of macrocosm and microcosm according to a system of correspondences and hierarchies, sympathies and harmony, allowing initiates to manipulate the material world by intervening in the spirit realm, and vice versa.

8 Burton, p. 129.

9 William Shakespeare, *The Tempest, c.* 1610, I.2.404.

10 Giovanni Pico della Mirandola, *De hominis dignitate, Heptaplus, de ente et uno e scritti vari*, Florence, 1949, p. 380.

11 Bacon, *The Great Instauration*, in *The Works*, vol. III, 1857, pp. 345–60.

12 Quoted in Aldofo Venturi, 'Zur Geschichte der Kunstsammlungen Kaiser Rudolf II', in *Repertorium für Kunstwissenschaft* 8, 1885, p. 15.

13 A. Grindely, *Rudolf II. Und seine Zeit, 1600–1612*, Prague, 1868, p. 27.

An Ark Abducted

1 Here quoted in Allen, p. 34.

2 State Papers Domestic, vol. IV, ch. 1, pp. 155–6.

3 P. Mundy, *The Travels of Peter Mundy, in Europe and Asia, 1608–1667*, London, 1914, vol. III.

4 Topsell, p. 91.

5 Stirn visited Tradescant in 1638. His account is preserved in manuscript in the Bodleian Library, Oxford: 'An Illustrated Account in German of the Travels of a Student of Altdorf, 1632–40', MS ADD 438 B.67.

6 Elias Ashmole, *Diary*, quoted in Allen, p. 192.

7 Ibid., Appendix.

The Exquisite Art of Dr Ruysch

1 Bacon, vol. III, 1857, pt III, bk 2, p. 330.

2 A. M. Luyendijk-Elshout 'Death Enlightened', in *Jama* 212, 1970, p. 121.

3 In the words of the collection's first Librarian and Keeper of Rarities, Johann Schumacher, *Pis 'ma I bumagi imperatora Petra Velikogo I*, St Petersburg, 1887, p. 240.

4 Gottfried Wilhelm Leibnitz in a memorandum to Peter the Great, in V. Gerje, *Otnoschenije Leibinitza k Rossii I Petru Velikomu*, St Petersburg, 1871, p. 76.

5 Johann Schumacher on his instructions, in P. Petarskij, *Nauka I Literatura pri Petri Velikom*, St Petersburg, 1862.

6 F. de la Neuville, *A Curious and New Account of Muscovy in the Year 1689*, ed. L. Hughes, London, 1994, p. 59.

7 Peter I to Andrei Vinius, quoted in Schumacher (see note 3 to this chapter), pp. 649ff.

II   A Complete History of Butterflies

This Curious Old Gentleman

1 Hans Sloane, *A Voyage to the Islands of Madera, Barbados, Nieves, S. Christophers, and Jamaica . . .* , 2 vols, London, 1707–25, vol. I, Preface.

2 Thomas Birch, 'Memoirs Relating to the Life of Sir Hans Sloane Bart formerly President of the Royal Society', British Library, Additional MS 4241, pp. 3–4.

3 Ibid., pp. 4–5.

4 Sloane (see note 1 to this chapter), vol. I, Preface.

5 *The Diary of John Evelyn*, ed. E. S. de Beer, London, 1959, p. 48.

6 On Courten's collection and intellectual outlook see also: 'Classification

and Value in a 17th-century Museum: William Courten's Collection', in *Journal of the History of Collections* 9.1, 1997, pp. 61–77.

7 Joseph Hunter, ed., *The Diary of Ralph Thoresby, FRS*, London, 1830, vol. I, p. 343.

8 Quoted in MacGregor, *Sir Hans Sloane*, pp. 28–9. While the headings of the categories are by Sloane himself and published in the Introduction of his *A Voyage* in 1725, the numbers of items relate to the final size of the collection as it appears in the 1753 inventory.

9 Quoted in Jean Jacquot, 'Sir Hans Sloane and French Men of Science', in *Notes and Records of the Royal Society* 10, 1953, pp. 91–3. The original manuscript is kept at the Institute de France, Paris, MS 1797.

10 Quoted in MacGregor, *Sir Hans Sloane*, p. 71.

11 Ibid., p. 86.

12 Ibid.

13 Ibid.

14 Ibid.

15 John Coleman to C. Hutton, in C. Hutton Beale, ed., *Catherine Hutton and her Friends*, Birmingham, 1895, p. 112.

16 Quoted in Alma S. Wittlllin, *The Museum, Its History and Its Tasks in Education*, London, 1949, p. 113.

17 A similar fate, incidentally, befell the last surviving specimen of a stuffed dodo that used to be in the Pitt Rivers Museum in Oxford. Once in the Tradescant Collection, the precious and long-extinct bird was consigned to the storerooms since it was no longer in very good condition. Some decades later a museum employee came across the somewhat mottled exhibit and thought that it was beyond repair. Unaware that this was not just any old bird he threw it away. Today the Pitt Rivers Museum is the proud exhibitor of a dodo foot and skull.

18 The hapless German scholar was not alone in his revulsion against the intrusion of eroticism into the innocence of nature, nor was he the last. In 1874 John Ruskin, horrified by the idea of some plants being hermaphrodite, wrote: 'With these obscene processes and prurient apparitions the gentle and happy scholar of flowers has nothing whatever to do.' See: Keith West, *How to Draw Plants: The Techniques of Botanical Illustration*, New York, 1987, p. 59.

The Mastodon and the Taxonomy of Memory

1 In Elsner and Cardinal, Susan Stewart gives a good account of the programme of the Peale Museum.
2 Charles W. Peale, *Discourse Introductory to a Course of Lectures on the Science of Nature with Original Music composed for, and Sung on, the Occasion. Delivered in The Hall of the University of Pennsylvania*, November 8, 1800, Philadelphia, 1800, p. 34.
3 I am indebted for this reading of the works to Stewart (see note 1 to this chapter).

Angelus Novus

1 Browne, p. 74.
2 Bauer, p. 82.
3 Ibid., p. 83.
4 Ibid.
5 Ibid., p. 99.

The Greatness of Empires

1 Bruno Schulz, *Sklepy cynamonowe, Sanatorim Pod Kepsydrą*, Cracow, 1957, p. 139; trans. PB.
2 J. Stählin, *Originalanekdoten von Peder dem Grossen*, Leipzig, 1785/1988, p. 58.
3 On the organization of early modern collections, see also: Minges.
4 Quoted in Andrew McClellan, *Inventing the Louvre*, Cambridge, 1994, p. 108.
5 Quoted in Jean Chatelain, *Dominique Vivant Denon et le Louvre de Napoléon*, Paris, 1973, pp. 50–51.
6 Ibid., pp. 62–3.
7 Ibid., p. 102.
8 Quoted in Eilean Hooper-Greenhill, *Museums and the Shaping of Knowledge*, London, 1992, p. 174.
9 In *Bulletin de la Société de l'Histoire de l'Art français*, 1920, pp 204–10, here p. 206.

10 Quoted after McClellan (see note 4 to this chapter), p. 108.

11 Quoted after Chatelain (see note 5 to this chapter), p. 169.

12 There were precedents to this chronological approach, of course, though Denon's arrangement proved the most influential. Already in 1726 the German Johann Friedrich Christ had identified different stages in German art, while the galleries of Johann Wilhelm of the Palatinate and the Vienna Belvedere, discussed in the text, were other examples. See: Minges, pp. 155, 159, *passim*.

13 Johann Joachim Winckelmann, *Gedanken über die Nachahmung der griechischen Werke . . .*, p. 54. Digitale Bibliothek Band 1: Deutsche Literatur, S. 102298 (vgl. Winckelmann-BDK, S. 35–6); trans. PB.

14 Chatelain (see note 5 to this chapter), p. 272.

15 In another twist of museum history the former imperial stables have been converted into a new Museum Quarter in 2001. It comprises two new buildings containing important collections of modern and contemporary art (the Sammlung Ludwig and the Sammlung Leopold), as well as artists' studios and workshops, a concert hall and exhibition spaces. Together with the Museums of Natural History and of the History of Art across the road this new institution now forms the largest museum complex in Europe. The design of the Museum Quarter, with its workshops and flexible exhibition spaces, emphasizes change and the mutability of a new museum concept, away from the monumental universality of former times and back, perhaps, to a more experimental spirit.

16 Sir William Henry Flower, *Essays on Museums and Other Subjects Connected with Natural History*, London, 1898, p. 18.

17 'On the Principles of Classification Adopted in the Arrangement of His Anthropological Collections, Now Exhibited in the Bethnal Green Museum', in *Journal of the Anthropological Institute* 4, 1875, pp. 293–4.

An Elevator to the Heavens

1 Quoted in Strouse, p. 38.

2 Ibid., p. 486.

3 Ibid., p. 492.

4 Quoted in Berman, p. 68.

5 Ibid., p. 82.

6 Ibid., p. 73.

7 Ibid., p. 106.

8 See: Swanberg, p. 415.
9 Ibid., p. 324.
10 *The New York Times*, 10 and 24 August 1924.

III   Incantations

Epigraph

1 The original reads: 'Et tout d'un coup le souvenir m'est apparu. Ce goût, c'était celui du petit morceau de madeleine que le dimanche matin à Combray . . . quand j'allais lui dire bonjour dans sa chambre, ma tante Léonie m'offrait après l'avoir trempé dans son infusion de thé ou de tilleul . . . Mais, quand d'un passé ancien rien ne subsiste, après la mort des êtres, après la destruction des térielles, plus persistantes, plus fidèles, l'odeur et la saveur restent encore longtemps, comme les âmes, à se rappeler, à attendre, à espérer, sur la ruine de tout le reste, à porter sans fléchir, sur leur gouttelette presque impalpable, l'édifice immense du souvenir.' (Marcel Proust, *Du côté de chez Swann*, Paris, 1954, pp. 46–7. The translation is quoted in: *Swann's Way*, trans. C. K. Scott Moncrieff, London, 1960, p. 41.
2 In *Die Zeit*, no. 22, 28 May 1993.

Why Boiling People is Wrong

1 Browne, p. 75.
2 Quoted in Cronin, pp. 428, 438.
3 This theory received new currency after research conducted by two French scientists, Pascal Kintz and Paul Fornes, and by the historian Ben Weider; see: the *Guardian*, 5 May 2000. Weider himself believes that the emperor's murderer was the Compte de Montholon, a member of Napoleon's St Helena entourage, who had personal grudges against his master. See: *The Assassin of Napoleon*, address given at the 3rd Conference of the International Napoleonic Society, on the WWW.
4 *Book of Suger Abbot of St Denis on What was Done during his Administration*, in Michel Bur, trans. and ed., *La geste de Louis VI et autres œuvres de Suger*, Paris, 1994, p. 10.
5 Ibid., p. 11.

6 *Inventory St Denis*, 1634, Bibliotheque Nationale, Paris, f. fr. 4611, folio 260.

7 A. C. Kruijt, 'Het Koppensnellen der Toradja's van Midden-Celebes', in *Verslagen en Mededelingen, afd. Letterkunde*, 4th series, III, Netherlands, 1899, pp. 164ff.

Three Flying Ducks

1 New York, 1998, p. 237.

2 This and the following extracts are taken from 'Unless you do these crazy things . . .', interview with Robert Opie, in Elsner and Cardinal, pp. 25–48.

3 The profile of Arnold de Wit is taken from Thomas Leeflang, *Verzamelen is ook een kunst*, Utrecht, 1982.

4 The Polish-French historian Krzysztof Pomian calls collected objects 'semiphores', 'carriers of meaning'. See: Pomian, *Der Ursprung des Museums*.

Anglers and Utopias

1 Pearce in her statistical study of collecting puts the value at about 51 per cent. See: Pearce, *Museums*.

2 For a clinical definition of Asperger's Syndrome, see: A. Klin and F. R. Volkmar, *Asperger's Syndrome: Guidelines for Assessment and Diagnosis*, Washington, DC, 1995; and U. Frith, ed., *Autism and Asperger Syndrome*, Cambridge, 1991.

3 E. Newson, M. Dawson and P. Everard, 'The Natural History of Able Autistic People: Their Management in Social Context', in *Communication*, Nottingham, 1982, pp. 1–19, here p. 18.

A Theatre of Memories

1 Erasmus, *Epistolae*, ed. P. S. Allen et al., Oxford, 1906, X, pp. 29–30.

2 Ibid., IX, p. 479.

3 Not everyone in France was enamoured of mnemonic systems, though. While Erasmus and Melanchton pontificated about it from on high, Rabelais punctured its pretensions with more direct weapons, letting Gargantua

undergo a gruelling course in the art of memory during which he has to commit to memory various absurd grammatical works with commentaries by scholars whose names alone are insults. As a result of this, he could indeed 'recite them backward', and was 'as wise as any man baked in an oven'. His understanding of the world, however, was still somewhat limited, and those expecting enlightenment from him found that 'it was no more possible to draw a word from him than a fart from a dead donkey'. François Rabelais, *The Histories of Gargantua and Pantagruel*, trans. J. M. Cohen, London, 1970, pp. 70–72.

4 Quoted in Janet Coleman, *Ancient and Medieval Memories: Studies in the Reconstruction of the Past*, Cambridge, 1992, pp. 17–22.

5 Bruno had a passion for long and august titles that outdid even those used by the authors of the Baroque. One of his main works on the art of memory is called, less than succinctly: *Ars reminiscendi et in phantastico campo exarandi; Explicatio triginta sigillorum ad omnium scientiarum et artium inventionem dispositionem et memoriam; Sigillus Sigillorum ad omnes animi operationes comparandas et earundem rationes habendas maxime conducens; hic enim facile invenies quidquid per logicam, metaphysicam, cabalam, naturalem magicam, artes magnas atque breves theorice inquiruntur* (printed in England, 1583).

6 This is the opinion of Frances Yates, as set out in *The Art of Memory*, Chicago, IL, 1966, and, in more detail, in *Theatre of the World*, London, 1969.

7 The following reference would seem a tempting lead in a continuing search for theories of memory: Geoffrey Sonnabend, *Obliscence: Theories of Forgetting and the Problem of Matter*. It would, however, be barking up an entirely wrong tree. This obscure academic publication by Sonnabend, who had been conducting research into the memory pathways of the carp in South America, might illuminate further the problem of artificial memory and the conservation of meaning in our world but for the fact that it cannot be found in any library. It was supposedly published in Chicago in 1946, but no American institution holds even a single copy or catalogue reference. Despite this omission Sonnabend has an entire room devoted to himself and to his work at the Museum for Jurassic Technology in Los Angeles, an intriguing institution masterfully brought to the attention of the world by Lawrence Weschler in an elegant little book, *Mr Wilson's Cabinet of Wonder*. The museum is the closest thing our day has got to the great *Wunderkammer* of centuries gone by. Visitors who make it into the suburban isolation of the MJT can marvel at now extinct French and Flemish moths, the life and death of the Cameroonian Stink Ant (*Megaloponera*

foetens), a model of Noah's Ark (1 inch = 12.5 cubits), a horn grown on the head of a woman in the seventeenth century and originally exhibited in John Tradescant's Ark, an illustration of the efficient but sadly neglected duck-breath therapy, a micro-sculpture of a pope inside the eye of a needle, and other wonders of the world. Familiarity breeds discontent, and doubts about the exhibits soon assert themselves. All of them are beautifully and competently displayed and documented, too beautifully perhaps. There is the story of father and son Owen Thum, two gardeners in South Platte in south-western Nebraska, who gathered together some of the collections shown here and whose photographs grace the display texts. They were cheated out of their treasures, David Wilson, the museum's director and guiding spirit explains, by a certain Gerard Billius, who after the death of Owen Thum junior showed great cruelty to his wife, Hester. The coincidence seems too remarkable: father and son Tradescant, the English gardeners and the fight of Hester, John the younger's wife, with Elias Ashmole – does history really repeat itself with quite such remarkable accuracy? Can it be an accident that the address of the Society for the Diffusion of Useful Information Press (9091 Divide Place, West Covina, California OX2 6DP), the publisher of the museum's monographs, shares a postcode with Oxford University Press and with no known Californian postal area? Those tempted to dismiss the museum altogether and to declare as pure fiction the Cameroonian Stinking Ant and the fascinating series of quasi-occult 'Letters to the Mount Wilson Observatory 1915–1935' and the zinc-inlaid black onyx box used for holding sacrificial human hearts will find the exposition of Athanasius Kircher's life and collection scholarly and accurate. Jurassic Technology, it seems, lives on the intersection between fact and fiction but right in the heart of curiosity, in the same place occupied by the cabinets of the seventeenth century. The pamphlet of the museum itself explains: 'The Museum of Jurassic Technology in Los Angeles, California, is an educational institution dedicated to the advancement of knowledge and the public appreciation of the Lower Jurassic. Like a coat of two colors, the museum serves dual functions. On the one hand the museum provides the academic community with a specialized repository of relics and artifacts from the Lower Jurassic, with an emphasis on those that demonstrate unusual or curious technological qualities. On the other hand the museum serves the general public by providing the visitor with a hands-on experience of "life in the Jurassic".' The Lower Jurassic, a definition exclusive to David Wilson's museum, is alive in Los Angeles, and with it the memory of the sense of the cabinet of curiosities, a memory reinterpreted and put on display, dramatized on a stage of its very own.

8 Bacon, vol. III, 1857, pp. 156, 164.

9 Francis Bacon, *The New Atlantis*, Wheeling, IL, 1989, p. 42.

10 Ibid., p. 79.

11 Bacon, *Gesta grayorum*, in *The Works*, vol. VIII, 1862, pp. 329–42, here p. 335.

12 Francis Bacon, *Distributio operis*, in *The Complete Essays of Francis Bacon*, New York, 1963, p. 173.

13 *A Catalogue of the Libraries of Sir Thomas Browne and Dr Edward Browne, His Son: A Facsimile Reproduction*, Leiden, 1986.

14 Sir Thomas Browne, 'To the Reader', in *Pseudodoxia Epidemica*, London, 1646.

15 *The Works of Sir Thomas Browne*, ed. Geoffrey Keynes, 4 vols, repr. London, 1964, vol. III, pp. 158f.

16 Ibid., p. 278. The *Commonplace Books*, in which this remark appears, was presumably written for Browne's eldest son, Edward. Considering the unorganized form in which these aphorisms appear, Arno Löffler writes rather revealingly in a fine Internet essay: 'The order in which his thoughts and observations occur is left to chance. His so-called *Commonplace Books*, in short, are a literary cabinet of rarities.' See: A. Löffler, 'The Problem of *Memoria* and Virtuoso Sensibility in Sir Thomas Browne's *The Garden of Cyrus*', http://webdoc.gwdg.de/edoc/ia/eese/artic97/loeffler/1b_97.html.

17 Browne, pp. 112–14. Browne was not the only man to invent entire libraries before Borges hit on this brilliant idea. The most famous instance of this kind was a catalogue sent to collectors in 1840 announcing the sale of the library of Jean-Nepomucene-Auguste Pichaud, Count Fortsas, a reclusive Belgian nobleman who had amassed a collection of books so rare that no other library had copies of them. The Preface of the publication explained his collecting philosophy as follows: 'With such a system, it is easy to conceive that the collection formed by him – although during forty years he devoted considerable sums to it – could not be very numerous. But what it will be difficult to believe is, that he pitilessly expelled from his shelves books for which he had paid their weight in gold – volumes which would have been the pride of the most fastidious amateurs – as soon as he learned that a work, up to that time unknown, had been noticed in any other catalogue.' Bids were invited by post to be sent to M Em. Hoyois, Printer and Bookseller, with a deposit from those with whom the auctioneer had done no previous business. The catalogue entries were meticulous and the titles so tempting to many collectors that bids came flooding in. The Princesse de Ligne recognized in one of them, bound, it said, in 'green chagrin, with a lock of silver gilt' the work of her own grandfather, who

had had a considerable reputation as a womanizer. It was a memoir entitled *My Campaigns in the Low Countries, with the List, Day by Day, of the Fortresses That I have Lifted to the White Arm*, and bearing the bibliographic information 'Printed by Me Alone, for Me Alone, in One Sole Copy, and for a Reason.' Eager to avoid terrible embarrassment, the princess was willing to pay any price. Other volumes, however, were no less intriguing. Lot Number 47, the *Philosophical Disputation, in Which the Anonymous Author Attempts to Show that Man before Sin Did Not Have Sex*, Cologne, 1607, 4to, excited considerable interest, as did Number 43, *The Aftermaths of Pleasure or the Discomfiture of the Great King in the Low Countries*, At Ponent, Holland, 1686, 12mo, further described as a 'libel of disgusting cynicism on the occasion of the fistula of Louis XIV. One of the plates represents the "royal behind" under the form of a sun surrounded with rays with the famous motto: *Nec pluribus impar*.' Just before the sale was due to take place bibliophiles from across Europe who had converged upon the small town of Binche in Belgium found a short notice in the local papers announcing that the collection was not to be sold after all, but had been bought by the town itself as a memorial to its native son. The entire affair later turned out to be the brainchild of Renier Chalons, President of the Société des Bibliophiles Belges in Brussels. (Quoted in Basbanes, pp. 116–120.)

18 *The Diary of John Evelyn*, ed. E. S. de Beer, London, 1959, p. 562.

19 Browne, p. 73.

20 Ibid., p. 105.

21 Ibid., p. 76.

22 Ibid., pp. 74–5.

23 Ibid., p. 88.

24 Browne, p. 55.

25 Another lovely collection deserves an honorary mention here. Its only claim to existence is a newspaper article but, considering its subject, that seems oddly appropriate. Peter Haffner collects, he writes, exclusively the names of objects he does not understand. Among his proudest possessions are: 'reservist jugs', 'Bumble Bee Children', 'Whole Objects on the Motive Peter Paul Rubens' and 'United States of America without Rubber' (stamps, may we guess?). The apex of the collection is, for the time being, 'Australia by the Kilo, 1966'. See: *NZZ Folio*, December 2000, p. 15.

26 I had the opportunity of interviewing Vilar myself at the Dorchester Hotel, London, in December 2000.

27 The connection between money and collecting has, naturally, always been intimate. Misers are, arguably, collectors of money; people for whom

the fortune they possess has lost its value as a means of exchange and has assumed an existential value beyond its purchase power. The security their balance sheets represent would be injured by taking away one single penny more than is absolutely necessary, for this balance is no longer a potential of exchangeable goods and services, but the metaphysical entity between them and poverty, unhappiness or powerlessness.

IV   The Tower of Fools

A Veritable Vello-Maniac

1 Norman D. Weiner, 'On Bibliomania', in *Psychoanalytic Quarterly* 35, 1966, pp. 217–32, here p. 217. His radical claim, incidentally, is borne out by Richard Heber, an early nineteenth-century English bibliophile, whose private library went into the hundreds of thousands, and whose homosexual relationship with a protégé caused a scandal in the 1820s. This trifle, however, did not keep him from proposing marriage to Richardson Currer, a great book collector in her own right, whose copy of *The Book of St Albans*, first published in 1486, he coveted greatly. Currer wisely kept her books to herself and never married.

2 Munby, *Portrait of an Obsession*, p. 267.

3 Ibid.

4 A. N. L. Munby, *Phillipps Studies* III, 1954.

5 Munby, *Portrait of an Obsession*, p. 283.

6 A. N. L. Munby, 'The Family Affairs of Sir Thomas Phillipps', in *Phillipps Studies* II, 1953.

7 Ricci, p. 119.

8 Ibid., pp. 119–20.

9 Basbanes, p. 2.

10 I hesitate to quote Benjamin and do so only after overcoming considerable misgivings: so many trendy academics have found it necessary to cannibalize his writings in pursuit of post-modernist theory and interesting jargon that there should be a moratorium on any quotations from him. The fact, however, is that he is one of the most sensitive and most insightful commentators on this passion and that it would be a gross omission not to let him speak.

11 Benjamin, pp. 169–78, here p. 169; trans. PB.

12 Ibid.

13 Ibid., p. 170.

14 Ibid.

15 Ibid., p. 171.

16 Ibid., pp. 177–8.

17 Walter Benjamin, *Das Kunstwerk im Zeitalter der technischen Reproduzierbarkeit*, Frankfurt, 1986, pp. 93, 105.

18 Ibid., p. 107.

19 Walter Benjamin, *Das Passagenwerk*, Frankfurt, 1972, vol. V, p. 280.

20 Petrarch, *Letters*, trans. James Harvey Robinson and Henry Winchester Rolf, New York, 1909, pp. 239–51.

21 Jorge Louis Borges, 'The Library of Babel', in *The Book of Sand*, various translators, ed. D. A. Yates and J. E. Irby, London, 1970, p. 80.

22 Ibid., pp. 81–2.

Leporello and His Master

1 Prince Charles de Ligne, *Mélanges militaire, littéraires et sentimentaires*, Dresden, 1807, vol. XXXIX, quoted in Masters, pp. 280–81.

2 Casanova's final occupation as a librarian has itself been the cause of many psychologizing comments seeking to equate the conquest of women with the collecting of books. The psychoanalyst Norman D. Weiner put a rather pitilessly Freudian interpretation on the occupation of book collecting when he wrote that bibliomaniacs were condemned never to rest but to 'set out on another quest for a great book as soon as his anxiety returns. The quality of the boasting, the constant search for new conquest, and the delight in recounting tales of acquisition and success brings to mind the activities of the hypersexual male hysteric who must constantly reassure himself that he has not been castrated. It seems germane to this point that Casanova, after his many amatory adventures, settled down as a librarian in the castle of Count Waldstein at Dux, in Bohemia'. 'On Bibliomania', in *The Psychoanalytic Quarterly* 35, 1966, pp. 217–32.

3 Masters, p. 221.

4 That same collector devotes much of his day to recording musical broadcasts from across the world via a digital receiver. Frequently, four tape recorders will run at one time, capturing, say, a chamber music recital from Czech radio, an opera on the BBC and a symphony concert each from Spain and Austria. He has long since lost count of how many tapes he possesses, or how many recordings of one particular work. Moreover, his relentless recording schedule leaves him hardly any time to listen to any of his treasures,

much less to catalogue them. Some collectors, it seems, collect for an anticipated hereafter, collect as if death would not exist, or perhaps in order to convince themselves that it does not.

5 Quoted in Rheims, p. 28.

6 Maurice Rheims, *La vie étrange des objects*, Paris, 1956, p. 28.

7 Jacques Attali, *Mémoire de Dablier: Collections, mode d'emploi*, Paris, 1997, pp. 44, 51, *passim*. Attali makes his observation in an especially interesting context. The book describes his own collection of hourglasses, *mementi mori* and symbols of impending death since their inception. Eros and Thanatos are never far apart. Rheims (p. 29, *passim*) has made the same point.

8 Muensterberger makes a valiant attempt at formulating a comprehensive psychoanalytical picture of the collector, but the result illustrates, if anything, the impossibility of doing so.

9 *Minutes of the Vienna Psychoanalytic Society*, trans. M. Nunberg, ed. Herman Nunberg and Ernst Federn, New York, 1962, 19 Febraury 1908, vol. I, p. 321.

10 *The Complete Letters of Sigmund Freud to Wilhelm Fleiss, 1887–1907*, ed. J. M. Masson, Cambridge, MA, 1984, 24 January 1895, p. 110.

11 Rheims (see note 6 to this chapter), p. 50. Another French author, Jean Baudrillard, takes this erotic analogy between pets and objects one mercilessly psychoanalysing step further. To be domesticated pets are frequently castrated, just as objects are rendered neutral in a collection: 'Let us observe in passing that pets are never sexually distinct (indeed they are occasionally castrated for domestic purposes): although alive, they are as sexually neutral as any inert object. Indeed this is the price one has to pay if they are to be emotionally comforting, given that castration, real or symbolic, is what allows them to play, on their owner's behalf, the role of regulating castration anxiety.' 'The System of Collecting', in Elsner and Cardinal, pp. 10–11.

Mr Soane is Not at Home

1 Louis-Henri de Loménie, Comte de Brienne, *Mémoires*, ed. Paul Bonnefon, Paris 1916–19, vol. III, pp. 88–90.

2 Quoted in Arthur T. Bolton, *The Portrait of Sir John Soane RA*, London, 1927, p. 12.

3 Alexander Penrose, ed., *The Autobiography and Memoirs of Benjamin Robert Haydon*, London, 1927, pp. 305–7.

4 Sir John Soane, *Memoirs of the Professional Life of an Architect*, London, 1835.

5 Sir John Soane, *Description of the House and Museum on the North Side of Lincoln's Inn Fields*, London, 1835, p. 88.

6 Browne, p. 55.

7 Anonymous, *Le danse macabre*, Paris, 1485, after a *danse macabre* painted in 1424 in the arcades of the ossiarium of the Franciscan Cimetière aux SS. Innocents by the rue de la Ferronerie in Paris. It seems worth noting that it is the bourgeois who is seen as the amasser and collector of things. This new creature in the social universe was soon to dominate collecting and to bring it into its own after it had languished at princely palaces for so long.

Bibliography

Aldrovandi, Ulisse, *Musaeum metallicum*, Bologna, 1648

——, *Serpentum et draconum historiae*, Bologna, 1640

Allen, M., *The Tradescants, Their Plants, Gardens and Museum, 1570–1662*, London, 1964

Allin, Michael, *Zarafa – The True Story of a Giraffe's Journey from the Plains of Africa to the Heart of Post-Napoleonic France*, London, 1998

Alsop, J., *The Rare Art Traditions: A History of Collecting and Its Linked Phenomena*, New York, 1982

Ariès, Philippe, *L'homme devant la mort*, Paris, 1978

Arnold, U. and Schmidt W., *Barock in Dresden. Kunst und Kunstsammlungen unter der Regierung des Kurfürsten Friedrich August I. von Sachsen und Königs August II. von Polen genannt August der Starke (1694–1733) und des Kurfürsten Friedrich August II. von Sachsen und Königs August III. von Polen (1733–1763)*, Leipzig, 1986

Bacon, Francis, *The Works of Francis Bacon*, ed. James Spedding et al., 14 vols, London, 1857–74

Balfe, H. J., *Paying.the Piper: Causes and Consequences of Art Patronage*, Chicago, 1993

Balsinger, B. J., *The Kunst- und Wunderkammern. A Catalogue Raisonné of Collecting in Germany, France and England, 1565–1750*, Pittsburgh, PA, 1970

Balzac, Honoré de, *Le cousin Pons*, Paris (1847), 1993

Barge, J. A. J., *De oudste inventaris der oudste academische anatomie in Nederland*, Leiden, 1934

Barker, Nicolas, *Portrait of an Obsession*, New York, 1967

Barker, Stephen, ed., *Excavations and Their Objects*, New York, 1996

Basbanes, Nicholas A., *A Gentle Madness*, New York, 1995

Bauer, Wilhelm A., *Angelo Soliman, der hochfürstliche Mohr*, Vienna, 1992, new edition, ed. Monika Firla-Forkl, Berlin, 1993

Baur, R. and Haupt H., *Das Kunstkammerinventar Kaiser Rudolf II., 1607–11 (Verzeichnis was in der Röm. Kay. May. Kunstkammer gefunden worden ist.)*, Vienna, 1977

Bazin, Germain, *The Museum Age, Brussels*, 1967

Becker, C., *Vom Raritäten-Kabinett zur Sammlung als Institution. Sammeln und Ordnen im Zeitalter der Aufklärung*, Hohenhausen, 1996

Bedini, S. A., 'Citadels of Learning. The Museo Kircheriano and Other Seventeenth-Century Italian Science Collections', in Maristella Casciato, ed., *Enciclopedismo in Roma barocca*, Venice, 1986, pp. 249–67

Belper, J., *Barocke Sammellust. Die Bibliothek und Kunstkammer des Herzogs Ferdinand Albrecht zu Braunschweig Lüneburg, 1636–1687*, Weinheim, 1988

Benjamin, Walter, 'Ich packe meine Bibliothek aus' [1931], in *Angelus Novus*, Frankfurt, 1966, pp. 169–78

Bennett, J. and Mandelbrote, S., *The Garden, the Ark, the Tower, the Temple: Biblical Metaphors of Knowledge in Early Modern Europe*, Oxford, 1998

Bennett, Tony, *The Birth of the Museum – History, Theory, Politics*, London, 1995

Bentley, J., *Restless Bones*, London, 1985

Bergvelt, Ellinoor and Kistemaker, R., *De wereld binnen handbereik. Nederlandse kunst- en rariteitenverzamelingen, 1578–1735*, Amsterdam, 1992

Bergvelt, Ellinoor, Meijers, D. J. and Rijnders, M., *Verzamelen. Van rariteitenkabinet tot kunstmuseum*, Heerlen, 1993

Berman, S. N., *Duveen*, New York, 1952

Berti, L., *Il principe dello studiolo. Francesco I dei Medici e la fine del rinascimento florentino*, Florence, 1967

Beurdeley, Michel, *The Chinese Collector through the Centuries*, Rugland, VT, 1966

Blair, A., *The Theater of Nature: Jean Bodin and Renaissance Science*, Princeton, NJ, 1997

Blumenthal, Walter, *Booksman's Bedlam*, New Brunswick, NJ, 1955

Bock, H., 'Fürstliche und öffentliche Kunstsammlungen im 18. und frühen 19. Jahrhundert in Deutschland' in Per Bjurström, ed., *The Genesis of the Art Museum in the 18th Century*, Stockholm, 1993, pp. 112–30

Bogenig, G. A. E., *Die großen Bibliophilen. Geschichte der Büchersammler und ihrere Sammlungen*, 3 vols, Hildesheim, 1984

Bolton, A. T., *Description of the House and Museum on the North Side of Lincoln's Inn Fields, the Residence of Sir John Soane*, London, 1930

Bonnaffé, Edmond, *Les collectionneurs de l'ancienne France*, Paris, 1869

————, *Les collectionneurs de l'ancienne Rome: Notes d'un amateur*, Paris, 1867

Bredekamp, H., *The Lure of Antiquity and the Cult of the Machine*, Princeton, NJ, 1995

Brieger, Lothar, *Das Kunstsammeln: Eine kurze Einführung in seine Theorie und Praxis*, Munich, [1918]

Brown, C. M., *Our Accustomed Discourse on the Antique. Cesare Gonzaga and Gerolamo Garimberto – Two Renaissance Collectors of Greco-Roman Art*, New York and London, 1993

Browne, Sir Thomas, *Urne Buriall*, in *Selected Writings*, ed. Claire Preston, Manchester, 1995

Burckhardt, Jacob, *Die Kultur der Renaissance in Italien*, Basle, 1860

Burk, C. F., 'The Collecting Instinct', in *Pedagogical Seminary* 7, 1900, pp. 179–207

Burke, Peter, *Tradition and Innovation in Renaissance Italy*, London, 1972

Burton, Robert, *The Anatomy of Melancholy* (1651), ed. Holbrook Jackson, London, 1977

Cabanne, P., *Die Geschichte großer Sammler*, Bern and Stuttgart, 1993

Caggill, M., *Nineteenth-Century Collecting and the British Museum*, ed. A. W. Franks, London, 1997

Calceolari, F. *Musaeum Calceolarium*, Verona, 1622

Céard, J., *La curiosité à la renaissance*, Paris, 1986

Cheles, L., *The Studiolo of Urbino: An Iconographic Investigation*, Wiesbaden, 1986

Clifford, J., 'Sich selbst sammeln', in G. Korff and M. Roth, eds, *Das historische Museum, Frankfurt*, New York, 1990, pp. 87–106

Constable, W. G., *Art Collecting in the United States of America*, London, 1964

Cooper, Douglas, ed., *Great Family Collections*, London, 1965

————, ed., *Great Private Collections*, New York, 1974

Cronin, Vincent, *Napoleon*, London, 1971

Cruz, Joan Carroll, *Relics*, Huntingdon, IN, 1983

DaCosta Kaufmann, Thomas, *Court, Cloister and City – The Art and Culture of Central Europe, 1450–1800*, London, 1995

Dance, S. P. A., *History of Shell Collecting*, Leiden, 1986

Darley, Gillian, *John Soane: An Accidental Romantic*, New Haven, CT, and London, 1999

Darlington, H. S., 'The Meaning of Head Hunting', in *Psychoanalytic Review* 26, 1939

Dekkers, Midas, *De vergankelijkheid*, Amsterdam, 1998

Demetz, Peter, *Prague in Black and Gold*, New York, 1997

Dibdin, Revd Thomas Frognall, *The Bibliomania; Or, Book-Madness; Containing Some Account of the History, Symptoms, and Cure of This Fatal Disease*, London, 1809

Donath, A., *Der Kunstsammler, Psychologie des Kunstsammelns*, Berlin, 1923

Dühring, Monika von, et al., eds, *Encyclopaedia Anatomica*, Cologne, 1999

Duncker, L., 'Mythos, Struktur und Gedächtnis. Zur Kultur des Sammelns in der Kindheit', in L. Duncker, F. Maurer and G. E. Schäfer, eds, *Kindliche Phantasie und ästhetische Erfahrung*, Langenau-Ulm, 1990

Durost, W., *Children's Collecting Activity Related to Social Factors*, New York, 1932

Eccles, Lord, *On Collecting*, London, 1968

Elshout, A. M., *Het Leidse Kabinet der Anatomie uit de achttiende eeuw. De betekenis van een wetenschappelijke collectie als cultuur-historisch monument*, Leiden, 1952

Elsner, John and Cardinal Roger, eds, *The Cultures of Collecting*, London, 1994

Eudel, Paul, *Collections et collectionneurs*, Paris, 1958

Evans, R. J. W., *The Making of the Habsburg Monarchy, 1550–1700*, Oxford, 1979

——, *Rudolf II and His World: A Study in Intellectual History, 1576–1612*, Oxford, 1953

Fabbrini, Fabrizio, ed., *Il collezionismo nel mondo romano: Dall'età degli Scipioni a Cicerone*, Arezzo, 2001

Fatke, R. and Flintner, A., 'Was Kinder sammeln. Beobachtungen und Überlegungen aus pädagogischer Sicht', in *Neue Sammlung. Zeitschrift für Erziehung und Gesellschaft. Studien- Texte- Entwürfe*, 23, 1983, pp. 600–611

Findlen, Paula, *Possessing Nature: Museums, Collecting and Scientific Culture in Early Modern Italy*, Berkeley, CA, 1994

Flintner, A., 'Steine, Muscheln, Zinnsoldaten. Besitzen und Sammeln im Kindesalter', in *Welt des Kindes*, 1984, pp. 276–81

Floerke, H., *Die Formen des Kunsthandels, das Atelier und die Sammler in den Niederlanden vom 15.–18. Jahrhundert*, Munich and Leipzig, 1905

Förster, Henrich, *Sammler & Sammlung oder das Herz in der Schachtel*, Cologne, 1998

Foucault, Michael, *The Order of Things: An Archaeology of the Human Sciences*, New York, 1994

Fučikova, Elisa, ed., *Prag um 1600: Kunst und Kultur am Hofe Rudolfs II.*, *(catalogue)*, Freren, 1988

——, ed., *Rudolf II and Prague: The Court and the City*, London, 1997

Gabhardt, A., *Treasures and Rarities: Renaissance, Mannerist and Baroque*, Baltimore, MD, Bradford and London, 1971

Gamber, Ortwin, *Curiositäten und Inventionen aus der Kunst- und Rüstkammer*, Vienna, 1978

Geary, Patrick J., *Furta Sacra*, New York, 1990

Georges, Chantal, ed., *La Jeunesse des Musées*, Paris, 1994

Gere, Charlotte and Vaizey, Marina, *Great Women Collectors*, London, 1999

Gould, Cecil, *Trophy of Conquest – The Musée Napoléon and the Creation of the Louvre*, London, 1965

Gould, Stephen Jay and Wolff Purcell, Rosamund, *Finders, Keepers: Eight Collectors*, London, 1992

Green, André, *On Private Madness*, Madison/Conn., 1986

Greenblatt, S., *Marvelous Possessions: The Wonder of the New World*, Chicago, 1991

——, 'Resonance and Wonder', in Ivan Karp and Stephen D. Lavine, eds, *Exhibiting Cultures: The Poetics and Politics of Museum Display*, Washington, DC, 1991

Greenfeld, Howard, *The Devil and Dr Barnes*, London, 1996

Grote, Andreas, ed., *Macrocosmos in Microcosmos*, Opladen, 1994

Groys, Boris, *Logik der Sammlung. Am Ende des musealen Zeitalters*, Munich and Vienna, 1997

Guiffrey, Jules, ed., *Inventories de Jean, duc de Berry (1401–1416)*, 2 vols, Paris, 1894–6

Hamann, G., 'Zur Wissenschaftspflege des aufgeklärten Absolutismus. Naturforschung, Sammlungswesen und Landesaufnahme', in Zöller, Erich, ed., *Österreich im Zeitalter des aufgeklärten Absolutismus*, Vienna, 1983, pp. 151–77

Händler, Gerhard, *Fürstliche Mäzene und Sammler in Deutschland von 1500–1620*, Strassburg, 1933

Hauser, Ernst, *Das pathologisch-anatomische Bundesmuseum im Narrenturm des alten Allgemeinen Krankenhauses in Wien*, Vienna, 1998

Herrmann, Frank, *The English as Collectors*, London, 1972/1999

Hibbert, Christopher, *The Rise and Fall of the House of Medici*, London, 1974

Hobsbawm, Eric and Ranger, Terence, eds, *The Invention of Tradition*, Cambridge, 1997

Holst, Niels van, *Creators, Collectors and Conoisseurs – The Anatomy of Artistic Taste from Antiquity to the Present Day*, London, 1967

Hunter, M., *Elias Ashmole and His World*, Oxford, 1983

Impey, Oliver and MacGregor, Arthur, eds., *The Origins of Museums: The Cabinet of Curiosities in Sixteenth- and Seventeenth-Century Europe*, Oxford, 1985

Jackson, Holbrook, *The Anatomy of Bibliomania*, 2 vols, London, 1930

Jacobi, Franz, *Grundzüge einer Museographie der Stadt Rom zur Zeit des Kaisers Augustus*, Speier, 1884

Jansen, Dirk Jacob, 'Samuel Quiccheberg's "Inscripitones": De encycopedische verzameling als hulpmiddel voor de wetenschap', in Ellinoor Bergvelt, ed., *Verzamelen*, Heerlen, 1993

Jeudy, Henry Pierre, *Die Welt als Museum* (Paris, 1985), Berlin 1987

Johnson, Thomas, *Cornucopiae, or Divers Secrets: Wherein is contained the rare secrets in man, beasts . . . plantes, stones, and such like . . . and not before committed to be printed in English, newlie drawen out of divers Latine authors . . .*, London, 1595

Juel-Jensen, Bent, 'Musaeum Clausum, or Biblioteca Abscondita: Some Thoughts on Curiosity Cabinets and Imaginary Books', in *Journal of the History of Collections* 4.1, 1992

Kamen, Henry, *Philip of Spain*, New Haven, CT, and London, 1997

Kenseth, Joy, ed., *Age of the Marvelous*, Chicago, 1991

Kopplin, Monika, ' "Was frembd und seltsam ist": Exotica in Kunst- und Wunderkammern', in Tilman Osterwold and Herman Pollig, eds, *Exotische Welten-Europäische Phantasien*, Stuttgart, 1987

Kupperman, Karen Ordahl, *America in European Consciousness, 1493–1750*, London, 1995

Kurz, O., *Fakes: A Handbook for Collectors and Students*, New York, 1967

Lelièvre, Pierre, *Vivant Denon – Homme des lumières 'ministre des arts' de Napoléon*, Paris, 1993

Lhotsky, Alphons, *Festschrift des kunsthistorischen Museums zur Feier des Fünfzgjaehrigen Bestandes*, Vienna, 1941–5

Liebenwein, W., *Studiolo. Die Entstehung eines Raumtyps und seine Entwicklung bis um 1600*, Berlin, 1977

Lloyd, C., *The Queen's Pictures. Royal Collectors through the Centuries*, London, 1991

Lucius, Wulf D. von, *Bücherlust: Vom Sammeln*, Cologne, 2000

Lyons, J., *Exemplum: The Rhetoric of Example in Early Modern France and Italy*, Princeton, NJ, 1989

MacGregor, Arthur, *Ark to Ashmolean: The Story of the Tradescants, Ashmole and the Ashmolean Museum*, Oxford, 1983

——, *The Late King's Goods. Collections, Possessions and Patronage of Charles I in the Light of the Commonwealth Sale Inventories*, London, 1989

——, *Sir Hans Sloane: Collector, Scientist, Antiquary, Founding Father of the British Museum*, London, 1994

——, *Tradescant's Rarities. Essays on the Foundation of the Ashmolean Museum, 1683. With a Catalogue of the Surviving Early Collections*, Oxford, 1983

Major, Johann Daniel, *Unvorgreiffliches Bedencken von Kunst- und Naturalien-Kammern insgemein*, Kiel, 1662

Mandelartz, B., *Zur Psychologie des Sammelns*, 1981

Masson, Georgina, *Queen Christina*, London, 1968

Masters, John, *Casanova*, London, 1969

Menzhausen, J., *Dresdner Kunstkammer und Grünes Gewölbe*, Leipzig, 1977

Minges, Klaus, *Das Sammlungswesen in der frühen Neuzeit. Kriterien der Ordnung und Spezialisierung*, Münster, 1998

Muensterberger, Werner, *Collecting: An Unruly Passion*, Princeton, NJ, 1994

Munby, A. N. L., *The Formation of the Phillipps Library up to the Year 1840*, Cambridge, 1954

——, *Portrait of an Obsession: The Life of Sir Thomas Phillipps, the World's Greatest Book Collector*, London, 1967

Neickelius, C. F., *Museographia oder Anleitung zum rechten Begriff und nützlicher Anlegung der Museorum und Raritätenkammern*, 1727

Ohlsen, M., *Wilhelm v. Bode*, Berlin, 1995

Olmi, Giuseppe, *Ulisse Aldrovandi: Scienza e natura nel seconco Cinquecento*, Trent, 1976

Pearce, Susan M., *Interpreting Objects and Collections*, London, 1994

——, *Museums, Objects and Collectors*, Leicester, 1992

Petropoulos, Jonathan, *The Faustian Bargain: The Art World in Nazi Germany*, London, 2000

Pomian, Krzysztof, ed., *L'anticomanie*, Paris, 1992

——, *Collectors and Curiosities: Paris and Venice, 1500–1800*, Cambridge, 1990

——, 'Collezionisti d'arte e di curiosità naturali', in *Storia della cultura veneta dalla Controriforma alla fine della Repubblica. Il Settecento 2*, 1986, p. 5

——, *Der Ursprung des Museums: Vom Sammeln*, Berlin, 1998

Quiccheberg, Samuel, *Inscriptiones vel tituli. Theatri aplissimi, complectentis rerum universitatis singulas materias et imagines eximias* ... , Munich, 1565

Reitlinger, Gerald, *The Economics of Taste*, London, 1961

Rheims, Maurice, *Les collectionneurs: De la Curiosité, de la beauté, du goût, de la mode et de las spéculation*, Paris, 1981

Ricci, Seymour de, *English Collectors of Books and Manuscripts, 1530–1930, and Their Marks of Ownership*, New York and Cambridge, 1930

Ridley, Ronald, *Napoleon's Proconsul in Egypt: The Life and Times of Bernardino Drovetti*, London, 1998

Riedl-Dorn, Christa, *Wissenschaft und Fabelwesen ein kritischer Versuch über Conrad Gessner und Ulisse Aldrovandi*, Vienna, 1989

Roberts, Andrew, *Collections Management for Museums*, Cambridge, 1988

Roger, J. Buffon, *A Life in Natural History*, Ithaca, NY, 1997

Rufus, Anneli, *Magnificent Corpses*, New York, 1999

Rumphius, G. E., *D'Amboinsche Rariteitkammer*, Amsterdam, 1705

Ruysch, Frederik, *Thesaurus Animalium Primus*, Amsterdam, 1710

Savini Branca, Simona, *Il collezionismo veneziano nel 1600*, Florence, 1965

Schaffner, I. and Winzen, M., *Deep Storage: Arsenale der Erinnerung. Sammelns, Speichern, Archivieren in der Kunst*, Munich and New York, 1997

Schama, Simon, *The Embarrassment of Riches: An Interpretation of Dutch Culture in the Golden Age*, London, 1987

Scheicher, Elisabeth, et al., eds, *Die Kunstkammer: Sammlungen Schloss Ambras*, Innsbruck, 1977

——, *Die Kunst- und Wunderkammern der Habsburger*, Vienna, Munich and Zürich, 1979

Scheurleer, Lunsingh Th. H. and Meyjes, G. H. M., eds, *Leiden University in the Seventeenth Century: An Exchange of Learning*, Leiden, 1975

Schlosser, Julius von, *Die Kunst- und Wunderkammern der Spätrenaissance. Ein Beitrag zur Geschichte des Sammelwesens. Ein Handbuch für Sammler und Leibhaber*, 2 vols., Braunschweig, 1978

Scholler, Hubert: *Naturhistorisches Museum in Wien – Die Geschichte der Wiener naturhistorischen Sammlungen*, Vienna, 1958

Schwarzenfeld, Gertrude von, *Rudolf II, der Saturnische Kaiser*, Munich, 1960

Schubert, Karsten, *The Curator's Egg: The Evolution of the Museum Concept from the French Revolution to the Present Day*, London, 2000

Seligman, Germaine, *Merchants of Art*, New York, 1961

Sharpe, Kevin, *The Personal Rule of Charles I*, New Haven, CT, and London, 1992

Skeates, Robin, *The Collecting of Origins: Collectors and Collections of Italian Prehistory and the Cultural Transformation of Value (1550–1999)*, Oxford, 2000

Spence, Jonathan D., *The Memory Palace of Matteo Ricci*, New York, 1984

Strohl, Alfred, *Der Narrenturm – oder die dunkle Seite der Wissenschaft*, Vienna, 2000

Strouse, Jean, *Morgan – American Financier*, New York, 1999

Swanberg, W. A., *Citizen Hearst*, New York, 1961

Swann, Marjorie, *Curiosities and Texts: The Culture of Collecting in Early Modern England*, Philadelphia, PA, *c.* 2001

Taylor, F. H., *The Taste of Angels: A History of Collecting from Ramses to Napoleon*, Boston, 1948

Topsell, Edward, *The Elizabethan Zoo: A Book of Beasts Both Fabulous and Authentic*, ed. M. St Clare Byrne, London, 1926

Tradescant, J., *Musaeum Tradescantianum: Or A Collection of Rarities, Preserved at South-Lambeth near London*, London, 1656

Vaisey, David George, *The Foundations of Scholarship: Libraries and Collecting, 1650–1750: Papers Presented at a Clark Library Seminar, 9 March 1985*, Los Angeles, 1992

Wainwright, C., *The Romantic Interior: The British Collector at Home, 1750–1850*, New Haven, CT, and London, 1989

Welscher, Lawrence, *Mr Wilson's Cabinet of Wonders*, New York, 1998

Wenneker, Lu Beery, *An Examination of L'idea del theatro of Giulio Camillo . . .*, (dissertation) Pittsburgh, PA, 1970

Wolbert, Klaus, 'Die Kunst- und Wunderkammer: Ein Sammlungstyp zwischen Mythos und Wissenschaft', in *Sammeln: Eine Ausstellung zur Geschichte und zu den Formen der Sammeltägkeit*, Darmstadt, 1981

Worm, Ole, *Musaeum Wormianum*, Leiden, 1655

Zorzi, Marino, *Collezioni di antichità a Venezia: Nei secoli della Repubblica dai libri e documenti della Biblioteca Marciana: mostra 27 maggio-31 luglio 1988; catalogo a cura di; con un saggio di Irene Favaretto; schede di P. Bravetti*, Rome, 1988

Index

Page references in *italic* refer to illustrations